D0905050

STUDENT'S GUIDE TO LANDMARK CONGRESSIONAL LAWS
ON CIVIL RIGHTS

Recent Titles in
Student's Guide to Landmark Congressional Laws

Student's Guide to Landmark Congressional Laws on Education
David Carleton

Student's Guide to Landmark Congressional Laws on the First Amendment
Clyde E. Willis

Student's Guide to Landmark Congressional Laws on Youth
Kathleen Uradnik

Student's Guide to Landmark Congressional Laws on Social Security and
Welfare
Steven G. Livingston

STUDENT'S GUIDE TO LANDMARK CONGRESSIONAL LAWS
ON CIVIL RIGHTS

MARCUS D. POHLMANN
and LINDA VALLAR WHISENHUNT

STUDENT'S GUIDE TO
LANDMARK CONGRESSIONAL LAWS
John R. Vile, Series Adviser

Greenwood Press
Westport, Connecticut • London

342.085
P748

WITHDRAWN
LIBRARY
MILWAUKEE AREA TECHNICAL COLLEGE
Milwaukee Campus

Library of Congress Cataloging-in-Publication Data

Pohlmann, Marcus D., 1950–
    Student's guide to landmark congressional laws on civil rights / Marcus D. Pohlmann
and Linda Vallar Whisenhunt.
        p. ; cm.—(Student's guide to landmark congressional laws, ISSN 1537–3150)
    Includes bibliographical references and index.
    ISBN 0–313–31385–7 (alk. paper)
    1. Civil rights—United States—History—Sources. I. Whisenhunt, Linda Vallar.
II. Title. III. Series.
    KF4749.P626   2002
    342.73'085—dc21   2002276830

British Library Cataloguing in Publication Data is available.

Copyright © 2002 by Marcus D. Pohlmann and Linda Vallar Whisenhunt

All rights reserved. No portion of this book may be
reproduced, by any process or technique, without
the express written consent of the publisher.

Library of Congress Catalog Card Number: 2002276830
ISBN: 0–313–31385–7
ISSN: 1537–3150

First published in 2002

Greenwood Press, 88 Post Road West, Westport, CT 06881
An imprint of Greenwood Publishing Group, Inc.
www.greenwood.com

Printed in the United States of America

The paper used in this book complies with the
Permanent Paper Standard issued by the National
Information Standards Organization (Z39.48–1984).

10 9 8 7 6 5 4 3 2 1

This book is dedicated to

Lisa M. Pohlmann, who teaches by example every day.
—Marcus D. Pohlmann

Mark N. Whisenhunt, with love and appreciation.
—Linda Vallar Whisenhunt

Contents

Series Foreword by John R. Vile   xi

Acknowledgments   xv

Introduction   xvii

Timeline   xxiii

Part I: The Slavery Period   1

 1. Articles of Confederation (1776)   3

 2. Declaration of Independence (1776)   8

 3. Northwest Ordinance (1787)   13

 4. United States Constitution (1787)   16

 5. Fugitive Slave Act (1793)   22

 6. Slave Importation Act (1807)   27

 7. Missouri Compromise (1820)   35

 8. Compromise of 1850 (1850)   40

 9. Kansas-Nebraska Act (1854)   46

10. Constitution of the Confederate States of America (1861)   52

11. Confiscation Acts (1861 and 1862)   56

12.   Emancipation Proclamation (1863)   62

Part II: Postwar Reconstruction   **69**

13.   Freedmen's Bureau (1865)   71

14.   Thirteenth Amendment to the United States Constitution
(1865)   78

15.   Civil Rights Act (1866)   82

16.   Reconstruction Act (1867)   85

17.   Fourteenth Amendment to the United States Constitution
(1868)   92

18.   Fifteenth Amendment to the United States Constitution
(1870)   102

19.   Enforcement Act (1870)   106

20.   Klan Act (1871)   115

21.   Civil Rights Act (1875)   123

Part III: Civil Rights Era   **129**

22.   Executive Order 8802 (1941)   133

23.   Executive Order 9808 (1946)   139

24.   Executive Order 9980 (1948)   145

25.   Executive Order 9981 (1948)   152

26.   Executive Order 10730 (1957)   157

27.   Civil Rights Act (1957)   163

28.   Civil Rights Act (1960)   173

29.   Executive Order 10925 (1961)   183

30.   Executive Order 11053 (1962)   194

31.   Executive Order 11063 (1962)   199

32. Twenty-Fourth Amendment to the United States
Constitution (1964)   207

33. Civil Rights Act (1964)   210

34. Voting Rights Act (1965)   235

35. Executive Order 11246 (1965)   250

36. Fair Housing Act (1968)   261

Bibliography   275

Index   277

Series Foreword

Most of the Founding Fathers who met at the Constitutional Convention in Philadelphia in the summer of 1787 probably anticipated that the legislative branch would be the most powerful of the three branches of the national government that they created. For all practical purposes, this was the only branch of government with which the onetime colonists had experience under the Articles of Confederation. Moreover, the delegates discussed this branch first and at greatest length at the convention, the dispute over representation in this body was one of the convention's most contentious issues, and the Founding Fathers made it the subject of the first and longest article of the new Constitution.

With the president elected indirectly through an electoral college and the members of the Supreme Court appointed by the president with the advice and consent of the Senate and serving for life terms, the framers of the Constitution had little doubt that Congress—and especially the House of Representatives, whose members were directly elected by the people for short two-year terms—would be closest to the people. As a consequence, they invested Congress with the awesome "power of the purse" that had been at issue in the revolutionary dispute with Great Britain, where the colonists' position had been encapsulated in the phrase "no taxation without representation." The framers also entrusted Congress with the more general right to adopt laws to carry out a variety of enumerated powers and other laws "necessary and proper" to the implementation of these powers—the basis for the doctrine of implied powers.

Wars and the threats of wars have sometimes tilted the modern
balance of power toward the president, who has gained in a media
age from his position as a single individual. Still, Congress has ar-
guably been the most powerful branch of government over the long
haul, and one might expect its power to increase with the demise
of the Cold War. Especially in the aftermath of President Franklin
D. Roosevelt's New Deal and President Lyndon B. Johnson's Great
Society program, the number and complexity of laws have increased
with the complexity of modern society and the multitude of demands that citizens have placed on modern governments. Courts
have upheld expansive interpretations of federal powers under the
commerce clause, the war-powers provisions, and the power to tax
and spend for the general welfare, and in recent elections Democratic and Republican candidates alike have often called for expansive new federal programs.

It has been noted that there are 297 words in the Ten Com-
mandments, 463 in the Bill of Rights, 266 in the Gettysburg Address, and more than 26,000 in a federal directive regulating the
price of cabbage. Although the U.S. Constitution can be carried in
one's pocket, the compilation of federal laws in the *U.S. Code* and
the *U.S. Code Annotated* requires many volumes, not generally available in high-school and public libraries. Perhaps because of this
modern prolixity and complexity, students often consider the analysis of laws to be the arcane domain of lawyers and law reviewers.
Ironically, scholars, like this author, who focus on law, and especially constitutional law, tend to devote more attention to the language of judicial decisions interpreting laws than to the laws
themselves.

Because knowledge of laws and their impact needs to be made
more widely accessible, this series on Landmark Congressional Laws
presents and examines laws relating to a number of important topics. These currently include education, First Amendment rights,
civil rights, the environment, the rights of young people, women's
rights, and health and social security. Each subject is a matter of
importance that should be of key interest to high-school and college students. A college professor experienced in communicating
ideas to undergraduates has compiled each of these volumes. Each
author has selected major laws in his or her subject area and has
described the politics of these laws, considering such aspects as
their adoption, their interpretation, and their impact.

The laws in each volume are arranged chronologically. The entry on each law features an introduction that explains the law, its significance, and its place within the larger tapestry of legislation on the issues. A selection from the actual text of the law itself follows the introduction. This arrangement thus provides ready access to texts that are often difficult for students to find while highlighting major provisions, often taken from literally hundreds of pages, that students and scholars might spend hours to distill on their own.

These volumes are designed to be profitable to high-school and college students who are examining various public policy issues. They should also help interested citizens, scholars, and legal practitioners needing a quick, but thorough and accurate, introduction to a specific area of public policy-making. Although each book is designed to cover highlights of the entire history of federal legislation within a given subject area, the authors of these volumes have also designed them so that individuals who simply need to know the background and major provisions of a single law (the Civil Rights Act of 1964, for example) can quickly do so.

The Founding Fathers of the United States devised a system of federalism dividing power between the state and national governments. Thus, in many areas of legislation, even a complete overview of national laws will prove inadequate unless it is supplemented with knowledge of state and even local laws. This is duly noted in entries on laws where national legislation is necessarily incomplete and where powers are shared among the three layers of government. The U.S. system utilizes a system of separation of powers that divides authority among three branches of the national government. Thus, while these volumes keep the focus on legislation, they also note major judicial decisions and presidential initiatives relating to the laws covered.

Although the subjects of this series are worthy objects of study in their own right, they are especially appropriate topics for students and scholars in a system of representative democracy like the United States where citizens who are at least eighteen years of age have the right to choose those who will represent them in public office. In government, those individuals, like James Madison, Abraham Lincoln, and Woodrow Wilson, who have acquired the longest and clearest view of the past are frequently those who can also see the farthest into the future. This series is presented in the hope that it will help students both to understand the past and to equip themselves for future lives of good citizenship.

This editor wishes to thank his friends at Greenwood Press, his colleagues both at his own university and at other institutions of higher learning who have done such an able job of highlighting and explaining the laws that are the focus of this series, and those students, scholars, and citizens who have responded by reading and utilizing these volumes. When the Founding Fathers drew up a constitution, they depended not only on a set of structures and rights but also on the public-spiritedness and education of future citizens. When Benjamin Franklin was asked what form of government the Founding Fathers had created, he reportedly responded, "A republic, if you can keep it." When we inform ourselves and think deeply about the government's role in major areas of public policy, we honor the faith and foresight of those who bequeathed this government to us.

John R. Vile
Middle Tennessee State University

Hope Franklin and Alfred A. Moss, *From Slavery to Freedom: A History of African Americans* (1994); Hanes Walton, Jr., and Robert C. Smith, *American Politics and the African American Quest for Universal Freedom* (2000); Albert Blaustein and Robert Zangrando, *Civil Rights and the Black American* (1968); Jeffrey Schultz et al., *Encyclopedia of Minorities in American Politics: African Americans and Asian Americans* (2000); and Bernard Schwartz, ed., *Statutory History of the United States: Civil Rights* (1970).

FOCUS

The book's focus is on the civil rights laws that emerged from the struggle of African Americans to attain equality. This perspective was chosen given the unique history of African Americans in the United States, as well as their central place in the movement for the extension of civil rights. Many of these laws apply to other groups as well because the basic principle remains equal protection under the law regardless of the characteristics of one's birth.

It should be noted that, although the book focuses on congressionally passed legislation, it also considers key related components of constitutional law and pivotal executive orders. The constitutional laws provide an important legal underpinning for the subsequent statutory laws. Presidential executive orders were of particular importance from 1875 to 1957. During this period, Congress was divided in a manner that precluded virtually any civil rights legislation from emerging. From Franklin D. Roosevelt to Richard Nixon, executive orders filled the legislative void, slowly advancing civil rights in the face of mounting protests and the intense lobbying conducted by such organizations as the National Association for the Advancement of Colored People (NAACP). No discussion of American legislation on civil rights would be complete without the inclusion of these executive orders.

POLITICAL AND ECONOMIC CONTEXT

After more than two centuries, the institution of slavery was finally abolished following the Civil War. Nonetheless, the legacies of slavery endured. Integration and equal justice met with considerable opposition, and nearly another century had passed before even the legal foundations of this discrimination began to be dismantled. Decades of struggle for civil rights, however, finally did

Introduction

This book describes thirty-six separate laws that have been integral in the effort to secure civil rights and civil liberties for African Americans. The list is not exhaustive; nonetheless, each law covered is a "landmark" in that it has had a significant impact on this endeavor.

The entries in this book are discussed in chronological order and are subdivided into three primary eras. The slavery period began with the arrival of black indentured servants in 1619 and culminated in the Emancipation Proclamation of 1863. The period of postwar reconstruction occurred from the end of the Civil War until the turn of the century. The civil rights era spanned the entire twentieth century and peaked with the adoption of the nation's three most sweeping civil rights laws in the 1960s. A historical timeline has been included at the outset to indicate how the laws coincide with other significant events.

The chapters begin with a synopsis of the law under consideration, followed by a brief discussion of the historical context within which each arose. This context includes the impetus for the law, the issues at hand, the political battles fought to attain passage, major judicial interpretations of the law, and the law's subsequent impact. Finally, the specifics of the law itself are outlined and described, and select excerpts are provided, including brief definitions of the more difficult legal terms.

The book benefited greatly from information contained in several classic historical accounts as well as other excellent legal compilations. In particular, these secondary sources included John

Acknowledgments

No project can be successful without the help of many individuals. This book is no exception. We are grateful for the students, colleagues, friends, and family members who have supported us in this endeavor. In particular, Jennifer Keirce, Anna Smith, and Mitchell Ryan were outstanding research assistants. Russell Wigginton, Kenneth Goings, and Brian Murphy were invaluable resource people. We thank our editors, John Vile, Kevin Ohe, and Frank Saunders, for all their help and patience. Rhodes College generously provided grant and travel monies through its Faculty Development Fund. And last, but certainly not least, we thank Barb Pohlmann and Mark Whisenhunt, Katherine and Meredith Whisenhunt, and Justin Pohlmann for all their unwavering love and support.

begin to succeed following World War II. The right to register and vote came to be enforced directly by the U.S. Department of Justice. Schools were forcibly desegregated. Housing discrimination was outlawed. Not only were employers barred from discriminating openly, many were compelled to search for qualified black applicants when positions were available. Such legal gains have only recently begun to eradicate centuries of political and economic inequities.

Political Participation

For nearly a century after the abrupt end of Reconstruction in 1877, the majority of African Americans were effectively denied their constitutionally guaranteed right to vote. With the assistance of civil rights and voting rights acts passed in the 1960s and 1970s, however, blacks finally were able to register and vote more easily. The results were dramatic. For example, whereas there were fewer than 500 black elected officials in the entire country in 1965, that number increased to more than 8,000 in the subsequent thirty years.[1]

Blacks in Congress

From the founding of the nation until 1869, not one African American served in the U.S. Congress. From 1869 until 1901, only twenty blacks served in the House of Representatives and two in the Senate, all of whom represented reconstructed Southern states. Black congresspersons reappeared on Capitol Hill in 1929, however, and their numbers grew steadily beginning in the 1940s. Chicago sent the only blacks to Congress in the period from 1929 to 1944, although the black contingent gradually increased to nine members in 1969 and reached a peak of forty in the early 1990s.[2]

The Congressional Black Caucus, which normally includes all of these members, collects data, formulates budgetary proposals, and initiates investigations—for example, the investigation of the 1971 police killings of Chicago Black Panthers Mark Clark and Fred Hampton. They also have lobbied presidents on both domestic and foreign policy matters—for example, pressing for aggressive civil rights enforcement at home and justice for predominantly black populations in nations such as Haiti and South Africa.[3] In addition, the Black Caucus orients new black congresspersons prior to their arrival on Capitol Hill.[4]

Education

An area of marked gain has been in education. For example, whereas more than 80 percent of all African Americans were completely illiterate in 1870, very few are today.[5] In addition, racial differentials in school years completed and college enrollment have been reduced considerably. The black high school dropout rate, for instance, has been reduced and is now only marginally higher than the corresponding white dropout rate.[6]

Income

Although black unemployment has remained roughly twice the white rate, college-educated blacks and younger, two-parent black families are now doing nearly as well or better than comparable whites.[7] Nevertheless, despite affirmative action efforts, approximately half of the black managers and professionals continue to be employed either directly or indirectly by government.[8] Meanwhile, the story is not nearly as encouraging for the large majority of black males without a college education. In addition, black households are more than three times as likely as white households to earn less than $5,000 per year, and they are more than twice as likely to earn between $5,000 and $10,000.[9]

Wealth

During the era of slavery, millions of blacks were denied the right to own property, and even free blacks faced a dual wage system and other forms of racial discrimination that made it quite difficult for them to accumulate wealth. By the 1990s, the median white household possessed wealth worth $44,408; the figure for the median black household was $4,604.[10] Although African Americans represented 13 percent of the U.S. population, they held less than one-half of 1 percent of the nation's wealth[11]; 2 percent of the nation's capital stock[12]; and, although they owned 3 percent of the businesses, those businesses tended to be small and received only 1 percent of all gross receipts.[13]

Poverty

Whereas 55 percent of all blacks were officially poor in 1959, a growing economy and a federal War on Poverty helped reduce that figure to 32 percent by 1969; and it reached an all-time low of 27 percent in 1997.[14] Compared to whites, however, blacks are three times more likely to be poor, and the median income of poor black families is about 20 percent lower than of poor white families.[15]

NOTES

1. David A. Bositis, *Black Elected Officials* (Washington, D.C.: Joint Center for Political and Economic Studies, 2002).

2. Ibid.

3. For an example of foreign policy influence, see Steven Holmes, "With Persuasion and Muscle, Black Caucus Reshapes Haiti Policy," *New York Times,* July 14, 1994, p. A18. Also see the Anti-Apartheid Act of 1986.

4. For example, see Graeme Browning, "Strength in Numbers for Hill Group?" *National Journal,* November 28, 1992, pp. 2732–33.

5. Department of Commerce, Bureau of the Census, *Statistical Abstracts of the United States* (Washington, D.C.: U.S. Government Printing Office, various years); Department of Commerce, Bureau of the Census, Current Population Reports, P-23, No. 80, *The Social and Economic Status of the Black Population in the United States: A Historical Overview, 1790–1978* (Washington, D.C.: U.S. Government Printing Office, 1978); Department of Education, Office of Civil Rights, periodic reports (Washington, D.C.: U.S. Government Printing Office, various years); *American Council of Education Reports* (Washington, D.C.: American Council of Education, various years).

6. Department of Commerce, Bureau of the Census, *The Black Population in the United States* (Washington, D.C.: U.S. Government Printing Office, 2001); Department of Commerce, Bureau of the Census, *Characteristics of the Black Population* (Washington, D.C.: U.S. Government Printing Office, 2001); Department of Commerce, Bureau of the Census, Current Population Reports, P-20, No. 476, *Educational Attainment in the United States: March 1993 and 1992* (Washington, D.C.: U.S. Government Printing Office, 1994).

In 2000, the Associated Press reported that the comparative dropout rates were 16.3% for blacks and 8.2 percent for whites. See Greg Toppo, "High School Graduation Hits Record Rate of 86.5%," in the Memphis *Commercial Appeal,* November 16, 2001, P. A20.

7. Department of Commerce, Bureau of the Census, *Money Income of Families: Aggregate, Mean and Per Capita, by Family Characteristics* (Washington, D.C.: U.S. Government Printing Office, various years); Alan Krueger, "Equality in Hiring Remains the Key to Civil Rights Goals," *New York Times,* June 22, 2000, p. C2.

8. For example, see Morton Kondracke, "The Two Black Americas," *New Republic,* February 6, 1989, p. 18.

9. Department of Commerce, Bureau of the Census, *Money Income of Families,* various years.

10. Department of Commerce, Bureau of the Census, *Household Wealth and Asset Ownership* (Washington, D.C.: GPO, various years).

11. Jude Wanniski, "To Aid the Poor, Cut Capital Gains Taxes,"*New York Times,* July 25, 1989.

12. See Jeremiah Cotton, "Towards a Theory and Strategy for Black Economic Development," in *Race, Politics, and Economic Development*, ed. (New York: Verso, 1992), p. 13.

13. Eugene Carlson, "The No. 1 State?" *Wall Street Journal*, April 3, 1992, p. R6.

14. Robert Pear, "Black and Hispanic Poverty Falls, Reducing Overall Rate for Nation,"*New York Times*, September 25, 1998, p. A1; Department of Commerce, *Income, Poverty, and Valuation of Noncash Benefits: 1993* ('Washington, D.C.: GPO, 1993), Tables K and 20; Department of Commerce, Bureau of the Census, *Statistical Abstracts of the United States* (Washington, D.C. GPO, yearly); Cynthia Rexroat, *The Declining Economic Status of Black Children* (Washington, D.C.: Joint Center for Political and Economic Studies, 1994).

15. Billy Tidwell, ed., *State of Black America* (New York: National Urban League: various years); Pear, "Black and Hispanic Poverty Falls."

Timeline

1619   The first twenty black indentured servants arrive in Jamestown, Virginia.

1637   The first American-based slave ship, the *Desire*, begins transporting black Africans for sale in the New World.

1641   Slavery begins to be sanctioned by American law.

1688   German Mennonites join British-born residents and others in pressing for the abolition of slavery.

1776   The Articles of Confederation are passed.

       The Declaration of Independence is signed.

1777   Vermont is the first U.S. territory to abolish slavery, followed by the Northwest Territories a year later.

1787   The Northwest Ordinance calls for the eventual outlawing of slavery in the new territories but allows for the capture and return of runaway slaves apprehended therein.

1787   The United States Constitution is ratified.

       Revolutionary America finds 92 percent of its roughly 750,000 blacks still enslaved. Free blacks constitute about 2 percent of the national population, and very few of them are allowed to vote.

1793   The Fugitive Slave Act requires the federal government to assist in the return of runaway slaves.

       The Tenth Amendment lays the legal groundwork for claims of states' rights.

1800   Slaves number over one million and reside almost exclusively in the South. They are bound by slave codes that strictly limit their rights to such privileges as owning property and learning to read. Meanwhile, approximately 60,000 free blacks reside about equally in the North and South, and some of them even own slaves. Their rights have been eroding since the American Revolution, and many face being enslaved as a result of kidnapping or a judicial reversal of their status.

1807 The Slave Importation Act prohibits any further legal importation of slaves.

1819 The Missouri Compromise establishes a boundary line to delineate whether newly admitted states are to be free states or slave states.

1829 Free black David Walker begins publishing *Walker's Appeal,* which calls for blacks to rise up against slavery, using violence if necessary. Soon there are nearly fifty black abolitionist groups.

1831 As slave resistance escalates, Nat Turner leads a major slave revolt in Virginia. In just two days, approximately seventy slaves rise up and execute about that many whites. Other forms of slave resistance include arson, sabotage, work slowdowns, running away, and suicide.

The first National Negro Convention convenes in Philadelphia.

With the number of slaves topping the 2 million mark, white reformer William Lloyd Garrison uses his publication, the *Liberator,* to press for an immediate and total end to slavery. The white abolition movement, calling primarily for nonviolent passive resistance, is beginning to become a significant force. A variety of tactics are pursued, including the formation of the Liberty Party.

1834 As the black presence increases in Northern cities, racism flourishes. In one of the worst racial riots of the 1830s and 1840s, white mobs storm black neighborhoods in Philadelphia.

1838 Frederick Douglass escapes his enslavement, ultimately to become an important national leader and spokesperson for his race. He uses his publication, the *North Star,* to press for an end to slavery and later an antilynching law, advises presidents, and voluntarily recruits blacks for the Union Army when the Civil War erupts.

1850 J.W. Loguen, Harriet Tubman, and others organize and operate the Underground Railroad, which by this time helps roughly 1,000 blacks a year to escape slavery.

The Compromise of 1850 allows California to be admitted as a free state and Utah to make the decision for itself. It also ends the slave trade in Washington, D.C., in return for a stricter enforcement of the Fugitive Slave Act.

1852 Harriet Beecher Stowe's novel *Uncle Tom's Cabin* dramatizes some of the abject cruelty imposed by slavery.

1853 Sojourner Truth rises to speak at the Fourth National Women's Rights Convention. Posing the question, "Ain't I a woman?," and fending off racist jeers, she speaks of what it means to be black and female at that time.

The National Council of Colored People is formed, conducting some of the many black political conventions held prior to the Civil War.

1854   The Kansas-Nebraska Act nullifies a significant portion of the Missouri Com-
       promise, allowing Kansas and Nebraska to decide their own slave status
       despite lying north of the line of demarcation established by the earlier
       Missouri Compromise.

1855   Wilberforce University is founded as an extension of the African Methodist
       Episcopal Church, and it reflects the growing effort on the part of blacks
       to provide their own education for black children.

1857   In *Dred Scott v. Sanford*, the U.S. Supreme Court explicitly declares that the
       now nearly 4 million slaves are property of their masters and not citizens;
       they have no standing to sue, they have no constitutional rights, and their
       owners' possession of them is protected by the due process clause of the
       Fifth Amendment. The decision also challenges the federal government's
       right to regulate slavery in the territories.

1859   Discrimination continues in the North. Only six states allow blacks to vote;
       public schools are generally segregated, with black public schools being
       inferior; some states preclude black testimony if a white is a party in the
       legal case; and others bar black immigration altogether.

       Radical abolitionist John Brown unsuccessfully leads twenty-two men in a
       raid on a federal arsenal in Harpers Ferry, Virginia. The goal was to use
       the captured weapons to help set off a general slave revolt across the South.

1860   The Civil War begins following the election of Abraham Lincoln as presi-
       dent and the Confederate attack on Fort Sumter, South Carolina.

1861   The Constitution of the Confederate States of America is adopted in Mont-
       gomery, Alabama.

       The Federal Confiscation Act allows for the seizure of slaves in all but the
       loyal border states where even the Fugitive Slave Act would continue to be
       enforced. Seized slaves are to be emancipated but subject to being con-
       scripted into the service of the Union's war effort.

1863   The Emancipation Proclamation frees all slaves dwelling in states that had
       seceded from the Union.

1865   The Freedmen's Bureau is created to provide former slaves and displaced
       Southern whites with education, relief assistance, and resettlement, and to
       assist in the disposition of abandoned property.

       The Thirteenth Amendment bans slavery and involuntary servitude in the
       United States and its territories, unless the involuntary servitude is part of
       a legitimate punishment for a crime.

       President Abraham Lincoln is assassinated.

       In Savannah, Georgia, General William T. Sherman expropriates thirty
       miles of Southern coastline and grants it to former slaves as an exclusive
       black settlement. Allotted forty acres per family, some 40,000 blacks quickly
       move there. Within months, however, President Andrew Johnson has re-

turned it all to its Confederate owners. Throughout the South, recently freed blacks find themselves without property and are often forced to depend on former slave masters for employment.

1866   Reactionary race riots resume. In Memphis, Tennessee, for instance, a white rampage leaves forty-six blacks and two white sympathizers dead, and ninety homes, twelve schools, and two churches burned.

The Civil Rights Act attacks Southern "black codes" by guaranteeing blacks equal protection under the law, essentially overturning the Dred Scott decision, which had affirmed the legality of slavery.

1867   The Reconstruction Act provides a mechanism by which ex–Confederate states can reconstitute their governments in order to be readmitted into the Union.

The Ku Klux Klan is founded as one of a number of reactionary white organizations.

1868   The Fourteenth Amendment prohibits states from abridging federal "privileges and immunities"; denying life, liberty, or property without "due process of law"; and denying "equal protection of the laws."

1869   The National Negro Labor Union is formed because blacks are generally excluded from the early white labor movement, a practice that would continue well into the twentieth century.

1870   The Fifteenth Amendment declares that the right to vote is "not to be denied or abridged by the United States or by any State on account of race, color, or previous condition of servitude."

1871   The Enforcement Acts establish federal sanctions for interfering with another person's civil rights, especially a black's right to vote. They also allow for federal election supervisors to oversee registration and voting procedures.

The Klan Act establishes federal criminal sanctions and enforcement mechanisms to be used against those denying others equal protection under the law.

1874   The Democratic Party, based in the South, wins control of the House of Representatives and makes significant gains in the Senate.

1875   The Civil Rights Act attempts to outlaw racial segregation in public accommodations, and it prohibits the exclusion of blacks from jury duty.

1876   Reconstruction officially ends when President Rutherford B. Hayes trades it for enough Southern votes in the House to win an extremely close presidential election over Samuel Tilden. Northern troops will no longer remain in the South to protect the rights of former slaves.

1896   In *Plessy v. Ferguson*, the U.S. Supreme Court declares that legal separation of the races is not a violation of blacks' constitutional rights: "separate but equal" is equal.

1900   By this time, all Southern states have changed their laws and constitutions in order to create the legal disenfranchisement and segregation of blacks, 90 percent of whom still reside in the South. In terms of voting, a combination of grandfather clauses, literacy tests, poll taxes, all-white Democratic primaries, administrative discrimination, and violence or threats of violence have disenfranchised over 95 percent of all Southern black voters.

Some of the first direct action begins when blacks boycott segregated streetcars in more than twenty-five cities over the following six years. Although boycotting is a non-violent technique, some violent confrontations do occur.

1905   W.E.B. Du Bois, Monroe Trotter, and other black leaders organize the Niagara Movement, designed to press for equal rights and black solidarity. This movement gives rise to a number of black political conferences including a major one held in Amenia, New York, in 1916.

1909   Growing out of the Niagara Movement, the NAACP is created primarily to press for black rights by means of lobbying and court cases. W.E.B. Du Bois edits its official publication, the *Crisis*.

1910   The National Urban League is founded.

1914   Marcus Garvey founds the Universal Negro Improvement Association in Jamaica and soon brings it to the United States. It is grounded in the principles of black pride and a separatism that ultimately involves renewed efforts to help blacks return to Africa.

1915   The U.S. Supreme Court, siding with the NAACP, declares the grandfather clause unconstitutional. No longer is it to be more difficult for blacks to vote simply because their grandfathers were not registered.

Spawned by acts of violence, the mechanization of Southern agriculture, and industrial job opportunities in the North, the first major wave of the Great Migration begins, and migrating blacks are assisted in adjusting to their new environment by the National Urban League and a variety of black newspapers. By 1970, some 6.5 million blacks will have migrated to the North, resulting in half of the black population residing there.

1917   Racial rioting occurs in East Saint Louis. Typical of such rioting at the time, mobs of whites attack black ghettos in retaliation for alleged incidents.

1920   The Nineteenth Amendment legally enfranchises half the black population—women.

1921   An antilynching bill is finally introduced in Congress. Despite the fact that more than 3,000 blacks have been the victims of lynch mobs since 1884, the bill is stopped by a filibuster in the Senate.

1925   A. Philip Randolph founds the Brotherhood of Sleeping Car Porters and Maids, a black labor union created as a result of continuing racial discrimination on the part of white unions. Such segregation would persist for another three decades.

1929   The Great Depression hits blacks particularly hard, leaving them three to four times as likely as other Americans to be receiving public assistance.

1932   The U.S. Supreme Court strikes down whites-only primary elections.

1934   The newly created Federal Housing Administration openly sanctions racial segregation in housing for its first ten years of existence.

1936   The shift of black voters to the national Democratic Party, first noticeable in 1928, is cemented when Franklin D. Roosevelt receives a majority of black votes.

   The National Negro Congress emerges as an umbrella organization for the civil rights struggle, which would include the formation of groups such as the Southern Conference for Human Welfare.

1941   Despite the beginning of U.S. involvement in World War II, A. Philip Randolph threatens a huge, all-black march on Washington to protest racial discrimination. He ultimately calls it off in return for the establishment of the Fair Employment Practices Commission.

   President Roosevelt's Executive Order 8802 prohibits racial discrimination in defense-related industries and in government, and it creates the Fair Employment Practices Commission to monitor these employment decisions.

   The U.S. Supreme Court rules that the federal government can step in and regulate primary elections, as they are an "integral part" of the right to vote.

1942   The Congress of Racial Equality (CORE) is formed and is soon organizing freedom rides, sit-ins, boycotts, rent strikes, and other protest actions as a way of challenging continuing racial discrimination.

1943   The Detroit riots are some of the most destructive of a series of black ghetto revolts, including a major one in Harlem, New York, in 1935.

1946   President Harry S Truman's Executive Order 9808 establishes the President's Committee on Civil Rights to investigate the status of civil rights in the United States.

1948   President Truman's Executive Order 9980 promises blacks fair treatment in federal employment and establishes a Fair Employment Board to monitor and enforce it.

   President Truman's Executive Order 9981 desegregates the military.

   The Democratic Party adopts a civil rights plank at its presidential nominating convention, prompting a number of Southern delegates to bolt and form the States' Rights Party, nearly costing Truman the election.

1954   In *Brown v. Board of Education*, the U.S. Supreme Court reverses its 1896 decision and strikes down "separate but equal" as "inherently unequal." The same legal issues will be addressed again thirty-two years later, however, as racially segregated schools will continue to be a problem.

1955   Martin Luther King, Jr., helps organize the successful Montgomery bus boy-
        cott.

1957   Out of King's Montgomery Improvement Association is formed the South-
        ern Christian Leadership Council (SCLC) to continue to organize direct
        action against racial discrimination in the South.

        The Civil Rights Act establishes a nonpartisan Civil Rights Commission to
        monitor civil rights progress.

        President Dwight D. Eisenhower's Executive Order 10730 authorizes use of
        the National Guard to assist in the desegregation of schools in Little Rock,
        Arkansas.

1960   Black students sit at a segregated lunch counter in Greensboro, North Car-
        olina, touching off a wave of such sit-ins across the South. Ultimately, their
        arrests and convictions are struck down by the U.S. Supreme Court.

        The Civil Rights Act empowers federal referees to facilitate voting.

1961   School segregation persists, and South Carolina, Alabama, Georgia, Missis-
        sippi, and Louisiana still do not have a single integrated public school.

        Federal troops are dispatched to protect civil rights demonstrators engaged
        in freedom rides on interstate buses.

        President John F. Kennedy's Executive Order 10925 creates the President's
        Equal Employment Opportunity Committee.

1962   President Kennedy's Executive Order 11053 authorizes the use of federal
        troops to restore order after riots occur at the University of Mississippi.

        President Kennedy's Executive Order 11063 prohibits discrimination in
        housing either loaned or directly financed by the federal government.

1963   Alabama's Governor George Wallace stands defiantly "in the schoolhouse
        door" to prevent black students from enrolling at the University of Alabama.

        With more than 200,000 in attendance and capped by Martin Luther King's
        famous "I Have a Dream" speech, the march on Washington is probably
        the most dramatic of a number of nonviolent protest marches that have
        been occurring across the South and are beginning to appear in the North
        as well.

        As the world watches escalating violence against peaceful black protesters,
        President Kennedy warns of impending federal action. Civil rights activist
        Medgar Evers is gunned down on the day of that speech, and the president
        is assassinated within two months.

1964   The Twenty-fourth Amendment bars poll taxes.

        The Civil Rights Act directly involves the federal government in the enforce-
        ment of an extensive list of civil rights, including voting, public accommo-
        dations, public facilities, federally assisted programs, education, and
        employment.

1965   Black mobs riot in the Watts ghetto of Los Angeles, the worst racial unrest since 1943 and one of 164 such outbreaks to occur between 1962 and 1968. These revolts leave more than 100 people dead, thousands wounded, thousands more arrested, and hundreds of millions of dollars' worth of property damage.

The Voting Rights Act prohibits literacy tests and comparable vote-impeding devices and provides federal examiners to conduct registration and observe voting as needed.

President Lyndon B. Johnson declares a War on Poverty, which ultimately leads to the creation of a host of federal programs, including Head Start, VISTA, the Job Corps, and Legal Aid.

President Johnson's Executive Order 11246 prohibits discrimination by federal contractors and requires them to take positive steps to hire and promote qualified minorities and women.

1966   The term "black power" is first used by Stokely Carmichael and CORE's Floyd McKissick. Black power conferences begin in Newark, New Jersey, and spread to other large cities during the next two years.

A U.S. Supreme Court's decision eliminates poll taxes in state elections as well as federal elections.

1967   Thurgood Marshall is the first African American ever appointed to the U.S. Supreme Court.

Cleveland's Carl Stokes is the first black mayor elected in a major U.S. city.

1968   Martin Luther King, Jr., is assassinated.

The Fair Housing Act bars racial discrimination in the advertising, sale, rental, or financing of most housing units.

Richard M. Nixon and George Wallace together receive more than two-thirds of the presidential vote, marking what now appears to be the beginning of the end of the governing New Deal electoral coalition.

A tent city is erected as part of the Poor Peoples' March on Washington, D.C.

1970   The 1965 Voting Rights Act is renewed.

1971   The U.S. Supreme Court rules that busing is a legitimate tool for fighting school segregation, although it is later limited to exclude busing across city-suburb boundaries.

1972   The first National Black Political Convention is held the same year that Shirley Chisholm becomes the first black candidate to mount a formidable campaign for the office of president of the United States.

The 1964 Civil Rights Act is amended to enhance the enforcement power of the Equal Employment Opportunity Commission.

1974   The U.S. Supreme Court determines that heavy reliance on neighborhood property taxes is not a discriminatory way to fund public schools, despite tremendous disparities in neighborhood wealth. A few individual states have found otherwise and have introduced a more redistributive method of school funding.

1975   The 1965 Voting Rights Act is renewed.

1978   *University of California v. Bakke* is the first in a series of Supreme Court decisions clarifying the scope of allowable "affirmative action."

1980   The census confirms black majorities in large cities such as Baltimore, Detroit, Newark, and Washington, D.C., and impending majorities in Chicago, Cleveland, Memphis, Philadelphia, and Saint Louis.

        Ronald Reagan is elected president of the United States, with implications for the enforcement of civil rights laws. For example, his administration ceases to enforce affirmative action regulations and argues against them in federal court.

        Ghetto unrest in Miami includes beatings, maimings, burning, looting, and sniper fire, leaving eighteen dead, more than 200 seriously wounded, 750 arrested, and more than $100 million in property damage. Smaller incidents occur in Wichita, Kansas; Chattanooga, Tennessee; and Orlando, Florida.

1981   Blacks and laborites join in a massive march on Washington, D.C., as they do again two years later.

1982   The 1965 Voting Rights Act is renewed.

1984   The U.S. Supreme Court declares that existing federal law does not allow the federal government to cut financial aid to an entire institution when only one of its branches has violated federal guidelines. The decision poses dilemmas for federal enforcement of a variety of civil rights provisions.

1988   Congress passes the Civil Rights Restoration Act over President Reagan's veto. Its primary purpose is to allow entire institutions to be denied federal assistance if any of their parts is found to be illegally discriminating.

1989   Virginia's L. Douglas Wilder becomes the nation's first black governor.

        The U.S. Supreme Court's *Richmond v. Croson* decision severely limits the lower courts' ability to require affirmative action quotas on the basis of clear statistical evidence of prior discrimination.

1991   An amendment of the 1964 Civil Rights Act addresses portions of several Supreme Court opinions, most notably requiring employers to justify their job performance criteria if clear statistical evidence of job discrimination is found.

I

THE SLAVERY PERIOD

Recognized as legal by constitutional provision, statutes, and case law, the institution of slavery continued in the United States and its territories until the Civil War. The Articles of Confederation (1) and later the United States Constitution (4) allowed for the existence of slavery, while the Declaration of Independence (2) carefully avoided the subject. The Northwest Ordinance (3), passed in 1787, called for the eventual outlawing of slavery in the new territories but allowed for the capture and return of runaway slaves apprehended therein. The 1793 Fugitive Slave Act (5) even required the federal government to assist in the return of runaway slaves. Meanwhile, free blacks were barred from such institutions as the militia, navy, marines, and postal service.

The Slave Importation Act (6), passed in 1807, prohibited any further legal importation of slaves, and the 1820 Missouri Compromise (7) set up a boundary line to delineate whether newly admitted states were to be free states or were to be permitted to have slavery. The Compromise of 1850 (8) allowed California to be admitted as a free state and Utah to make the decision for itself; it also ended the slave trade in Washington, D.C., in return for stricter enforcement of the Fugitive Slave Act. The Kansas-Nebraska Act (9) nullified a significant portion of the Missouri Compromise, however, allowing Kansas and Nebraska to decide their own slave status despite lying north of the line of demarcation established by the earlier Missouri Compromise.

It was not long before the Southern states were in complete rebellion, as exemplified by the Constitution of the Confederate

States of America (10). Soon the nation was locked in the throes of the Civil War. The Confiscation Acts (11) allowed for the seizure of slaves in all but the loyal border states where even the Fugitive Slave Act would continue to be enforced. Seized slaves were to be emancipated, but they remained subject to being conscripted into the service of the Union's war effort. Finally, the Emancipation Proclamation (12) freed all slaves dwelling in states that had seceded from the Union.

1

Articles of Confederation

1776

HISTORICAL CONTEXT

Once the colonies had decided on a course of independence from Great Britain, the Continental Congress formed primarily for the purposes of mutual self-defense, and its earliest actions focused on preparing the fledgling combined colonies for an impending war of independence. One of the first requirements, however, would be for the Congress to legitimize its own existence. Meanwhile, the thirteen original states fashioned their own constitutions and political institutions, proceeding to carve out their own bastions of sovereignty, independent of the Continental Congress.

In May 1776, the Congress appointed a committee to construct a plan for a confederation of states. The committee was to be chaired by John Dickinson, a lawyer who had written an important revolutionary pamphlet entitled *Letters from a Farmer in Pennsylvania.* Dickinson's initial draft, presented on July 12, 1776, created a far stronger and more centralized government than most had anticipated. It apportioned one representative per state, even though states like Massachusetts and Virginia had considerably larger populations. It also recommended assessing taxes by the total number of persons in the state, black as well as white, angering Southerners who did not feel slaves should be counted for that purpose.

The document passed by the Continental Congress bore little resemblance to Dickinson's initial plan. In the end, the Articles of Confederation and Perpetual Union, somewhat hastily pieced together, passed on November 15, 1777. Ratification, however, would be considerably slower, given heated disagreement over whether the new Congress was to be authorized to settle disputes about ownership of western territories. Maryland, the final holdout, did not ratify the Articles until March 1, 1781, when the British military began to pose a serious threat to the Chesapeake region. Finally the Articles became the nation's first actual constitution.

This document was not a philosophical treatise setting out conceptions of freedom and governmental power; instead, it focused on creating a national government with the wherewithal to wage a war, while leaving virtually all else to the several states. Consequently, the individual states retained considerable sovereignty under the Articles of Confederation, as very little independent authority was delegated to a national government, and the role of the president was severely constrained as well.

As Edward Rutledge, a delegate from South Carolina, put it, the new national government had been delegated "no more Power than is absolutely necessary."[1]

This understanding was quite clearly stated in Article II, proposed by Thomas Burke of North Carolina and passed by eleven of the thirteen delegations. Each state was to "retain its sovereignty, freedom, independence, and every power, jurisdiction and right, which is not by this Confederation expressly delegated to the Congress." The word "expressly" is very important, as demonstrated by the fact that the subsequent United States Constitution would omit it in the Tenth Amendment and by so doing open the door to an expansive myriad of "implied powers" of the federal government. In racial terms, those implied powers would allow the federal government more leeway in coercing recalcitrant states equally to protect black and white persons under their laws.

Meanwhile, one of the advantages to the more decentralized approach, especially in a fledgling nation gearing up to fight a war of independence, was that it allowed the delegates to avoid potentially divisive issues like the future of the institution of slavery.

As for the issue of slavery, without explicitly mentioning the word, the Articles did distinguish between "free" as opposed to non-free persons.[2] Also, there was a provision for capturing and returning fugitives from justice, but such fugitives were limited to those guilty of or at least charged with "treason, felony, or other high misdemeanor." The only explicit mention of race concerned the mustering of land forces, whereby each state could be asked to fill a said quota "in proportion to the number of white inhabitants in such State."

In 1787, after the revolutionary war, the Congress, under these Articles, outlawed slavery and involuntary servitude in the Northwest Territories, one of the legislature's only major legislative accomplishments. At almost the same time, however, the new nation's founding fathers were meeting in Philadelphia and crafting a new constitution that would allow for a stronger national government, deemed necessary if the "united states" were to survive and prosper. It would also essentially legitimate the institution of slavery for at least two decades, in part to maintain national unity.[3]

THE LAW

The Articles of the Confederation was a compact agreed upon by the original thirteen states. This agreement formally named the confederacy the United States of America. The states retained all rights not expressly delegated by Congress, although "every State shall abide by the determination of the United States in Congress assembled."

Among other things, the Articles encouraged social and economic interaction among residents of different states by stating that "free" individuals traveling in any state be provided the same rights offered by that state to its own residents.

To maintain order among the states, the Articles contained a provision for capturing and returning fugitives to the state from which they had fled. In addition, each state was to give full faith and credit to other states' judicial proceedings.

In regard to the mustering of land forces, each state could be asked to fill a said quota "in proportion to the number of white inhabitants in such State." Aside from the provisions explained above that indirectly referred to race or enslaved persons, this was the only portion of the Articles that specifically distinguished people on the basis of race.

1. Articles of Confederation

[B]etween the states of New Hampshire, Massachusetts Bay, Rhode Island and Providence Plantations, Connecticut, New York, New Jersey, Pennsylvania, Delaware, Maryland, Virginia, North Carolina, South Carolina, and Georgia. . . .

ARTICLE II

Each state retains its sovereignty, freedom, and independence, and every power, jurisdiction, and right, which is not by this Confederation expressly delegated to the United States, in Congress assembled. . . .

ARTICLE IV

The better to secure and perpetuate mutual friendship and intercourse among the people of the different States in this Union, the free inhabitants of each of these States, paupers, vagabonds and fugitives from justice excepted, shall be entitled to all privileges and immunities of free citizens in the several States; and the people of each State shall free ingress and regress to and from any other State, and shall enjoy therein all the privileges of trade and commerce, subject to the same duties, impositions, and restrictions as the inhabitants thereof respectively, provided that such restrictions shall not extend so far as to prevent the removal of property imported into any State, to any other State, of which the owner is an inhabitant; provided also that no imposition, duties or restriction shall be laid by any State, on the property of the United States, or either of them.

If any person guilty of, or charged with, treason, felony, or other high misdemeanor in any State, shall flee from justice, and be found in any of the United States, he shall, upon demand of the Governor or executive power of the State from which he fled, be delivered up and removed to the State having jurisdiction of his offense.

Full faith and credit shall be given in each of these States to the records, acts, and judicial proceedings of the courts and magistrates of every other State. . . .

The United States in Congress assembled shall have authority . . . to agree on the number of land forces, and to make requisitions from each State for its quota, in proportion to the number of white inhabitants in such State. . . .

ARTICLE XIII

Every State shall abide by the determination of the United States in Congress assembled, on all questions which by this confederation are submitted to them. And the Articles of this Confederation shall be inviolably observed by every State, and the Union shall be perpetual; nor shall any alteration at any time hereafter be made in any of them; unless such alteration be agreed to in a Congress of the United States, and be afterwards confirmed by the legislatures of every State. . . .

NOTES

1. Quoted in David Goldfield et al., *The American Journey* (Upper Saddle River, N.J.: Prentice-Hall, 1998), p. 202.

2. It should be noted that several years earlier the Continental Congress had passed an agreement not to import slaves after December 1, 1775; however, this understanding was not written into the Articles of Confederation.

3. For example, see Merrill Jensen, *The Articles of Confederation* (Madison: University of Wisconsin Press, 1970); J.N. Rakove, "The Articles of Confederation, 1775–1783," in *The Blackwell Encyclopedia of the American Revolution* ed. J.P. Green and J.R. Pole (New York: Blackwell, 1991).

2

Declaration of Independence

1776

HISTORICAL CONTEXT

Thomas Paine called for complete and unconditional independence from Great Britain in his widely circulated and fiery 1776 pamphlet *Common Sense*, but there was still significant local opposition to revolution. Many such opponents argued instead for reaching a compromise solution with King George III. Some were simply not ready to take such a radical step; others feared the protracted bloody struggle that was likely to ensue. There were also those who feared that internal strife among the several colonies would dissolve the union. The most vexing of these potentially divisive issues was the institution of slavery. It would take a ringing and universally appealing declaration to unite the various factions sufficiently to wage a revolutionary war.

Representatives of the states assembled defiantly as the Continental Congress. Their Declaration of Independence reflects a mounting frustration on the part of the thirteen colonial states with the policies of the British throne. This was clearly a call to revolt. Carefully avoided in the document, however, was any direct mention of slavery: "We hold these truths to be self-evident, that all men are created equal, that they are endowed by their Creator with certain unalienable rights. . . ."

Those words would not have rung nearly so hollow in the ears of 600,000 enslaved blacks had it not been for the deletion of the following paragraph from Thomas Jefferson's initial draft of the Declaration. Jefferson's initial draft had contained this rather scathing attack on the institution of slavery, presented in the context of stirring opposition to the king of England for his ongoing support of that institution.

> He [George III] has waged cruel war against human nature itself, violating its most sacred rights of life and liberty in the persons of a distant people who never offended him, captivating and carrying them into slavery in another hemisphere, or to incur miserable death in their transportation thither. This piratical warfare, the opprobrium of INFIDEL powers, is the warfare of the CHRISTIAN King of Great Britain. Determined to keep open a market where MEN should be bought and sold, he has prostituted his negative for suppressing every legislative attempt to prohibit or restrain this execrable commerce.

Besides condemning George III in no uncertain terms for supporting the practice of slavery, Jefferson accused him of fomenting slave revolts in America. As Jefferson put it,

> And that this assemblage of horrors might want no fact of distinguished die, he is now exciting those very people to rise in arms among us and to purchase that liberty of which he has deprived them, by murdering the people on whom he also obtruded them; thus paying off former crimes committed against the LIBERTIES of one people with crimes which he urges them to commit against the LIVES of another.

The purpose of the Declaration of Independence was to set forth the very premises of a free nation. In the process, it also defined a revolutionary view of individual equality. At the same time, however, it left important questions unanswered. What was the standing of the 600,000 enslaved colonists? Were they, too, "created equal . . . [and] endowed by their Creator with certain unalienable rights"?

In the deleted passage, Jefferson, a slaveholder himself, spoke out against the institution of slavery, both as a reflection of his own moral indignation as well as an attempt to rouse the sentiments of colonists who yearned for personal liberty in all its forms.[1] He called the institution a "cruel war against human nature," which "violat[ed] its most sacred rights of life and liberty." At the same time, he was careful to blame the institution on King George and not domestic slave owners and traders. Then, on an even more practical level, he noted that King George had been inciting those same slaves to rise up and murder their local slave masters, posing a significant threat to domestic tranquility. That admonition was the only one retained in the final text, when it stated (without the above context), "He has excited domestic insurrections amongst us."

The latter more practical warning, however, was not enough to secure the support of those members of the Continental Congress who represented slave-holding states. They could not endorse a proposition that condemned outright a practice upon which their local economies depended. Such a collective statement could very well sow the seeds of a future wholesale attack on this economically essential form of labor. In addition, a host of social and religious beliefs and practices had evolved to justify and support the institution.

Representatives from slave and non–slave holding states also feared the nationalization of politics. It would be pointless to fight for independence from the tyranny of a distant king in England, only to have such tyranny replaced by a comparably oppressive national governmental system here. As much as possible, the desire was to have political, economic, and certainly social issues resolved locally.

Beyond that, condemning the king of England for an "inhuman" practice that was to continue legally in an independent United States would appear hypocritical. As Abigail Adams noted to her husband, John, at the time, "It always appeared a most ubiquitous scheme to me to fight ourselves for what we are daily robbing and plundering from those who have as good a right to freedom as we have."[2]

The issue of slavery was the only major point of substantive contention among the delegates in terms of the Declaration's wording. In the end, in order to maintain the unity that would no doubt be necessary to follow through with an armed rebellion against the crown, most of the slavery paragraph was deleted. Yet, the words "all men are created equal" survived in this Unanimous Declaration of the Thirteen United States of America. In retrospect, it would serve as a blatant reminder that meshing the principles of liberty and equality with the institution of slavery remained an issue far from resolved. Slavery was being maintained for a combination of economic and political reasons. Yet, it was also clearly a moral issue, but a moral issue that would have to wait until after the Revolutionary War to be addressed.

THE LAW

The drafters of the Declaration of Independence obviously believed that in declaring their independence they were required to set forth their reasons for taking such bold action. In the Declaration itself, the United States declared its independence from Great Britain. In absolving itself of allegiance to the British crown, the document set out the new nation's many grievances with King George.

2. The Declaration of Independence

When, in the course of human events, it becomes necessary for one people to dissolve the political bonds which have connected them with another, and to assume among the powers of the earth, the separate and equal station to which the laws of nature and of nature's God entitle them, a decent respect to the opinions of mankind requires that they should declare the causes which impel them to the separation.

We hold these truths to be self-evident, that all men are created equal, that they are endowed by their Creator with certain unalienable rights, that among these are life, liberty and the pursuit of happiness. That to secure these rights, governments are instituted among men, deriving their just powers from the consent of the governed. That whenever any form of government becomes destructive to these ends, it is the right of the people to alter or to abolish it, and to institute new government, laying its foundation on such principles and organizing its powers in such form, as to them shall seem most likely to effect their safety, and happiness. Prudence, indeed, will dictate that governments long established should not be changed for light and transient causes; and accordingly all experience hath shown that mankind are more disposed to suffer, while evils are sufferable, than to right themselves by abolishing the forms to which they are accustomed. But when a long train of abuses and usurpations, pursuing invariably the same object evinces a design to reduce them under absolute despotism, it is their right, it is their duty, to throw off such government, and to provide new guards for their future security. Such has been the patient sufferance of these colonies; and such is now the necessity which constrains them to alter their former systems of government. The history of the present King [George III] of Great Britain is a history of repeated injuries and usurpations, all having in direct object the establishment of an absolute tyranny over these states. To prove this, let facts be submitted to a candid world. . . .

He has excited domestic insurrections amongst us. . . . [one of the more than two dozen specific grievances cited]

We, therefore, the representatives of the United States of America, in General Congress, assembled, appealing to the Supreme Judge of the world for the rectitude of our intentions, do, in the name, and by the authority of the good people of these colonies, solemnly publish and declare, that these united colonies are, and of right ought to be free and independent states; that they are absolved from all allegiance to the British Crown, and that all political connection between them and the state of Great Britain, is and ought to be totally dissolved; and that as free and independent states, they have full power to levy war, conclude peace, contract alliances, establish commerce, and to do all other acts and things which independent states may of right do. And for the support of this declaration, with a firm reliance on the protection of Divine Providence, we mutually pledge to each other our lives, our fortunes and our sacred honor.

NOTES

1. For more on Jefferson and his own views of slavery, see David Brian Davis, *The Problem of Slavery in the Age of Revolution, 1770–1823* (Ithaca, N.Y.: Cornell University Press, 1975), pp. 171–84.

2. Quoted in Robert Divine et al., *America: Past and Present* (New York: Longman, 1997), p. 198.

3

Northwest Ordinance

1787

Among other things, the Northwest Ordinance called for the eventual outlawing of slavery in the new territories, but meanwhile it allowed for the capture and return of runaway slaves apprehended therein.

HISTORICAL CONTEXT

Quaker committees, who had been encouraging slave owners to free their slaves as early as the 1750s, formed the first formal antislavery society in 1775. Their lobbying efforts soon began to pay legislative dividends at the state level, especially after the revolutionary war had been won. As early as 1780, for instance, Pennsylvania provided for the gradual prohibition of slavery; Connecticut and Rhode Island followed four years later. Virginia enacted a 1782 law allowing individual slave owners to emancipate their own slaves. In 1783 the state of Maryland banned slave trading within its boundaries, and North Carolina substantially increased its duty on imported slaves in 1786. South Carolina banned slave importation in 1787, although it rescinded that law in 1803 when it was deemed to be unenforceable. Thereafter, emancipation laws were passed in New York in 1799 and New Jersey five years later.

Meanwhile, at the national level, when President Thomas Jefferson managed to purchase the Louisiana Territories from France, the United States immediately doubled in geographic size. How would the slavery issue be managed as these territories developed and sought entry into the nation as sovereign states? About the only legal guidance was provided by the Northwest Ordinance, fashioned under the Articles of Confederation and covering all land north of the Ohio River.

As western populations increased and conflicting land claims proliferated, the Continental Congress had passed a series of "land ordinances" that began the process of settling, governing, and finally gradually absorbing these lands into the United States. The Northwest Ordinance created a governmental structure to be supervised by the Congress, with the understanding that the Northwest Territories would ultimately be admitted as anywhere from three to five states, on "equal footing with the original states in all respects whatsoever." This process would set precedent for other future admissions to statehood as well.

As for slavery, it was declared illegal in the new territories. On the other hand, the ordinance allowed the recapture and return of any runaway slaves who happened to venture into those territories. Such a compromise worked its way into law in part with the support of Southern representatives who had reason to fear that planters in the new territories might employ slaves and begin to compete with them in the production of economic staples such as tobacco. They also correctly anticipated that slavery would be allowed south of the Ohio River, as it indeed was by the Southwest Ordinance of 1790.

Having declared a prohibition against slavery in the Northwest Territories, however, this law was far from self-implementing in a region whose governmental structures were just taking form. By the 1830 census, for instance, 16,000 blacks were officially residing in the states of Ohio, Indiana, Illinois, and Michigan. Yet, despite the Northwest Ordinance, there were also 788 officially listed "slaves."

THE LAW

The Northwest Ordinance[1] addressed a myriad of issues related to the governance of this newly acquired region. The law provided that the new territory would be deemed one district and that Congress would appoint a governor, a secretary, and a court consisting of three judges. The governing officials of the new territory were directed to adopt the laws of the original United States as needed. Once the population of the area had increased to 5,000 free male residents, the ordinance provided for the means to establish a general assembly for the district. All legislation produced was nevertheless subject to the governor's absolute veto. The governor was given other powers under the ordinance to ensure peace and order.

The Ordinance set forth six articles of "compact," or agreement, between the original United States and the new territory. The articles of agreement mandated that territories guarantee to respect such principles as religious freedoms, trial by jury, and educational opportunity. Further, the articles set forth the requirements and procedures for portions of the territory to apply for formal statehood. The most relevant article regarding the rights of blacks was Article 6. This article prohibited slavery or involuntary servitude, except in the case of convicted criminals. The law specifically provided, however, that any enslaved person escaping into the new territory from one of the original United States could be reclaimed by the owner.

3. Northwest Ordinance

ARTICLE 6

There shall be neither slavery nor involuntary servitude in the said territory, otherwise than in the punishment of crimes whereof the party shall have been duly convicted; Provided always, That any person escaping into the same, from whom labor or service is lawfully claimed in any one of the original States, such fugitive may be lawfully reclaimed and conveyed to the person claiming his or her labor or service as aforesaid.

NOTE

1. *Statutes at Large of the United States* (Washington D.C.: GPO), vol. 1, pp. 51–53.

4

United States Constitution

1787

HISTORICAL CONTEXT

Fifty-five delegates to the Constitutional Convention sat in Philadelphia from May to September of 1787 framing the governmental structure for the new United States of America. From the "Notes" taken by James Madison, it is clear that one of the dilemmas the Founding Fathers could not avoid was how to appease slave-dependent states and, at the same time, mesh that reality with the new nation's revolutionary language of "liberty and equality."

One such compromise was that the term "slavery," at the urging of James Madison, never did appear in the original United States Constitution.[1] In addition, the document was careful nearly always to use the term "persons" as opposed to "citizens" when allocating rights and privileges, especially clear when the Bill of Rights (the first ten amendments) were added in order to codify basic rights and liberties. Among other things, this helped avoid the issue of whether slaves were to be considered citizens.

In terms of taxation and representation, however, the implications of the status of slaves could not be disguised. The reality was that 90 percent of all slaves lived in the South, and slaves made up some 30 percent of at least six Southern states (North Carolina, South Carolina, Maryland, Delaware, Virginia, and Georgia). If slaves were ignored, the South would have gotten roughly 41 percent of the original seats in the United States House of Representatives. By contrast, if they were counted fully, the South would have had half the original seats. In addition, until the Sixteenth Amendment allowed Congress to tax incomes directly, the federal government taxed states in proportion to their populations. Thus, counting slaves as persons for these purposes would severely increase the tax burden of slave-heavy states.

Hugh Williamson of North Carolina first proposed the "3/5 compromise," counting slaves as three-fifths of a person both for determining taxes owed and for apportioning national representation. This would leave the South with roughly 46 percent of the congressional representatives and a comparable share of the federal tax burden. The only real opposition came from the Georgia and South Carolina delegates who wanted slaves counted as full individuals for the purpose of state representation in Congress. In the end, however, when the three-fifths formula was to be used for taxation and representation purposes, only Delaware and New Jersey dissented.

James Madison attempted to summarize the compromise from a Southern perspective in his Federalist Paper Number 54 when he stated,

> The Federal Constitution, therefore, decides with great propriety on the case of our slaves, when it views them in the mixed character of persons and property. . . . Let the compromising expedient of the Constitution be mutually adopted which regards them as inhabitants, but as debased by servitude below the equal level of free inhabitants; which regards the slave as divested as of two fifths of the man.[2]

The truth is that this three-fifths compromise was nothing new and actually was not a major issue at the convention. It had already been adopted by the Congress of the Confederation in the revenue amendment of 1783; it was embodied in the New Jersey Plan; amended to the Virginia Plan by a vote of 9–2; and included in the Great Compromise between the Virginia and New Jersey Plans as "the ratio recommended by Congress in their resolution of April 18, 1783." Delegates regularly referred to it as the "Federal ratio" as if it was well understood. A few months later at the Massachusetts state convention, Rufus King stated, "This rule . . . was adopted because it was the language of all America." In point of fact, it came up early in the representation debate, and there was far more concern with the monied states in the East losing control of the government to the expansion states of the West than there was between slave and free states.[3]

Slavery actually received little discussion at the Philadelphia convention.[4] There was some moral objection to slavery's being sanctioned by the Constitution, raised by a few Northern delegates as well as by George Mason of Virginia. But, just as strong was the concern of the delegates from North Carolina, South Carolina, and Georgia who knew they would need the labor and argued that "their right to import slaves be untouched." In between these two sides, Benjamin Franklin opted not to stir the waters further by simply reading a moral pleading he carried with him as a member of the Pennsylvania Society for Promoting the Abolition of Slavery. Oliver Ellsworth of Connecticut seemed to speak for many of the other delegates when he supported letting "every state import what it pleases. The morality or wisdom of slavery are considerations belonging to the states themselves—What enriches a part enriches the whole, and the states are the best judges of their particular interest."[5]

Sensing that the importation issue could well bog down the entire proceedings, the matter was tabled and sent to a special committee, which would have a representative from each state. The committee promptly reported back a proposal that would allow full importation until 1800 (later changed to 1808) of "the migration or importation of such persons that the several states now existing shall think proper to admit," and also allowing such persons to be taxed at a rate not to exceed the average import duty (later changed to $10, calculated as a 5 percent duty). When the term "several states" was seen as too vague, possibly allowing the taxation of freemen outside the slave-holding states, Governour Morris proposed that it be changed to "North Carolina, South Carolina, and Georgia." That motion failed, and the language remained as it was originally proposed. The motion carried by a vote of 6–4, with New Jersey, Pennsylvania, Delaware, and Virginia in dissent.[6]

Two underlying assumptions are of particular note. First of all, there was a presumption that "under the power to regulate commerce, Congress would be authorized to abridge [the principle of slaves as legitimate private property] in favor of the great principles of humanity and justice."[7] Yet, at the same time, "such persons" were still not viewed by the Founders as "citizens" either.[8]

During the convention, General Charles Cotesworth Pinckney of South Carolina argued fervently against any such restrictions. He even went so far as to assert that South Carolina would never ratify a constitution that would prohibit the slave trade. But, it was at the

South Carolina convention thereafter that he spoke most frankly, justifying to his home state the 1808 limit.

> "Show some period" said the members of the Eastern states "when it may be in our power to put a stop, if we please, to the importation of this weakness, and we will endeavor, for your convenience, to restrain the religious and political prejudices of our people on this subject." . . . In short, considering all circumstances, we have made the best terms for the security of this species of property it was in our power to make. We would have made better if we could; but, on the whole, I do not think them bad.[9]

Once the importation compromise was finally adopted in the waning days of the convention, a clause was added providing for the return of fugitive slaves. This was adopted to keep fugitive slaves from claiming freedom once they reached a free state. The provision was adopted unanimously and without significant debate, although the Framers did reject an initial draft that would have required runaways to "be delivered up as criminals," in that this would have obligated state governments to do it even if morally opposed.[10] Roger Sherman of Connecticut argued that he saw "no more propriety in public seizing and surrendering a slave or servant, than a horse"; but most of his colleagues, even those from the more liberal Northeast, were already packing their bags for home.[11]

The mandatory returning of runaway slaves and the three-fifths compromise remained in effect for nearly a century. Meanwhile, even after Congress banned slave importation in 1807, some 250,000 still managed to come in thereafter.[12]

In addition, at least two other race-related issues would continue to challenge the new constitution as it was put into practice. First, it was debatable whether the "privileges and immunities" clause meant slaveholders would have their rights protected, should they decide to move and take their slaves with them to a free state. Conversely, would slaves automatically become free when they experienced freedom in a free state?[13] A second issue was exactly what authority Congress had to determine the status of slavery in the western territories as those territories approached statehood.

THE LAW

The United States Constitution formally established the general purposes and governmental structure of the country. Most specifically, it set forth how the federal government was to be organized, and it outlined the relationship between the federal government and the individual states. It also contained several slavery-related passages, without mentioning the term directly.

4. United States Constitution

PREAMBLE

We the people of the United States, in Order to form a more perfect Union, establish Justice, insure domestic Tranquility, provide for the common defense, promote the general Welfare, and secure the Blessings of Liberty to ourselves and our Posterity, do ordain and establish this Constitution for the United States of America.

ARTICLE I

Section 2. Clause 3. Representatives and direct Taxes shall be apportioned among the several States which may be included within this Union, according to their respective Numbers, which shall be determined by adding the whole Number of free Persons, including those bound to Service for a Term of Years, and excluding Indians not taxed, three-fifths of all other Persons. . . .

Section 9. Clause 1. The Migration or Importation of such Persons as any of the States now existing shall think proper to admit, shall not be prohibited by the Congress prior to the year 1808, but a Tax or duty may be imposed on such Importation not exceeding 10 dollars for each Person. . . .

ARTICLE IV

Section 2. Clause 1. The Citizens of each State shall be entitled to all Privileges and Immunities of Citizens in the several States. . . .

Section 2. Clause 3. No Person held to Service or Labour in one State, under the Laws thereof, escaping into another, shall, in Consequence of any Law or Regulation therein, be discharged from such Service or Labour, but shall be delivered up on Claim of the Party to whom such Service or Labour may be due. . . .

Section 3. Clause 2. The Congress shall have Power to dispose of and make all needful Rules and Regulations respecting the Territory or other Property belonging to the United States; and nothing in this Constitution shall be so construed as to Prejudice any Claims of the United States, or of any particular State.

NOTES

1. See Lance Banning, *The Sacred Fire of Liberty: James Madison and the Founding of the Federal Republic* (Ithaca, N.Y.: Cornell University Press, 1995).
2. Clinton Rossiter, ed., *The Federalist Papers* (New York: New American Library, 1961), p. 337.
3. See Max Farrand, *The Framing of the Constitution of the United States* (New Haven, Conn.: Yale University Press, 1913), pp. 107–8. Also see Floyd B. McKissick, *Three-Fifths of a Man* (New York: Macmillan, 1969).
4. Farrand, *Framing the Constitution*, p. 110.
5. Ibid., p. 149.
6. Ibid., p. 150.
7. Quoted from the U.S. Supreme Court in *United States v. The William*, 28 Fed. Cas. No. 16700 (1808).
8. For example, see *Dred Scott v. Sandford*, 19 How. (60 U.S.) 393, 411 (1857).
9. Quoted in Farrand, *Framing the Constitution*, p. 151.
10. For example, see Donald Robinson, "The Constitutional Legacy of Slavery," *National Political Science Review* 4 (1994): 12.
11. For further discussion of the proslavery aspects of the U.S. Constitution, see Donald Nieman, *Promises to Keep: African-Americans and the Constitutional Order, 1776 to the Present* (New York: Oxford University Press, 1991), ch. 1. Also see Howard Zinn, *Declarations of Independence: Cross-Examining American Ideology* (New York: HarperCollins, 1990), ch. 9; Mervyn Dymally, ed., *The Black Politician: His Struggle for Power* (Belmont, Calif.: Wadsworth, 1971); Derrick Bell, "The Elusive Quest for Racial Justice: The Chronicle of the Constitutional Contradiction," in *The State of Black America, 1995*, ed. Paulette Robinson and Billy Tidwell (New York: National Urban League, 1995), pp. 225–39; Leslie Carr, *Color-Blind Racism* (Beverly Hills, Calif.: Sage, 1997).
12. See Jeffrey Schultz et al., *Encyclopedia of Minorities in American Politics: African Americans and Asian Americans*, vol. 1 (Westport, Conn.: Oryx Press, 2000), p. 9.
13. Much of this controversy would be sorted out, at least for the moment, by the U.S. Supreme Court in its Dred Scott decision.

5

Fugitive Slave Act

1793

The Fugitive Slave Act required the federal government to assist in the return of runaway slaves and included mechanisms for enforcement and fines for interference.

HISTORICAL CONTEXT

Runaways posed a challenge to slave owners from the onset of the practice of slavery.[1] The problem was multiplied significantly by the establishment of a series of stations and safe houses to harbor fugitive slaves as they escaped north—a practice that dates back at least to the eighteenth century. In 1787, for instance, Isaac Hopper of Philadelphia began to create a relatively elaborate set of such sanctuaries across the states of Pennsylvania and New Jersey. By 1804 the Underground Railroad had officially taken form.

The original United States Constitution was drafted in 1787. In Article IV, Section 2, Clause 3, it states that "No person held to Service or Labour in one state, under the Laws thereof, escaping into another, shall, in consequence of any Law or Regulation therein, be discharged from such Service or Labour, but shall be delivered up on Claim of the Party to whom such Service or Labour may be due." As Charles Cotesworth Pinckney reassured the planters of South Carolina upon his return from the Constitutional Convention in Philadelphia, "[We have] a right to recover our slaves in whatever part of America they may take refuge, which is a right we had not before."[2]

Like the rest of the Constitution, however, such clauses were not self-implementing. Consequently, Congress needed to pass legislation to facilitate their implementation. On February 12, 1793, led by several Southern congresspersons, the Congress of the United States passed the Fugitive Slave Act in order to enable enforcement. The act allowed runaways to be returned to slavery, and it became a crime to harbor fugitive slaves or interfere with their recapture. Tested in federal court, the law was held to be constitutional by the United States Supreme Court in its *Prigg v. Pennsylvania* decision.[3]

Nonetheless, often transporting runaways by the light of the moon, more than 3,000 abolitionists came to operate the Underground Railroad in nearly open defiance of federal fugitive slave laws. Initially they were dealing almost exclusively with young, single men who traveled largely by foot. As more women and children joined the ranks, carriages and wagons were employed to traverse the ten to twenty miles between safe havens, dodging determined slave patrols and federal marshals. Quakers and other abolitionists constantly raised money to provide the necessary food, clothing, and transportation for those escaping in this manner.

Levi Coffin, the so-called president of the Underground Railroad, recalled having assisted more than 3,000 runaways through his station in southern Indiana. Yet, much of the Underground Railroad was manned by free blacks. John Mason, a former slave, claimed to have helped as many as 1,300 fugitive slaves reach Canada. Meanwhile, former slaves such as Harriet Tubman and Josiah Henson actually made forays into the South to lead slaves north through the clandestine labyrinth. Free blacks also organized "vigilance committees" to shield fugitives and confound slave catchers; at times, they forcefully rescued recaptured runaways.

Governor John Quitman of Mississippi estimated that the South lost as many as 100,000 slaves between 1810 and 1850 alone, at a cost of more than $30 million.[4] Nevertheless, it should be remembered that this figure represents only a small portion of the total slave population. In the 1850s, for example, there were still more than 3 million slaves in the United States.

THE LAW

While commonly referred to as the Fugitive Slave Act,[5] this act was actually broader in scope. The act provided states and territories with the authority to demand from another state or territory the return of any "fugitives from justice." Fugitives from justice included any escaped persons who had fled after being arrested and charged. In order to facilitate the return of escaped slaves, on the other hand, the act set forth the manner in which a slave owner could make a claim regarding an escaped slave. The act provided the manner of transporting both fugitives and escaped slaves back to the state or territory from which the person had fled. Anyone attempting to interfere with the return of fugitives from justice could be fined and imprisoned. By contrast, anyone obstructing the arrest of an escaped slave could be punished only by fine.

5. Fugitive Slave Act

CHAP. VII

An Act respecting fugitives from justice, and persons escaping from the service of their masters.

SECTION 1. Be it enacted . . . That whenever the executive authority of any state in the Union, or of either of the territories northwest or south of the river Ohio, shall demand any person as a fugitive from justice, of the executive authority of any such state or territory to which such person shall have fled, and shall moreover produce the copy of an indictment found, or an affidavit made before a magistrate of any state or territory as aforesaid, charging the person so demanded, with having committed treason, felony or other crime, certified as authentic by the governor or chief magistrate of the state or territory from whence the person so charged fled, it shall be the duty of the executive authority of the state or territory to which such person shall have fled, to cause him or her to be arrested and secured, and notice of the arrest to be given to the executive authority making such demand, or to the agent of such authority appointed to receive the fugitive, and to cause the fugitive to be delivered to such agent when he shall appear: But if no such agent shall appear within six months from the time of the arrest, the prisoner may be discharged. And all costs or expenses incurred in the apprehending, securing, and transmitting such fugitive to the state or territory making such demand, shall be paid by such state or territory.

SECTION 2. And be it further enacted, That any agent, appointed as aforesaid, who shall receive the fugitive into his custody, shall be empowered to transport him or her to the state or territory from which he or she shall have fled. And if any person or persons shall by force set at liberty, or rescue the fugitive from such agent while transporting, as aforesaid, the person or persons so offending shall, on conviction, be fined not exceeding five hundred dollars, and be imprisoned not exceeding one year.

SECTION 3. And be it also enacted, That when a person held to labour in any of the United States, or in either of the territories on the northwest or south of the river Ohio, under the laws thereof, shall escape into any other of the said states or territory, the person to whom such labour or service may be due, his agent or attorney, is hereby empowered to seize or arrest such fugitive from labour, and to take him or her before any judge of the circuit or district courts of the United States, residing or being within the state, or before any magistrate of a county, city or town corporate, wherein such seizure or arrest shall be made, and upon proof to the satisfaction of such judge or magistrate, either by oral testimony or affidavit taken before and certified by a magistrate of any such state or territory, that the person so seized or arrested, doth, under the laws of the state or territory from which he or she fled, owe service or labour to the person claiming him or her, it shall be the duty of such judge or magistrate to give a certificate thereof to such claimant, his agent or attorney, which shall be sufficient warrant for removing the said fugitive from labour, to the state or territory from which he or she fled.

SECTION 4. And be it further enacted, That any person who shall knowingly and willingly obstruct or hinder such claimant, his agent or attorney in so seizing or arresting such fugitive from labour, or shall rescue such fugitive from such claimant, his agent or attorney when so arrested pursuant to the authority herein given or declared; or shall harbor or conceal such person after notice that he or she was a fugitive from labour, as aforesaid, shall, for either of the said offences, forfeit and pay the sum of five hundred dollars. Which penalty may be recovered by and for the benefit of such claimant, by action of debt, in any court proper to try the same; saving moreover to the person claiming such labour or service, his right of action for or on account of the said injuries or either of them.

APPROVED, February 12, 1793.

NOTES

1. For example, see Gerald Mullin, *Flight and Rebellion: Slave Resistance in 18th Century Virginia* (New York: Oxford University Press, 1972).

2. Robert Divine et al., *America: Past and Present* (New York: Longman, 1999), p. 190.

3. *Prigg v. Pennsylvania,* 41 U.S. 539 (1842).

4. John Hope Franklin and Alfred A. Moss, Jr., *From Slavery to Freedom: A History of African Americans* (New York: Knopf, 1994), pp. 183–188.

5. *Statutes at Large of the United States* (Washington, D.C.: GPO), vol. 1, pp. 302–5.

6

Slave Importation Act

1807

The Slave Importation Act prohibited any further legal importation of slaves.

HISTORICAL CONTEXT

In the decade from 1776 to 1786, most states in the union either outlawed or heavily taxed international slave trading. The only exceptions were South Carolina and Georgia, and it was the adamancy of these two states that prompted the Constitutional Convention to delay even the possibility of a federal ban on slave importation for twenty years. After a notoriously successful slave revolt was staged in Haiti in 1791, every Southern state proceeded to ban any further importation of foreign slaves, in part fearing the influx of Caribbean revolutionaries who might lead their own slaves into revolt.[1]

In 1794 Eli Whitney patented his cotton engine (subsequently shortened to "cotton gin"), and cotton soon became America's primary exported good.[2] Before this invention, the price of slaves had been falling. Between 1775 and 1800, for instance, the price had dropped some 50 percent. The expanded cotton trade now required some ten to twenty slaves for every 100,000 acres of cotton fields, and the price of slaves soon soared. The cost, roughly $50 per slave at the turn of the century, rose to between $800 and $1,000 by the middle of the nineteenth century.[3]

The final years of the eighteenth century and the first few years of the nineteenth witnessed a continuing influx of imported slaves despite state laws to the contrary. In 1803 alone the states of Georgia and South Carolina saw some 20,000 slaves reach their shores. Unable to enforce its legal ban effectively, South Carolina rescinded it that year. New England traders, defying their state laws as well, imported slaves and then sold them to Southern plantation owners.[4]

Meanwhile, the original United States Constitution stated in Article I, Section 9, Clause 1, "The Migration or Importation of such Persons as any of the States now existing shall think proper to admit, shall not be prohibited by the Congress prior to the year one thousand eight hundred and eight." To that end, antislavery groups began lobbying Congress for a national prohibition. In January 1800, the free blacks of Philadelphia led the way, pressing Congress for new laws on both slave importation and the forcible return of runaway slaves.

Congress did little, however, until December 1805 when Senator Stephen Bradley (Rep., Vt.) introduced a bill to prohibit further importation of slaves after 1807. The following December, President Thomas Jefferson used the occasion of his annual message to Congress to urge a congressional ban on slave importation and to call for measures to "prevent expeditions to Africa that could not be completed before January 1, 1808."[5] Representative Barnabas Bidwell (Rep., Mass.) introduced such a bill that same month.

The first two months of 1807 marked a period of heated congressional debate on virtually every one of the importation ban's provisions. Some even advocated the death penalty for slave traders. Many were ambivalent about what to do with poor and uneducated blacks seized by customs agents. Meanwhile Southern congressmen openly doubted that local planters would abide by a ban on a practice they did not regard as immoral.[6]

On March 2, 1807, the Congress of the United States finally exercised its right under Article I, Section 9. It passed and President Jefferson signed An Act to Prohibit the Importation of Slaves into any Port or Place Within the Jurisdiction of the United States, to take effect on January 1, 1808, the first day such a prohibition was constitutionally permissible. The act contained several compromises, most notably that captured slaves were to be turned over to local authorities for disposition.

In the end, the significance of this particular federal law was in many ways symbolic. All states had already outlawed the importation of slaves by 1803, and such laws had failed to arrest the slave trade. According to historians John Hope Franklin and Alfred Moss, "The

first underground railroad was not that established by the abolitionists to transport slaves to freedom but the one used by mer-
chants and others to introduce more blacks into slavery."[7] In
addition, Congress and the states had only banned the importation
of slaves, not slavery itself. Subsequently, the ban actually served to
increase the value of slaves born in the United States. In states such
as Virginia, Georgia, and the Carolinas, where land rapidly became
depleted and thus less conducive to the production of cotton, what
essentially amounted to the breeding of slaves became a primary
industry.[8]

The act would be further tailored and strengthened by the subsequent Slave Importation Acts of 1818 and 1820.[9] But, in the
meantime, slavery continued to flourish, and the importation of
slaves did not stop. As a matter of fact, even more slaves would have
arrived had Great Britain not outlawed the slave trade in 1807 and
had Her Majesty's Navy not captured a number of American slave
smugglers off the coast of Africa.

THE LAW

The Slave Importation Act[10] specifically outlawed the importation
of slaves and provided penalties for those involved in slave trading.
Each section of the act provided that it was not effective until January 1, 1808.

The language in the act prohibiting slave trading was clear. The
act made it unlawful to import into the United States "any negro,
mulatto, or person of colour" with the intention of holding that
person as a slave or selling that person into slavery.

It also contained specific enforcement provisions designed to
control the importation of slaves. Strong penalties for violating the
enforcement provisions were clearly set forth. The first enforcement provision addressed shipbuilders. The act made it illegal to
build a ship for the purpose of slave trading. If violated, the act
provided that the ship would be forfeited to the United States and
the shipbuilder fined.

There was a fine for anyone transporting or assisting in the transport of slaves from foreign countries for the purpose of slave trading. Again, the act specified that the ship used in the transport
would be forfeited to the United States. The act further provided
that the importer had no right to the persons imported and

granted that the state legislatures had the power to determine what to do with the imported persons.

The act set forth the penalty for any individual found selling persons into slavery. The penalty included both a fine and imprisonment. Likewise, the act provided for a fine for those found purchasing slaves.

The enforcement provisions of the Slave Importation Act set forth procedures for monitoring ships in the jurisdictional limits of the United States. The act granted the president authority to deploy armed vessels to enforce the act and provided for a fine and imprisonment for commanders of ships found in violation of the act.

Finally, the act provided specific means to monitor the transportation of "negro, mulatto, or persons of colour" aboard ships. The act required all ships to complete a detailed manifest regarding those on board. Violators of the provisions were subject to fines.

6. Slave Importation Act

An Act to prohibit the importation of slaves into any port or place within the jurisdiction of the United States, from and after the first day of January, in the year of our Lord one thousand eight hundred and eight. . . .

Be it enacted . . . That . . . it shall not be lawful to import or bring into the United States or the territories thereof from any foreign kingdom, place, or country, any negro, mulatto, or person of colour, with intent to hold, sell, or dispose of such negro, mulatto, or person of colour, as a slave, or to be held to service or labour.

SEC. 2. And be it further enacted, That no citizen or citizens of the United States, or any other person, shall . . . build, fit, equip, load . . . any ship . . . in any port or place within the jurisdiction of the United States, nor shall cause any ship . . . to sail from any port or place within the same, for the purpose of procuring any negro, mulatto, or person of colour, from any foreign kingdom, place, or country, to be transported to any port or place whatsoever, within the jurisdiction of the United States, to be held, sold, or disposed of as slaves, or to be held to service or labour: and if any ship . . . shall be so fitted out for the purpose aforesaid . . . every such ship . . . , her tackle, apparel, and furniture, shall be forfeited to the United States, and shall be liable to be seized, prosecuted, and condemned. . . .

SEC. 3. And be it further enacted, That all and every person so building, fitting out, equipping, loading . . . any ship . . . knowing or intending that the same shall be employed in such trade or business . . . shall severally forfeit and pay twenty thousand dollars. . . .

SEC. 4. And be it further enacted, If any citizen or citizens of the United States, or any person resident within the jurisdiction of the same, shall . . . take on board, receive or transport from any of the coasts or kingdoms of Africa, or from any other foreign kingdom, place, or country, any negro, mulatto, or person of colour, in any ship . . . for the purpose of selling them in any port or place within the jurisdiction of the United States as slaves, or to be held to service or labour, or shall be in any ways aiding or abetting therein, such citizen or citizens, or person, shall severally forfeit and pay five thousand dollars, . . . and every such ship . . . shall be forfeited to the United States. . . . And neither the importer, nor any person or persons claiming from or under him, shall hold any right or title whatsoever to any negro, mulatto, or person of colour, nor to the service or labour thereof, who may be imported or brought within the United States, or territories thereof, in violation of this law. . . .

SEC. 5. And be it further enacted, That if any citizen or citizens of the United States, or any other person resident within the [United States], shall . . . take on board any ship . . . from any of the coasts or kingdoms of Africa, or from any other foreign . . . country, any negro, mulatto, or person of colour, with intent to sell him, her, or them, for a slave, or slaves, or to be held to service or labour, and shall transport the same to any port or place within the jurisdiction of the United States, and there sell such negro, mulatto, or person of colour . . . for a slave, or to be held to service or labour, every such offender shall be deemed guilty of a high misdemeanor, and being thereof convicted before any court having competent jurisdiction, shall suffer imprisonment for not more than ten years nor less than five years, and be fined not exceeding ten thousand dollars, nor less than one thousand dollars.

SEC. 6. And be it further enacted, That if any person . . . shall . . . purchase or sell any negro, mulatto, or person of colour, for a slave, or to be held to service or labour, who shall have been imported, or brought from any foreign . . . country . . . into any port or place within the jurisdiction of the United States, after the last day of December, one thousand eight hundred and seven, knowing at the time of such purchase or sale, such negro, mulatto or person of colour, was so brought within the jurisdiction of the Unified States, . . . such purchaser and seller shall severally forfeit and pay for every negro, mulatto, or person of colour, so purchased or sold as aforesaid, eight hundred dollars. . . .

SEC. 7. And be it further enacted, That if any ship . . . shall be found . . . in any river, port, bay, or harbor, or on the high seas, within the jurisdictional limits of the United States, or hovering on the coast thereof, having on board any negro, mulatto, or person of colour, for the purpose of selling them as slaves, . . . in any port or place within the jurisdiction of the United States, contrary to the prohibition of this act, every such ship . . . , together with her tackle, apparel, and furniture, and the goods or effects which shall be found on board the same, shall be forfeited to the use of the United States, and may be seized, prosecuted, and condemned, in any court of the United States. . . . And it shall be lawful for the President of the United States, and he is hereby authorized, should he deem it expedient, to cause any of the armed vessels of the United States to be manned and employed to cruise on any part of the coast of the United States . . . where he may judge attempts will be made to violate the provisions of this act, and to instruct and direct the commanders of armed vessels of the United States, to seize . . . all such ships . . . and moreover to seize . . . all ships . . . of the United States, wheresoever found on the high seas, [violating] the provisions of this act, to be proceeded against according to law, and the captain . . . of every such ship . . . so found and seized . . . shall be deemed guilty of a high misdemeanor, and shall be liable to be prosecuted before any court of the United States . . . and being thereof convicted, shall be fined not exceeding ten thousand dollars, and be imprisoned not less than two years, and not exceeding four years. . . . [And] every . . . negro, mulatto, or person of colour [from the ship shall be delivered] to such person or persons as shall be appointed by the respective states, to receive the same, and if no such person or persons shall be appointed by the respective states, they shall deliver every such negro, mulatto, or person of colour, to the overseers of the poor of the port or place where such ship . . . may be brought or found, and shall immediately transmit to the governor or chief magistrate of the state. . . .

SEC. 8. And be it further enacted, That no captain . . . of any ship . . . of less burden than forty tons, shall . . . take on board and transport any negro, mulatto, or person of colour, to any port or place whatsoever, for the purpose of selling or disposing of the same as a slave, or with intent that the same may be sold or disposed of to be held to service or labour, on penalty of forfeiting for every such negro, mulatto, or person of colour, so taken on board and transported, as aforesaid, the sum of eight hundred dollars. . . . Provided however, That nothing in this section shall extend to prohibit the taking on board or transporting on any river, or inland bay of the sea, within the jurisdiction of the United States, any negro, mulatto, or person of colour, (not imported contrary to the provisions of this act) in any vessel or species of craft whatever.

SEC. 9. And be it further enacted, That the captain . . . of any ship . . . of the burden of forty tons or more . . . from any port in the United States, to any port or place within the jurisdiction of the same, having on board any negro, mulatto, or person of colour, for the purpose of transporting them to be sold or disposed of as slaves, or to be held to service or labour, shall, previous to the departure of such ship . . . , make out and subscribe duplicate manifests of every such negro, mulatto, or person of colour, on board such ship . . . therein specifying the name and sex of each person, their age and stature, as near as may be, and the class to which they respectively belong, whether negro, mulatto, or person of colour, with the name and place of residence of every owner or shipper of the same, and shall deliver such manifests to the collector of the port, if there be one, otherwise to the surveyor, before whom the captain, . . . together with the owner or shipper, shall severally swear . . . that the persons therein specified were not imported or brought into the United States, from and after the first day of January, one thousand eight hundred and eight, and that under the laws of the state, they are held to service or labour; whereupon the said collector or surveyor shall certify the . . . manifests, . . . which he shall return to the . . . captain . . . , with a permit, specifying . . . the number, names, and general description of such persons, and authorizing him to proceed to the port of his destination. And if any ship . . . , being laden and destined as aforesaid, shall depart from the port where she may then be, without the captain . . . having first made out and subscribed duplicate manifests, . . . and without having previously delivered the same to the said collector . . . and obtained a permit . . . or shall, previous to her arrival at the port of her destination, take on board any negro, mulatto, or person of colour, other than those specified in the manifests, . . . every such ship . . . , together with her tackle, apparel and furniture, shall be forfeited to the use of the United States, and may be seized, prosecuted and condemned in any court of the United States having jurisdiction thereof; and the captain . . . of every such ship . . . , shall moreover forfeit, for every such negro, mulatto, or person of colour, so transported, or taken on board, contrary to the provisions of this act, the sum of one thousand dollars. . . .

SEC. 10. And be it further enacted, That the captain . . . of every ship . . . of the burden of forty tons or more . . . sailing coastwise, and having on board any negro, mulatto, or person of colour, to sell or dispose of as slaves, or to be held to service or labour, and arriving in any port within the jurisdiction of the United States . . . shall, previous to the unloading or putting on shore any of the persons aforesaid, or suffering them to go on shore, deliver to the collector, if there be one, or if not, to the surveyor residing at the port of her arrival, the manifest certified by the collector or surveyor of the port from whence she sailed . . . to the truth of which . . . he shall . . . affirm, and if the collector or surveyor shall be satisfied therewith, he shall thereupon grant a permit for unloading or suffering such negro, mulatto, or person of colour, to be put on shore, and if the captain . . . of any such ship . . . shall neglect or refuse to deliver the manifest at the time and in the manner herein directed, or shall land or put on shore any negro, mulatto, or person of colour, for the purpose aforesaid, before he shall have delivered his manifest as aforesaid, and obtained a permit for that purpose, every such captain . . . shall forfeit and pay ten thousand dollars. . . .

APPROVED, March 2, 1807.

NOTES

1. See John Mack Faragher et al., *Out of Many* (Upper Saddle River, N.J.: Prentice-Hall, 2000), pp. 298–99.

2. For example, see Jeannette Mirsky and Allan Nevins, *The World of Eli Whitney* (New York: Macmillan, 1952).

3. Paul Johnson, *A History of the American People* (New York: HarperCollins, 1997), p. 310.

4. See John Hope Franklin and Alfred A. Moss, Jr., *From Slavery to Freedom: A History of African Americans* (New York: Knopf, 1994), p. 90.

5. Ibid., p. 91.

6. Robert Divine et al., *America: Past and Present* (New York: Longman, 1999), pp. 248–249.

7. Franklin and Moss, *From Slavery to Freedom*, p. 92.

8. See Jan Lewis, *The Pursuit of Happiness, Family, and Values in Jefferson's Virginia* (New York: Cambridge University Press, 1983); Henry Hobhouse, *Seeds of Change: Five Plants That Transformed the World* (New York: Harper & Row, 1987), p. 153; Peter Kolchin, *Unfree Labor* (New York: Cambridge University Press, 1987), p. 366.

9. *Statutes at Large of the United States* (Washington, D.C.: GPO), vol. 3, pp. 450, 532, and 600.

10. *Statutes at Large of the United States* (Washington, D.C.: GPO), vol. 2, pp. 426–430.

7

Missouri Compromise

1820

The Missouri Compromise set up a boundary line to delineate whether newly admitted states were to be free states or permitted to have slavery.

HISTORICAL CONTEXT

Since the 1760s, the line dividing slave and free states had been relatively clear. In order to settle a dispute between Maryland and Pennsylvania, British astronomers Charles Mason and Jeremiah Dixon were hired to draw a line of demarcation, later known as the Mason-Dixon line. By the early nineteenth century, the eleven states located north of a line that ran along the southern and western boundaries of Pennsylvania were considered free states, and the eleven situated south of that line remained slave states.

Following the 1803 Louisiana Purchase, which allowed the United States to acquire vast expanses of land on its western frontier, it was only a matter of time before populations would increase, states would form, and these states would then seek admittance into the Union. At that juncture, a major national issue would not be able to be avoided. The federal government would have to decide whether to admit them as slave or free states.

The state of Missouri provided one of the first test cases. In 1817, having attained the necessary population requirement of 60,000 people, Missouri petitioned for statehood. With numerous slave-holders already living and working there, and several thousand slaves in residence, the decision as to the slavery status of the new state of Missouri was anything but an abstract exercise. Heated debate soon arose in the region and the nation over the matter.

By 1819 the issue of Missouri statehood and the imbedded issue of slavery's status in such states were being openly debated in Congress. Representative James Tallmadge, Jr. (Rep., N.Y.) offered an amendment that would have prohibited any further importation of slaves into Missouri and eventually have granted freedom to those currently residing there. In the ensuing debate held on the floor of the United States House of Representatives, Tallmadge appeared to echo the sentiment of many Northerners when he attacked the very institution of slavery and also expressed concern about increasing the political power of the Southern states by adding a state to its ranks. His amendment passed in the House where free states held a 105–81 majority, but it was subsequently defeated in the United States Senate where the body was divided evenly. Among other things, it was argued that the United States Constitution granted states complete sovereignty in drafting their state constitutions; therefore, it was deemed unconstitutional for the federal government to set such conditions of statehood.

The often bitter debate marked at least two firsts for the fledgling nation. It was part of the first extended public debate over the issue of slavery, and it was the first time Southern representatives openly threatened secession on the floor of the United States Congress. While highly emotional arguments were couched in the language of morality and fundamental rights, and while several votes followed closely along regional lines, many free blacks were observed listening intently to the debate from the Senate gallery.[1]

The badly divided Congress labored to find an alternative solution. A year later, they had worked out an uneasy compromise, assisted in the House by the efforts of the Speaker, Henry Clay (Rep., Ky.), the "Great Pacificator." Maine had long wanted to separate from Massachusetts and become a state in its own right. Thus, in a compromise approved on March 2, 1820, Missouri would be admitted as a state permitted to have slavery, and Maine, in a far different region, would come in as a free state. Meanwhile, the remainder of the expansive Louisiana Territories would be partitioned. With the exception of Missouri, slavery would be outlawed in any new state north of the 36° 30' parallel, but it would be allowed in those south of that demarcation. In addition, provisions of the Fugitive Slave Act would continue to be operative: slaves escaping to the Northern territories were still subject to being captured and returned to their Southern owners.

A year later, former President Thomas Jefferson stated, almost prophetically, "All, I fear, do not see the speck on our horizon which is to burst on us as a tornado, sooner or later. The line of division lately marked out between the different portions of our confederacy is such as will never, I fear, be obliterated."[2]

The Missouri Compromise ran into difficulties almost immediately, beginning when the Missouri constitutional convention insisted that a clause be added to their constitution prohibiting free blacks and mulattos from settling in the new state. At the time, however, there were already some 300,000 free black citizens in several states across both the North and South. Consequently, such a proviso appeared to run contrary to Article IV, Section 2 of the United States Constitution, which guarantees, "The citizens of each state shall be entitled to the privileges and immunities of citizens in the several states." As a way around this latest complication, Speaker Clay persuaded his colleagues to accept the Missouri constitution, as long as it "shall never be construed" to discriminate against citizens of other states. Since free blacks were already being treated differently under the law in the various states of the North and South, such an argument provided at least a temporary peace.

Nevertheless, the issue of "privileges and immunities" came to a head when Dred Scott, a Missouri slave, accompanied his master, army doctor John Emerson, to the free state of Illinois, as well as to Fort Snelling in the Wisconsin Territory. Upon his return to Missouri four years later, Scott sued for his freedom, as well as the freedom of his wife, Harriet, whom he had met and married while in Wisconsin, and a daughter, Eliza, born while the couple was residing there. He contended that the "privileges and immunities clause" allowed such a claim because they had essentially enjoyed free status for a significant period of time during their earlier travels.

Scott won at the trial level, but his legal victory was overturned by the Missouri Supreme Court. Then, in its now famous 1857 Dred Scott decision, the U.S. Supreme Court ruled, among other things, that the Missouri Compromise was unconstitutional, at least as it related to slavery north and south of the 36° 30' parallel. It had essentially denied slaveholders in free territories their property without due process of law, violating the Fifth Amendment to the United States Constitution.[3]

Republicans subsequently denounced the decision as "a wicked and false judgement" and "the greatest crime in the annals of the republic." Yet, rather than urging open defiance of the nation's highest court, they argued on technical grounds that it did not actually bind the United States Congress, and thus a ban on slavery in the territories could still be enacted.[4]

THE LAW

The Missouri Compromise[5] authorized the Missouri Territory to form a new state. The act delineated the boundaries of the new state. It provided that only free white male citizens were permitted to vote. It also contained specific provisions regarding the formation of a state convention and the objectives of that convention. The act addressed matters relevant to the proper functioning of the new state, such as establishing schools, funding roads, and providing land for government buildings. Most significantly, the act contained a provision that slavery was prohibited in the territory "north of thirty-six degrees and thirty minutes north latitude," except in Missouri. Finally, the act provided that fugitive slaves captured in this designated territory could be reclaimed by their owners.

7. Missouri Compromise

CHAP. XXII.

An Act to authorize the people of the Missouri territory to form a constitution and state government, and for the admission of such state into the Union on an equal footing with the original states, and to prohibit slavery in certain territories.

Be it enacted . . . That the inhabitants of that portion of the Missouri territory included within the boundaries hereinafter designated, be, and they are hereby, authorized to form for themselves a constitution and state government, and to assume such name as they shall deem proper; and the said state, when formed, shall be admitted into the Union, upon an equal footing with the original states, in all respects whatsoever. . . .

SEC. 3. And be it further enacted, That all free white male citizens of the United States, who shall have arrived at the age of twenty-one years, and have resided in said territory three months previous to the day of election, and all other persons qualified to vote for representatives to the general assembly of the said territory, shall be qualified to be elected, and

they are hereby qualified and authorized to vote, and choose representatives to form a convention. . . .

SEC. 8. And be it further enacted, That in all that territory ceded by
France to the United States, under the name of Louisiana, which lies
north of thirty-six degrees and thirty minutes north latitude, not included
within the limits of the state, contemplated by this act, slavery and involuntary servitude, otherwise than in the punishment of crimes, whereof the
parties shall have been duly convicted, shall be, and is hereby, forever
prohibited: Provided always, That any person escaping into the same, from
whom labour or service is lawfully claimed, in any state or territory of the
United States, such fugitive may be lawfully reclaimed and conveyed to
the person claiming his or her labour or service as aforesaid.

NOTES

1. John Mack Faragher et al., *Out of Many* (Upper Saddle River, N.J.: Prentice-
Hall, 2000), pp. 257–58.

2. As quoted in Robert Divine et al., *America: Past and Present* (New York: Longman, 1999), p. 282.

3. *Dred Scott v. Sandford*, 60 U.S. 393.

4. Divine, *America*, p. 427.

5. *Statutes at Large of the United States* (Washington, D.C.: GPO), vol. 3, pp. 544–
48.

8

Compromise of 1850

1850

The Compromise of 1850 allowed California to be admitted as a free state and Utah to make the decision for itself. It also ended the slave trade in Washington, D.C., in return for stricter enforcement of the Fugitive Slave Act.

HISTORICAL CONTEXT

Since the Northwest Ordinance prohibited slavery in the Northwest Territories, all subsequent states in that region entered the Union as free states. The Missouri Compromise at least temporarily settled how slavery was to be handled in the states that emerged from the recently acquired Louisiana Territories. Now, a similar issue developed surrounding how this matter would be resolved when parts of Texas and neighboring territories were annexed. These lands had been ceded by Mexico in the 1848 Treaty of Guadalupe Hidalgo, which ended the Mexican-American War. Within a year, both California and Utah had applied for statehood.

At the very outset of that war, in 1846, Representative David Wilmot (Rep., Pa.) introduced a relatively radical measure known as the Wilmot Proviso. Attached to one of President James Polk's appropriation bills, the proviso would have prohibited slavery in any territory gained as a result of the conflict. Some moderates countered with a proposal to extend westward the 36° 30' latitude set out in the Missouri Compromise; others argued for squatters' rights, essentially allowing settlers to decide the issue for them-

selves. Such moderate alternatives were opposed, however, by ide-
ologues from both the free and slave camps.[1]

Congressional exchanges, which became highly volatile, often
turned on fundamental ideological differences including whether
the federal government even had the constitutional authority to
make this determination for a state. For a period of six months, the
debate between such luminaries as Henry Clay (Rep., Ky.), John
Calhoun (Dem., S.C.), and Daniel Webster (Whig, Mass.) produced
some of the finest oratory ever to emanate from Capitol Hill. It also
contained a clear threat of secession by the South, posing a very
real possibility of a civil war.[2]

The fear of such dire developments finally prompted consideration of a compromise. A series of majorities gradually began to form
around a combination of proposals made by Representative Henry
Clay. Ultimately, Clay's Compromise of 1850 was passed one piece
at a time, lobbied through by younger senators such as Stephen
Douglas (Dem., Ill.). California had already applied to enter as a
free state, and it would be allowed to do so. The slave trade, but
not slavery, would be abolished in the District of Columbia. Territories that would become the states of Utah and New Mexico were
to decide the matter for themselves after they were admitted as
states. Finally, the Fugitive Slave Act would be revised and its provisions strengthened.

The Southern states chose not to quibble over the conversion of
Washington, D.C., primarily because it had always been conceded
that Congress had full reign over the District of Columbia and
could abolish the slave trade there at any time. In addition, there
was no real slavery presence or popular demand for it in California.
Southerners contented themselves with a real linchpin of the compromise: a significant bolstering of the Fugitive Slave Act.[3]

Given that the United States Supreme Court had ruled that state
officials were not compelled by Congress to assist in the enforcement of the 1793 Fugitive Slave Act,[4] the entire fugitive slave process was to be federalized. This would include the creation of federal
commissioners to adjudicate disputed claims. Those commissioners
would be granted the power to employ federal marshals, or even
temporarily conscript local citizens, for the purpose of capturing,
holding, and ultimately returning runaway slaves. Sworn testimony
by the owner would be considered sufficient evidence of ownership,
and the runaway would not be allowed to testify in his or her own
defense. To top it off, the commissioners stood to receive twice as

much ($10 as opposed to $5) per case if the fugitive slave were returned to the declared owner rather than set free. This entire process evoked fear of potential corruption and mistaken identity, not to mention the disdain many had for the idea that he or she might be coerced into becoming a slave hunter.

As with most issues that divide people on the basis of fundamental principles, resolving them in such a manner was destined to be an uneasy compromise. According to Salmon Chase, "The question of slavery in the territories has been avoided. It has not been settled."[5] Northern blacks and fugitive slaves, for example, would at times use violence to resist the recapture of runaways. Meanwhile, some abolitionists openly defied what they considered to be immoral fugitive slave laws. At times they rescued fugitive slaves directly out of the hands of United States marshals, and local juries refused to convict them. Such developments led Representative Cave Johnson (Dem., Tenn.) to warn, "If the fugitive slave bill is not enforced in the North, the moderate men of the South . . . will be overwhelmed by the 'fire-eaters' [secessionists]."[6] Even though the law generally was successfully enforced, at least initially, such resistance only further spurred discussion of secession in the South.[7]

Because California was added as a free state without also adding a corresponding slave state, there were now sixteen free states and only fifteen slave states. The slave state–free state balance in the United States Senate had been upset, and it remained that way. Future congresses contained antislavery majorities in both houses of Congress.

THE LAW

The Compromise of 1850 included several separate acts.[8] The first addressed the admittance of California as a state. Without reference to slavery, this act declared California a state and expressly set forth the specific conditions on which its admittance depended.

The second act included below established a governmental structure for Utah. The act specifically provided that when the territory was admitted into the Union it would be admitted "with or without slavery."

Another act included below amended the Fugitive Slave Act. Specifically, the new act provided for the appointment of commissioners to enforce the provisions of the Fugitive Slave Act. Powers and duties of the commissioners were specifically set forth. The new act granted commissioners the power to employ federal marshals or other suitable people to execute warrants. The act further provided the procedure for individuals to bring action to reclaim fugitive slaves. The act authorized fines and imprisonment for any person hindering the arrest of a fugitive slave or assisting in the escape of a fugitive slave. Finally, the act contained provisions for the compensation of marshals and others involved in the return of fugitive slaves.

A fourth act of the Compromise of 1850 declared slave trade illegal in the District of Columbia. No slave could be bought or sold in the district. Violation of the act resulted in freedom for the slave.

8. Compromise of 1850

ADMISSION OF THE STATE OF CALIFORNIA

An Act for the Admission of the State of California into the Union.

Be it enacted . . . That the State of California shall be one, and is hereby declared to be one, of the United States of America, and admitted into the Union on an equal footing with the original States in all respects whatever. . . .

APPROVED, September 9, 1850.

ESTABLISHING THE UTAH TERRITORY

An Act to Establish a Territorial Government for Utah.

Be it enacted . . . That all that part of the territory of the United States included within the following limits . . . is hereby, created into a temporary government, by the name of the Territory of Utah; and, when admitted as a State, the said Territory, or any portion of the same, shall be received into the Union, with or without slavery, as their constitution may prescribe at the time of their admission . . .

APPROVED, September 9, 1850.

AMENDING THE FUGITIVE SLAVE ACT

An Act to amend, and supplementary to, the Act entitled "An Act respecting Fugitives from Justice, and Persons escaping from the Service of their Masters," approved February twelfth, one thousand seven hundred and ninety-three.

Be it enacted . . . That the persons who have been . . . appointed commissioners . . . are authorized to exercise the powers that any justice of the peace, or other magistrate of any of the United States, may exercise in respect to offenders for any crime or offence against the United States, by arresting, imprisoning, or bailing the same . . . and are hereby, authorized and required to exercise and discharge all the powers and duties conferred by this act.

SEC. 2. And be it further enacted, That the Superior Court of each organized Territory of the United States shall have the same power to appoint commissioners to take acknowledgements of bail and affidavits, and to take depositions of witnesses in civil causes, which is now possessed by the Circuit Court of the United States; and all commissioners who shall hereafter be appointed . . . shall moreover exercise and discharge all the powers and duties conferred by this act. . . .

SEC. 4. And be it further enacted, That the commissioners above named shall have concurrent jurisdiction with the judges of the Circuit and District Courts of the United States . . . with authority to take and remove such fugitives from service or labor . . . to the State or Territory from which such persons may have escaped or fled. . . .

SEC. 6. And be it further enacted, That when a person held to service or labor in any State or Territory of the United States, has heretofore or shall hereafter escape into another State or Territory of the United States, the person or persons to whom such service or labor may be due . . . may pursue and reclaim such fugitive person, either by procuring a warrant from some one of the courts, judges, or commissioners aforesaid, of the proper circuit, district, or county, for the apprehension of such fugitive from service or labor, or by seizing and arresting such fugitive, where the same can be done without process, and by taking . . . forthwith before such court, judge, or commissioner, whose duty it shall be to hear and determine the case of such claimant in a summary manner. . . .

SEC. 7. And be it further enacted, That any person who shall knowingly and willingly obstruct, hinder, or prevent such claimant . . . from arresting such a fugitive from service or labor . . . or shall rescue . . . such fugitive from service or labor, from the custody of such claimant . . . or shall aid, abet, or assist such person so owing service or labor as aforesaid, directly or indirectly, to escape from such claimant . . . or shall harbor or conceal such fugitive . . . shall, for either of said offences, be subject to a fine not exceeding one thousand dollars, and imprisonment not exceeding six months. . . .

SEC. 8. And be it further enacted, That the marshals, their deputies and the clerks of the said District and Territorial Courts, shall be paid, for their services, the like fees as may be allowed to them for similar services in other cases. . . .

APPROVED, September 18, 1850.

SLAVE TRADING IN WASHINGTON, D.C.

Act to suppress the Slave Trade in the District of Columbia.

Be it enacted . . . That from and after the first day of January, eighteen hundred and fifty-one, it shall not be lawful to bring into the District of Columbia any slave whatever, for the purpose of being sold or for the purpose of being placed in depot, to be subsequently transferred to any other State or place to be sold as merchandize. And if any slave shall be brought into the said District by its owner, or by the authority or consent of its owner, contrary to the provisions of this act, such slave shall thereupon become liberated and free. . . .

APPROVED, September 20, 1850.

NOTES

1. For example, see Samuel Eliot Morrison and Henry Steele Commager, *The Growth of the American Republic* (Oxford, England: Oxford University Press, 1962), vol. 1, p. 618.

2. For example, see Elbert B. Smith, *The Presidencies of Zachary Taylor and Millard Fillmore* (Lawrence: Kansas University Press, 1988); Holman Hamilton, *Prologue to Conflict: The Crisis and Compromise of 1850* (Lexington: University of Kentucky Press, 1964).

3. For example, see Michael F. Holt, *The Political Crisis of the 1850s* (New York: Wiley, 1978).

4. *Prigg v. Pennsylvania*, 41 U.S. 539 (1842).

5. Quoted in John Mack Faragher et al., *Out of Many* (Upper Saddle River, N.J.: Prentice-Hall, 2000), p. 426.

6. Ibid., p. 428.

7. For example, see David Potter, *The Impending Crisis* (New York: Harper and Row, 1976).

8. *Statues at Large of the United States* (Washington, D.C.: GPO) vol. 9, pp. 452–53, 453–54, 462–65, 467–68.

9

Kansas-Nebraska Act

1854

The Kansas-Nebraska Act nullified a significant portion of the Missouri Compromise, allowing Kansas and Nebraska to decide their own slave status despite lying north of the line of demarcation established by the earlier compromise.

HISTORICAL CONTEXT

Northern business interests sought a transcontinental railroad that would run from Chicago, or one of the other major Midwestern cities, to the new state of California and the Pacific Ocean. To that end, legislation was devised that created the Nebraska Territory. The bill was initially conceived by Stephen Douglas, a Democratic senator from the state of Illinois who chaired the Senate Committee on the Territories. Besides advancing the economic interests of Illinois businessmen by fashioning a route that would increase the likelihood of a transcontinental railway terminus in Chicago, Douglas appeared to be trying to curry favor with both the North and South in order to bolster his own presidential aspirations.[1]

Nevertheless, any such legislation designed to assist the spread of commerce in this way also stood to create territories north of the 36° 30' line established by the Missouri Compromise, thereby laying the groundwork for the introduction of even more free states. This was a reality Southern congressmen were likely to oppose in principle; most of them believed that the states should decide this matter for themselves.

In order to appease those Southern congressmen, the proposal contained a provision that allowed for "popular sovereignty" on the slavery matter. The citizens of Nebraska would be allowed to determine the status of slavery for themselves. When that proposal was not enough in these volatile times, Douglas added the creation of the Kansas Territory with the same understanding. In the meantime, slaves could be brought into the new territories pending the local votes on that issue.

The main problem was that both Nebraska and Kansas lie north of the 36° 30' parallel: neither was supposed to have the option of slavery.

With the backing of President Franklin Pierce, and with both major political parties internally divided on the issue, the Kansas-Nebraska Act passed the House by a vote of 113–100; the Senate, 37–14. This was possible in part because many doubted that the geography of either Nebraska or Kansas was conducive to the introduction of a slave-based agriculture.

Nevertheless, the Missouri Compromise was essentially nullified, and with it went the tenuous peace it had created. Free Soilers of the North denounced the law, as did the ardent slaveholders of the South who contended that slavery could not constitutionally be excluded anywhere, even by state choice.

This latest legislative skirmish severely split the Democratic Party, to the point where a group of "independent Democrats," opposed to slavery or its spread, formed and denounced the legislation as "a gross violation of a sacred pledge" and "a criminal betrayal of precious rights."[2] It would also so divide the Whigs that they would soon give way to the Republicans as the other major political party in the nation's two-party political system. United States politics would come to be split cleanly along regional lines with the Democrats as the party of the South and the Republicans the party of the North.[3]

Meanwhile, Kansas quickly became the newest battleground of an emerging intranational war. Antislavery Senator William Seward (Whig, N.Y.) stated on the Senate floor, "We will engage in a competition for the virgin soil of Kansas, and God give this victory to the side which is strong in numbers as it is in right." In responding, South Carolina editor Barnwell Rhett urged Southerners to "send men to Kansas, ready to cast their lot with the pro-slavery party there and able to meet Abolitionism on its own issue, and with its own weapons."[4]

The battle for the soul of Kansas was fiercely contested. The New England Emigrant Aid Society, for example, sent more than 1,200 antislavery zealots in an attempt to sway the results of the initial elections. Meanwhile, pro-slavery legions gathered in Missouri. Led by Democratic Senator David Atchison of Missouri, they crossed over into Kansas on election day in March 1855 and swamped that election with Missouri votes. In one of several elections marred by the casting of ineligible votes by residents of other states, over 6,000 ballots were cast in a territory that had fewer than 3,000 eligible voters.[5]

In the end, the pro-slavery forces prevailed by sizable majorities. Soon they had taken over the Kansas legislature, expelled the elected free-staters, and passed legislation that not only legitimized slavery but also made it a capital offense to assist a fugitive slave and a felony even to question the legality of slavery.[6]

The response was just as emotional. The normally understated *New York Times* described these events as "part of this great scheme for extending and perpetuating the supremacy of Slave Power."[7] To combat these developments, the Kansas antislavery contingent held an unlawful constitutional convention in Topeka. At that convention, they drafted their own constitution, banned both slaves and free blacks from Kansas, applied for statehood, and elected their own governor and legislature. Meanwhile, challenged by crowds at several public appearances thereafter, Douglas himself was quoted as saying, "I could travel from Boston to Chicago by the light of my own [burning] effigy."[8]

Ironically, Kansas was actually a somewhat unlikely battleground because its climate all but precluded any serious possibility of plantation-type slavery. Nevertheless, the ideological battle lines had been drawn. By the spring of 1856, the disagreements had degenerated into bloodshed. By year's end, more than 200 people had been murdered by one side or the other in what came to be known as "Bleeding Kansas."[9]

The violence even bled over onto the floor of the United States Senate. In the spring of 1856, Charles Sumner (Whig, Mass.) delivered a fiery antislavery speech on the floor of the Senate entitled, "The Crime Against Kansas." Accusing the South of plotting to extend slavery into Kansas, the speech included insulting references to several Southern congressmen, especially elderly Democratic Senator Andrew Butler of South Carolina. On May 22, 1856, Butler's cousin, Representative Preston Brooks (Dem., S.C.), burst onto the Senate floor with a cane in his hand and beat the unsuspecting Sumner so severely that he did not return to his seat in that body for more than three years.

THE LAW

The Kansas-Nebraska Act[10] established the temporary territories of Nebraska and Kansas. This exceptionally long act contained numerous provisions relevant to establishing and governing the new territories. It also contained extensive detail regarding the formation and functioning of the executive, legislative, and judicial branches in the new territories.

In regard to race, the act authorized the new territories to decide the issue of slavery for themselves. It clarified that the Fugitive Slave Act was in full effect in these new territories. It restricted suffrage exclusively to white males. Finally, the act overturned provisions of the Missouri Compromise, that act "being inconsistent with the principle of non-intervention by Congress with slavery in the States and Territories."

9. Kansas-Nebraska Act

An Act to organize the Territories of Nebraska and Kansas.

Be it enacted . . . That . . . part of the territory of the United States included within the following limits . . . is hereby, created into a temporary government by the name of the Territory of Nebraska; and when admitted as a State or States, the said Territory or any portion of the same, shall be received into the Union with or without slavery, as their constitution may prescribe at the time of the admission. . . .

SEC. 5. And be it further enacted, That every free white male inhabitant above the age of twenty-one years who shall be an actual resident of said Territory, and shall possess the qualifications hereinafter prescribed, shall be entitled to vote at the first election, and shall be eligible to any office within the said Territory; but the qualifications of voters, and of holding office, at all subsequent elections, shall be such as shall be prescribed by the Legislative Assembly: Provided, That the right of suffrage and of holding office shall be exercised only by citizens of the United States. . . .

SEC. 9. . . . Provided, that nothing herein contained shall be construed to apply to or affect the provisions to the "act respecting fugitives from justice, and persons escaping from the service of their masters," approved

February twelfth, seventeen hundred and ninety-three, and the "act to amend and supplementary to the aforesaid act," approved September eighteen, eighteen hundred and fifty. . . .

SEC. 14. . . . That the Constitution, and all Laws of the United States which are not locally inapplicable, shall have the same force and effect within the said Territory of Nebraska as elsewhere within the United States, except the eighth section of the act preparatory to the admission of Missouri into the Union approved March sixth, eighteen hundred and twenty, which, being inconsistent with the principle of non-intervention by Congress with slaves in the States and Territories, as recognized by the legislation of eighteen hundred and fifty, commonly called the Compromise Measures, is hereby declared inoperative and void; it being the true intent and meaning of this act not to legislate slavery into any Territory or State, nor to exclude it therefrom, but to leave the people thereof perfectly free to form and regulate their domestic institutions in their own way, subject only to the Constitution of the United States: Provided, That nothing herein contained shall be construed to revive or put in force any law or regulation which may have existed prior to the act of sixth March, eighteen hundred and twenty, either protecting, establishing, prohibiting, or abolishing slavery. [This confirms that territories and states were authorized to determine the issue of slavery for themselves.]

Parallel provisions for the Territory of Kansas were codified in sections 19, 23, 27 and 32 of this Act.

NOTES

1. For example, see Robert Walter Johannsen, *Stephen A. Douglas* (New York: Oxford University Press, 1973).

2. Quoted in Robert Divine et al., *America: Past and Present* (New York: Longman, 1999), pp. 419–420; David Goldfield et al., *The American Journey* (Upper Saddle River, N.J.: Prentice-Hall, 1998), p. 443.

3. For example, see Allan Nevins, *Ordeal of the Union: A House Dividing, 1852–1857* (New York: Charles Scribner and Sons, 1947).

4. Quoted in Goldfield, *American Journey*, pp. 443–444.

5. John Mack Faragher et al., *Out of Many* (Upper Saddle River, N.J.: Prentice-Hall, 2000), p. 430.

6. For example, see P.W. Gates, *Fifty-Million Acres: Conflicts over Kansas Land Policy, 1854–1890* (Ithaca, N.Y.: Cornell University Press, 1954).

7. Cited in Faragher, *Out of Many*, p. 430.

8. Quoted in ibid.

9. For example, see James A. Rawley, *Race and Politics: Bleeding Kansas and the Coming of the Civil War* (Philadelphia: Lippincott, 1969); Stephen B. Oates, *To Purge*

This Land with Blood: A Biography of John Brown (Amherst: University of Massachusetts Press, 1984).

    10. *Statutes at Large of the United States* (Washington, D.C.: GPO), vol. 10, pp. 277–90.

10

Constitution of the Confederate States of America

1861

HISTORICAL CONTEXT

In November 1860, Abraham Lincoln won less than 40 percent of the popular vote in a bitterly contested four-way race. He nevertheless succeeded in gaining a majority of the electoral votes by winning all but one of the free states and splitting another. In nine of the Southern states, however, Lincoln failed to win a single vote.

In the months leading up to the 1860 election, the governors of South Carolina, Alabama, and Mississippi had committed their states to secession should Lincoln be the victor. In response to his election, several of the Southern states began almost immediately to move toward secession. None held referenda. Instead, they held secession conventions, and the delegates to those conventions were chosen by their respective state legislatures.

Within two months, seven Southern states had seceded from the Union. Besides the obvious need to protect slavery, an institution that had become vital to the Southern economy, the defense of slavery reflected a twin-edged philosophy on the part of many white Southerners. There was clearly a strong belief in both individualism and decentralized government. Individual slave owners had a right to their private property, which included their slave-holdings. As slaves were not regarded as being genetically equal to whites, this was not perceived to violate principles of individual liberty. In addition, it was believed, states had a right to make their own slavery-related policy without interference from the federal government.

South Carolina was the first to withdraw, seceding on December

20, 1860. Arguing at their secession convention that membership in the United States was a "compact" among sovereign states, they justified their withdrawal by arguing that Lincoln had been elected by a "sectional party whose opinions and purposes are hostile to slavery."[1] By February 1, South Carolina had been joined by Alabama, Mississippi, Florida, Georgia, Louisiana, and Texas.

Border states, such as Virginia, North Carolina, Tennessee, and Arkansas, continued to look for a compromise solution that would allow them to remain in the Union; the original seven seceding states chose not to wait for them. Instead, they met in Montgomery, Alabama, on February 4 for the purpose of forming the Confederate States of America. Those attending convened themselves as a provisional government, and they selected Jefferson Davis of Mississippi as their provisional president. They then moved quickly to design a permanent Confederate constitution.

As the Montgomery group debated, it was clear that the more radical factions were outnumbered. Radicals such as William Yancey of Alabama and Robert Barnwell Rhett of South Carolina were denied governance positions. Several of the most extreme propositions were defeated, including proposals to reinstitute the Atlantic slave trade, to abandon the three-fifths compromise, and to bar all free states from joining the Confederacy.

The final draft of the Constitution of the Confederate States was very similar to the existing United States Constitution, reflecting an allegiance to virtually all the primary principles upon which the United States had been founded. It also suggested a desire to attract wavering border states and ultimately many of the free states as well. The main differences involved writing Southern interpretations of the original document directly into constitutional law. Besides outlawing protective tariffs and strengthening the sovereignty of states from federal control, most of these differences had to do with protecting the institution of slavery.

Jefferson Davis was inaugurated at the state capitol in Montgomery, Alabama, on February 18, 1861. Speaking to a crowd of thousands, Davis declared in his inaugural address, "We have changed the constituent parts, but not the system of our government." Quoting the Declaration of Independence, he contended that secession "illustrates the American idea that governments rest on the consent of the governed . . . and that it is the right of the people to alter or abolish them at will whenever they become destructive of the ends for which they were established." He concluded that "a just perception of mutual interest [should] permit us peaceably to pursue our separate political [course]. . . . Obstacles may retard, but they cannot long prevent, the progress of a movement sanctified by its justice and sustained by a virtuous people."[2]

THE LAW

The Confederate constitution incorporated many of the provisions of the United States Constitution, including the manner in which slaves residing in each state should be counted for the purposes of calculating representation and taxation for the state. It prohibited the importation of slaves "from any foreign country" and gave the Confederate congress the authority "to prohibit the introduction of slaves from any State not a member of, or Territory not belonging to, this Confederacy." It also quite explicitly protected the right to own slaves as a form of private property, a right to be respected when traveling with them to other Confederate states. In addition there was a forceful fugitive slave provision. Such protections were also to apply to any territory the Confederate States happened to acquire.

10. Constitution of the Confederate States of America

ARTICLE I

Section 2. Clause 3. Representatives and direct taxes shall be apportioned among the several States, which may be included within this Confederacy, according to their respective numbers, which shall be determined by adding to the whole number of free persons, including those bound to service for a term of years, and excluding Indians not taxed, three-fifths of all slaves. . . .

Section 9. Clause 1. The importation of negroes of the African race from any foreign country other than the slaveholding States or Territories of the United States of America, is hereby forbidden; and Congress is required to pass such laws as shall effectually prevent the same.

Section 9. Clause 2. Congress shall also have power to prohibit the introduction of slaves from any State not a member of, or Territory not belonging to, this Confederacy. . . .

Section 9. Clause 4. No bill of attainder, ex post facto law, or law denying or impairing the right of property in negro slaves shall be passed. . . .

ARTICLE IV

Section 2. Clause 1. The citizens of each State shall be entitled to all the privileges and immunities of citizens in the several States; and shall have the right of transit and sojourn in any State of this Confederacy, with their slaves and other property; and the right of property in said slaves shall not be thereby impaired. . . .

Section 2. Clause 3. No slave or other person held to service or labor in any State or Territory of the Confederate States, under the laws thereof, escaping or lawfully carried into another, shall, in consequence of any law or regulation therein, be discharged from such service or labor; but shall be delivered up on claim of the party to whom such slave belongs, or to whom such service or labor may be due. . . .

Section 3. Clause 3. The Confederate States may acquire new territory; and Congress shall have power to legislate and provide governments for the inhabitants of all territory belonging to the Confederate States, lying without the limits of the several States; and may permit them, at such times, and in such manner as it may by law provide, to form States to be admitted into the Confederacy. In all such territory the institution of negro slavery, as it now exists in the Confederate States, shall be recognized and protected by Congress and by the Territorial government; and the inhabitants of the several Confederate States and Territories shall have the right to take to such Territory any slaves lawfully held by them in any of the States or Territories of the Confederate States. . . .

NOTES

1. Quoted in Robert Divine et al., *America: Past and Present* (New York: Longman, 1999), p. 443.

2. Quoted in John Mack Faragher et al., *Out of Many* (Upper Saddle River, N.J.: Prentice-Hall, 2000), p. 443.

11

Confiscation Acts

1861 and 1862

The Confiscation Acts allowed for the seizure of slaves in all but the loyal border states where even the Fugitive Slave Act would continue to be enforced. Seized slaves were to be emancipated, but they remained subject to being conscripted into the service of the Union's war effort.

HISTORICAL CONTEXT

Antislavery groups had been pressing for the emancipation of slaves at the state level since the first of these groups appeared in Pennsylvania in 1775. By 1792 there was at least one emancipation society in every Northern state. Vermont was the first state to emancipate, passing its law in 1777. By 1805 every Northern state had passed at least a gradual emancipation law, and legal slavery ceased to exist in the North as of July 4, 1827, when New York's legislation went into full effect.

The evolution of New York's law was similar to that found in several other states at the time. The 1790 census listed 21,000 slaves in the state. When New York passed its emancipation law in 1799, it was implemented gradually so as at least partially to appease existing slave owners. For example, all blacks born after the date the law was passed were free, but they owed service to their mother's owner until they reached a certain age. In other words, emancipation did not come into full force for another generation. In addition, compensation was paid to the state's slave owners.

It is important to remember that the gradual freeing of the slaves in the North was being matched by an acceleration of slavery in the South. From the formal termination of Northern slavery in 1827 until the end of the Civil War, the number of slaves in the United States increased from 1.8 million to more than 4 million.

When the Civil War began, many free blacks volunteered to fight for the Union; however, their enlistment was almost universally rejected. Meanwhile, Southern slaves were beginning to escape and seek refuge behind Union lines, although there was no federal policy outlining how they were to be handled. At least on paper, the Fugitive Slave Act remained in effect. Consequently, such fugitives were being returned or emancipated to one degree or another at the discretion of the Northern generals in the field.

In the summer of 1861, Congress adopted a resolution by a nearly unanimous vote that declared the war was being fought to preserve the union and not to change domestic institutions in any particular state. Nevertheless, the United States House of Representatives also passed a resolution declaring that Union troops did not have a responsibility to capture and return runaway slaves. That same summer, Congress as a whole passed the first of two Confiscation Acts, declaring that any property used in the Confederate war effort could be seized. This included slaves, who, if found to have been used in that manner, were to be immediately and forever set free.

The following summer, 1862, Congress passed the second of its Confiscation Acts, this time ordering the seizure of all land and property of disloyal Southerners. This included their slaves, who could then be employed in ways that advanced the federal war effort. In addition, as a concession to the loyal border states, fugitive slave laws would continue to be enforced as they applied to slaves held within the boundaries of those states.

As more and more fugitive slaves sought refuge behind advancing Union lines, their treatment continued to be inconsistent. Some were given small plots of confiscated land. Some were allowed to pursue employment on their own. Others were leased to loyal plantation owners. Meanwhile, some generals issued sweeping emancipation orders, far exceeding existing federal policy. Those orders then had to be rescinded by President Abraham Lincoln. There was a need for an even clearer federal emancipation policy, and President Lincoln would provide this in his Emancipation Proclamation.

THE LAW

The Confiscation Act,[1] passed in 1861, provided that property used in aiding an insurrection could be seized. The act set forth the jurisdiction for condemnation and delineated who could institute the proceedings. Furthermore, it provided that slave owners would forfeit any claim to a slave used in an insurrection.

The second Confiscation Act,[2] passed in 1862, bolstered its predecessor. It clearly set forth the punishment for treason. Punishment included death, imprisonment, fines, and freeing of slaves held by the person convicted of treason. This act also delineated punishment for insurrection or rebellion against the government. Punishment for this offense included imprisonment, fines, and liberation of any slaves owned. The second act specifically permitted the president to seize assets of those leading or assisting in the rebellion and contained a provision regarding the proceedings to be followed to secure condemnation of a seized property. It permitted those who were engaged in rebellion to have sixty days to cease aiding in the rebellion or risk seizure of property. In regard to slavery, certain slaves were deemed captives of war and freed, while other slaves would be set free unless the person claiming ownership of the slave made an oath of loyalty to the United States. The act allowed the United States to employ former slaves to assist in suppressing the rebellion. It condoned the colonization of freed slaves and authorized the president to offer amnesty and pardon to those who may have participated in the insurrection.

11a. Confiscation Act of 1861

CHAP. LX.

An Act to confiscate Property used for insurrectionary Purposes.

Be it enacted . . . That if, during the present or any future insurrection against the Government of the United States, after the President of the United States shall have declared, by proclamation, that the laws of the United States are opposed, and the execution thereof obstructed, by combinations too powerful to be suppressed by the ordinary course of judicial proceedings, or by the power vested in the marshals by law, any person or persons, his, her, or their agent, attorney, or employé, shall purchase or acquire, sell or give, any property of whatsoever kind or description, with intent to use or employ the same, or suffer the same to be used or employed, in aiding, abetting, or promoting such insurrection or resistance to the laws, or any person or persons engaged therein; or if any person or persons, being the owner or owners of any such property, shall knowingly use or employ, or consent to the use or employment of the same as aforesaid, all such property is hereby declared to be lawful subject of prize and capture wherever found; and it shall be the duty of the President of the United States to cause the same to be seized, confiscated, and condemned. . . . [Property used in aiding insurrection can be seized.]

SEC. 4. And be it further enacted, That whenever hereafter, during the present insurrection against the Government of the United States, any person claimed to be held to labor or service under the law of any State, shall be required or permitted by the person to whom such labor or service is claimed to be due, or by the lawful agent of such person, to take up arms against the United States, or shall be required or permitted by the person to whom such labor or service is claimed to be due, or his lawful agent, to work or to be employed in or upon any fort, navy yard, dock, armory, ship, entrenchment, or in any military or naval service whatsoever, against the Government and lawful authority of the United States, then, and in every such case, the person to whom such labor or service is claimed to be due shall forfeit his claim to such labor, any law of the State or of the United States to the contrary notwithstanding. And whenever thereafter the person claiming such labor or service shall seek to enforce his claim, it shall be a full and sufficient answer to such claim that the person whose service or labor is claimed had been employed in hostile service against the Government of the United States, contrary to the provisions of this act. [Slaves used in insurrection are forfeited.]

APPROVED, August 6, 1861.

11b. Confiscation Act of 1862

CHAP. CXCV.

An Act to suppress Insurrection, to punish Treason and Rebellion, to seize and confiscate the Property of Rebels, and for other Purposes.

Be it enacted . . . That every person who shall be adjudged guilty thereof, shall suffer death, and all his slaves, if any, shall be declared and made free; or, at the discretion of the court, he shall be imprisoned for not less than five years and fined not less than ten thousand dollars, and all his slaves, if any, shall be declared and made free; said fine shall be levied and collected on any or all of the property, real and personal, excluding slaves, of which the said person so convicted was the owner at the time of committing the said crime, any sale or conveyance to the contrary notwithstanding.

SEC. 2. And be it further enacted, That if any person shall hereafter incite, set on foot, assist, or engage in any rebellion or insurrection against the authority of the United States, or the laws thereof, or shall give aid or comfort thereto, or shall engage in, or give aid and comfort to, any such existing rebellion or insurrection, and be convicted thereof, such person shall be punished by imprisonment for a period not exceeding ten years, or by a fine not exceeding ten thousand dollars, and by the liberation of all his slaves, if any he have; or by both of said punishments, at the discretion of the court. . . .

SEC. 9. And be it further enacted, That all slaves of persons who shall hereafter be engaged in rebellion against the government of the United States, or who shall in any way give aid or comfort thereto, escaping from such persons and taking refuge within the lines of the army; and all slaves captured from such persons or deserted by them and coming under the control of the government of the United States; and all slaves of such persons found on [or] being within any place occupied by rebel forces and afterwards occupied by the forces of the United States, shall be deemed captives of war, and shall be forever free of their servitude, and not again held as slaves.

SEC. 10. And be it further enacted, That no slave escaping into any State, Territory, or the District of Columbia, from any other State, shall be delivered up, or in any way impeded or hindered of his liberty, except for crime, or some offence against the laws, unless the person claiming said fugitive shall first make oath that the person to whom the labor or service of such fugitive is alleged to be due is his lawful owner, and has not borne arms against the United States in the present rebellion, nor in any way given aid and comfort thereto; and no person engaged in the military or naval service of the United States shall, under any pretence whatever, assume to decide on the validity of the claim of any person to the service or labor of any other person, or surrender up any such person to the claimant, on pain of being dismissed from service.

SEC. 11. And be it further enacted, That the President of the United States is authorized to employ as many persons of African descent as he may deem necessary and proper for the suppression of this rebellion, and for this purpose he may organize and use them in such manner as he may judge best for the public welfare.

SEC. 12. And be it further enacted, That the President of the United

States is hereby authorized to make provision for the transportation, colonization, and settlement, in some tropical country beyond the limits of the United States, of such persons of the African race, made free by the provisions of this act, as may be willing to emigrate, having first obtained the consent of the government of said country to their protection and settlement within the same, with all the rights and privileges of freemen. . . .

APPROVED, July 17, 1862.

NOTES

1. *Statutes at Large of the United States* (Washington, D.C.: GPO), vol. 12, p. 319.
2. Ibid., pp. 589–92.

12

Emancipation Proclamation

1863

The Emancipation Proclamation freed all slaves dwelling in the states that had seceded from the Union.

HISTORICAL CONTEXT

Abraham Lincoln's position on emancipating the slaves was clear from early in his political career. In 1849, for example, he introduced a bill in Congress that would have gradually freed those slaves residing in Washington, D.C. In his Illinois senatorial campaign of 1858, he called for putting slavery on "the course of ultimate extinction."[1] Thereafter, the Republican Party adopted an antislavery plank in its 1860 party platform, and both Lincoln and a number of his fellow Republicans won election that year with the help of abolitionist support.

Nonetheless, Lincoln also made it clear that as president his goal was first and foremost to preserve the Union at all costs; and he could be very much a political pragmatist. As he responded to journalist Horace Greeley of the *New York Tribune*, "If I could save the Union without freeing any slave I would do it; and if I could save it by freeing all the slaves I would do it; and if I could save it by freeing some and leaving others alone, I would also do that."[2] Initially, this was the position most likely to keep the South from seceding. In his 1861 inaugural address, for instance, he declared that he had "no purpose, directly or indirectly, to interfere with the institution of slavery in the states where it exists."

Once the war had commenced, however, emphasizing the preservation of the Union, as opposed to freeing the slaves, was more likely to maintain the broadest Northern support for the war effort. The United States Congress echoed this sentiment when, in the summer of 1861, it voted almost unanimously for a resolution declaring that the purpose of the war was to save the Union and not to interfere with the social institutions of any state.

Yet, as the Civil War progressed, Lincoln found himself under increasing pressure. Abolitionists wanted all slaves emancipated immediately. At a minimum, Northern liberals wanted him to declare that ending slavery was the war's central purpose. Overly zealous generals were emancipating slaves without the president's knowledge or authorization, and those orders then had to be rescinded. Meanwhile, sizable numbers of slaves continued to flee into Union encampments, increasing the pressure to clarify their legal status. And time was becoming important, as Lincoln also faced skeptical European nations, morally opposed to slavery but losing trade because of the naval blockade of Southern seaports and thus trying to decide whether to grant diplomatic recognition to the Confederacy.

Rather than issuing a blanket emancipation, which threatened to alienate Northern Democrats and the border slave states (Delaware, Maryland, Kentucky, and Missouri) that had remained loyal to the Union, Lincoln first explored the possibility of a gradual emancipation whereby former slave owners would be compensated by the state and federal governments for their losses. In 1861, for instance, he encouraged allies in Delaware to propose such a measure. Given the political intensity surrounding the entire issue of slavery, however, no such proposal managed to make much progress at the state level.

In April 1862, the United States Congress did pass a joint resolution introduced by Congressman Roscoe Conkling (Rep., N.Y.) and ultimately signed by President Lincoln. It proposed that the federal government cooperate with any state passing a compensation plan, as many Northern states had done when they phased out the practice in that region. Nevertheless, this resolution met with considerable opposition from both extremes of the debate. Slave owners were not about to give up their slaves, especially at the behest of the federal government. Slaves had become a particularly integral part of the inland cotton industry.[3] Meanwhile, abolitionists were furious that the federal government was proposing to give money to slaveholders for "property" they had no right to possess.

That same month, April 1862, Congress passed and Lincoln signed an emancipation of all slaves in the District of Columbia, compensating owners up to $300 per slave. The law also contained $100,000 to help freed slaves who wished voluntarily to emigrate to such countries as Haiti, Panama, or Liberia. Lincoln even called a group of prominent free blacks to the White House in August and encouraged them to consider supporting emigration. Recognizing the level of racial prejudice that remained throughout the United States, Lincoln argued, "Your race suffer greatly, many of them, by living among us, while ours suffer from your presence. . . . If this is admitted, it affords a reason why we should be separated."[4] In addition, Lincoln's State Department sent inquiries to several South American and African nations looking for interest in creating colonies for freed American slaves.[5]

With the tide of the war beginning to turn in the Union's favor, federal emancipation efforts escalated rapidly, starting in the summer of 1862. Slavery was abolished in the territories, and any slave leaving a Confederate master and reaching Union territory was to be set free. Lincoln also approached representatives from loyal slave states, asking them to reconsider the possibility of a compensation plan in exchange for releasing their 800,000 slaves. They refused. Attention then turned to an emancipation proclamation that would free all the slaves in the Confederacy, but timing would be of the essence. Adhering to the advice of Secretary of State William Seward, Lincoln often reiterated, "We mustn't issue it until after a victory."[6] The proclamation was not to appear in any way to be to be a sign of weakness.

The initial Emancipation Proclamation was issued in September 1862 after General George McClellan's victory in the Battle of Antietam. Relying on his war powers under the United States Constitution, Lincoln's proclamation would free all slaves held in the Confederacy unless those states ceased their rebellion by the first day of January. As it became increasingly clear that the Confederate states were not going to accept such terms, Lincoln turned up the moral volume. In a December 1862 message to Congress, for example, he declared, "In giving freedom to the slave, we assure freedom to the free." Shortly thereafter, with the Confederacy still in revolt, the more famous version of the proclamation was delivered on January 1, 1863. It differed from the preliminary draft by omitting reference to compensation and to the colonization of freedmen outside the boundaries of the United States.[7]

Besides inciting additional slave revolts in the South and inspiring a number of liberal whites to join the Union cause, another tangible benefit for the Union was that the proclamation provided former slaves with a reason to join the fight. Black regiments of the U.S. Army, including many under the command of Martin Delany, made significant contributions to the war effort. More than 200,000 black men served; some of the best-known regiments were the 54th and 55th Massachusetts Infantries, as well as units later referred to as the United States Colored Troops.

Ironically, some of those freed during the war who did not opt to serve in the Union Army were conscripted to serve as contract laborers on cotton plantations within the occupied South. When abolitionists protested, the policy was justified as economically necessary for the war effort. Coincidentally, such a policy also appeased white urban immigrants, who feared further competition from blacks for the limited number of unskilled wage positions in preindustrial United States cities.[8]

The nature of this limited emancipation came under the scrutiny of many prominent critics. One London newspaper article noted, "The principle is not that a human being cannot justly own another, but that he cannot own him unless he is loyal to the United States."[9] Even Lincoln's own secretary of state, William Seward, noted sardonically, "We show our sympathy with slavery by emancipating slaves where we cannot reach them and holding them in bondage where we can set them free."[10]

Jefferson Davis addressed a joint session of the Confederate Congress in 1863. Referring to the proclamation as clear evidence of the North's "disposition to interfere with our social system," he went on to state,

> The people of this Confederacy, then, cannot fail to receive this proclamation as the fullest vindication of their own sagacity in foreseeing the uses in which the dominant party in the United States intended from the beginning to apply their power, nor can they cease to remember with devout thankfulness that it is their own vigilance in resisting the first stealthy progress of approaching despotism that they owe their escape from consequences now apparent to the most skeptical. . . . [T]he proclamation affords the fullest guarantee of the impossibility of [the reconstruction of the old Union]; it has established a state of things which can lead to but one of three possible consequences—the extermination of the slaves, the exile of

the whole white population from the Confederacy, or absolute and total separation of these States from the United States.

This proclamation is also an authentic statement by the Government of the United States of its inability to subjugate the South by force of arms, and as such must be accepted by neutral nations, which can no longer find any justification in withholding our just claims to formal recognition.[11]

There was also opposition in the North. A number of white soldiers resigned from the Union Army, for example, when they perceived the war to be more about freeing slaves than preserving the Union. Northern Democrats accused Lincoln of squandering soldiers' lives in the cause of the abolitionists. Meanwhile, the abolitionists thought it did not go far enough. Such discontent can be seen in the results of the 1864 national elections: the Democratic Party gained a sizable number of seats in both the House and Senate.[12]

THE LAW

The Emancipation Proclamation freed all slaves held in the states in rebellion against the United States and granted military and naval authority to enforce their freedom.

12. Emancipation Proclamation

. . . That on the 1st day of January, A.D. 1863, all persons held as slaves within any State or designated part of a State the people whereof shall then be in rebellion against the United States shall be then, thenceforward, and forever free; and the executive government of the United States, including the military and naval authority thereof, will recognize and maintain the freedom of such persons and will do no act or acts to repress such persons, or any of them, in any efforts they may make for their actual freedom. . . .

And I hereby enjoin upon the people so declared to be free to abstain from all violence, unless in necessary self-defence; and I recommend to them that, in all case when allowed, they labor faithfully for reasonable wages.

And I further declare and make known that such persons of suitable condition will be received into the armed service of the United States to garrison forts, positions, stations, and other places, and to man vessels of all sorts in said service.

And upon this act, sincerely believed to be an act of justice, warranted by the Constitution upon military necessity, I invoke the considerate judgment of mankind and the gracious favor of Almighty God.

NOTES

1. Quoted in Robert Divine, *America: Past and Present* (New York: Longman, 1999), p. 431.

2. Quoted in David Goldfield et al., *The American Journey* (Upper Saddle River, N.J.: Prentice-Hall, 1998), p. 486.

3. For example, see ibid., pp. 377–383.

4. John Hope Franklin and Alfred A. Moss, Jr., *From Slavery to Freedom: A History of African Americans* (New York: Knopf, 1994), p. 206.

5. For example, see George Fredrickson, "A Man Not a Brother: Lincoln and the Negro," *Journal of Southern History* 41 (1975): p. 48; Don Fehrenbacher, "Only His Stepchildren: Lincoln and the Negro," *Civil War History* 12 (1974): p. 307.

6. Paul Johnson, *A History of the American People* (New York: HarperCollins, 1997), p. 473.

7. For more discussion, see John Hope Franklin, *The Emancipation Proclamation* (Garden City, N.Y.: Doubleday, 1963).

8. See Divine, *America: Past and Present*, pp. 462–463.

9. Goldfield, *The American Journey*, p. 487.

10. Quoted in John Mack Faragher et al., *Out of Many* (Upper Saddle River, N.J.: Prentice-Hall, 2000), p. 463.

11. See James Richardson, *Messages and Papers of the Confederacy* (Nashville, Tenn.: U.S. Publishing Company, 1905), vol. 1, pp. 290–93.

12. See Franklin and Moss, *From Slavery to Freedom*, p. 207.

II

POSTWAR RECONSTRUCTION

In the aftermath of the Civil War, the Congress, devoid of much Southern opposition, moved quickly to strike down the legal vestiges of slavery. Reconstruction of the South began with legislation such as the Wade-Davis bill, marking Congress's efforts to be harsher on ex-Confederates than President Lincoln was being at the time. In particular, the bill sought to preclude a much larger number of ex-Confederates from voting, and it demanded more guaranteed loyalty from newly reconstructed Southern states. When Lincoln refused to sign the bill, the Congress was not able to override his veto.

Following Lincoln's death, however, Congress became even more responsive to black interests, and its majority Republican Party courted newly enfranchised black voters who faced racist violence, intimidation, and emerging black codes in the postwar South. The Freedmen's Bureau (13) was created to provide former slaves and displaced Southern whites with education, relief assistance, and resettlement and to assist them in the disposition of abandoned property.

The Civil War amendments to the U.S. Constitution were passed by the Congress and ratified by the states between 1865 and 1870. The Thirteenth Amendment (14) banned slavery and involuntary servitude in the United States and its territories, unless the involuntary servitude was part of a legitimate punishment for a crime. The Fourteenth Amendment (17) prohibited states from abridging federal "privileges and immunities"; denying life, liberty, or property without "due process of law"; and denying "equal protection of the laws." The Fifteenth Amendment (18) declared that the right to vote was "not to be denied or abridged by the United States or by any State on account of race, color, or previous condition of servitude."

Meanwhile, the 1866 Civil Rights Act (15) attacked Southern black codes by guaranteeing blacks equal protection under the law, essentially overturning the Dred Scott decision that had affirmed the legality of slavery. A year later, the Reconstruction Act (16) provided a mechanism by which ex–Confederate States could reconstitute their governments in order to be readmitted into the Union. The Enforcement Act (19) established federal sanctions for interfering with another person's civil rights, especially a black's right to vote, and it allowed for federal election supervisors to oversee registration and voting procedures. The Ku Klux Klan Act (20) established federal criminal sanctions and enforcement mechanisms to be used against those denying others equal protection under the law. The 1875 Civil Rights Act (21) outlawed racial segregation in public accommodations, and it prohibited the exclusion of blacks from jury duty. That law was struck down by the U.S. Supreme Court eight years later, and it would be nearly another century before those rights would be restored.

In the lull between the Hayes compromise in 1877 and the turmoil of the Great Depression of the 1930s, Congress proved incapable of doing much to protect Southern blacks from increasing oppression. Legalized segregation and disenfranchisement were tolerated, as was outright violence. In 1878 Congress prohibited the use of federal troops in elections and sixteen years later cut all appropriations for election marshals. This, of course, left black voters to fend for themselves. Final amnesty was granted to the remainder of the previously "disloyal" Southern Confederates in 1898. An antilynching bill never did emerge from the legislative maze. The 1883 Pendleton Act, however, did create a merit system for hiring federal bureaucrats, and that change inadvertently helped blacks by limiting opportunity for discriminatory federal hiring.

13

Freedmen's Bureau

1865

The Freedmen's Bureau was created to provide former slaves and displaced Southern whites with education, relief assistance, and resettlement and to dispose of abandoned property.

HISTORICAL CONTEXT

As the Civil War progressed, groups such as the New England Freedmen's Aid Society began sending volunteers into Union-occupied areas of the South to educate ex-slaves. A federal Freedmen's Bureau was then conceived by the American Freedmen's Inquiry Committee, an ad hoc investigative body set up by the War Department.

In 1863 the idea of a Freedmen's Bureau was introduced in Congress by Representative Thomas Dawes Eliot (Rep., Mass.). After a long debate, the bill ultimately was passed over the opposition of those who feared it would lead to even more federal intrusion, social disruption, and political corruption. After winning by only two votes in the House, the bill got bogged down when the Senate version insisted that the bureau be placed under the Treasury Department instead of the War Department.

In the end, a compromise bill was passed by both houses and signed by President Abraham Lincoln in March 1865, a month before he was assassinated. The Freedmen's Bureau was placed under the War Department and was initially headed by thirty-four-year-old General Oliver Otis Howard, known as "the Christian general" for his history of philanthropy and his active involvement in the Congregationalist church. The bureau was to remain in place during the war and for a year thereafter.

Officially entitled the Bureau of Refugees, Freedmen, and Abandoned Land, it came to be more commonly known as the Freedmen's Bureau. It was designed to assist the more than 4 million displaced Civil War refugees and former slaves. Specifically, it was assigned the "supervision and management of all abandoned lands, and the control of all subjects relating to refugees and freedmen from rebel states."

The commissioner, General Howard, had his headquarters in Washington, D.C. He created ten districts, each with its own assistant commissioner, all of whom were military officers. In the end, the bureau employed nearly a thousand military and civilian agents throughout the South, most of whom were white. For all intents and purposes, the commissioners were able to act with legislative, executive, and judicial authority. John Mercer Langston served as the bureau's inspector general.

The law was extended by an act of Congress in 1866, including a provision that allowed for punishing recalcitrant state officials. Despite mounting evidence of discrimination and outright violence against former slaves, President Andrew Johnson vetoed the extension. Johnson, himself from Tennessee, regarded it as an unconstitutional extension of federal authority. He was also sympathetic to the pleas of local plantation owners, who were chafing under this additional federal control. Beyond that, Johnson stated in his veto message, "Any legislation that shall imply that [former slaves] are not expected to attain a self-sustaining condition must have a tendency injurious alike to their character and their prospects."[1] Although his veto was sustained, a slightly modified version was later passed and implemented despite the president's continuing opposition.

The Freedmen's Bureau existed from 1865 to 1872, but most of its work was done by 1870. Although the legislation creating it was narrow in its language, the law was expanded considerably in its implementation. Among other things, it oversaw the emancipation of former slaves. The bureau provided them with food, clothing, and supplies, as well as medical assistance, job placement, educational facilities, and homestead land. It was an unprecedented expenditure of federal monies on individuals; in many ways, it was the first federal welfare program.

Faced with a black illiteracy rate of nearly 90 percent, one of the highest priorities was education. The bureau utilized abandoned buildings, shacks, basements, and churches to create schools, including schools to train black teachers after white teachers from the North repeatedly met with considerable hostility from embittered and wary local Southern whites.[2] Before it disbanded, the bureau spent some $5 million educating former slaves. It had more than 4,000 schools under its supervision, ranging from elementary grades to college and included industrial institutes as well. These schools employed more than 9,000 teachers and enrolled nearly 250,000 students.[3] Howard University, for example, was founded in large part due to the efforts of General Howard, and it came to bear his name as a result.[4]

The bureau dispensed many additional types of aid. Health services were provided for the ill, aged, and insane. By 1867, forty-six hospitals had been established, staffed by dozens of doctors and nurses. Their medical department alone would spend more than $2 million caring for more than 450,000 patients. Beyond that, the bureau distributed food. Between 1865 and 1869, for instance, it distributed some 21 million rations, three-quarters of which went to African Americans. The bureau also fought to gain legal rights for the freedmen, in particular the right to testify in court.[5]

Then, there was the matter of land. In May 1867, convention delegates at a Colored Convention held in Montgomery, Alabama, made a case for receiving portions of existing Southern farmland. They argued that plantation property owned by planters had been "nearly all earned by the sweat of our brows, not theirs. It has been forfeited to the government by the treason of its owners, and is liable to be confiscated whenever the Republican Party demands it."[6] Such a confiscation and disbursement of land, however, would not proceed smoothly.

By June 1865, some 40,000 freedmen had received property in coastal South Carolina and Georgia as "Sherman grants," the fruits of General William Sherman's Special Field Order 15. This had been done in large part to relieve his army of thousands of impoverished fugitive slaves who had retreated behind his lines. Congress also passed the Southern Homestead Act in 1866, giving former slaves preferential access to public lands in five Southern states. In addition, South Carolina's postwar government instituted its own land redistribution program, buying up land and selling it to freedmen who could buy these parcels with state-subsidized loans. General Howard attempted to deliver the much rumored "forty acres and a mule" to many other freedmen, parceling out more of the plantation land seized during the war. Congress went along, authorizing a limited land disbursement of this type.

Nevertheless, much of the land attained by the freedmen was small and of marginal quality. Freedmen found it difficult to get credit, making it hard to increase their holdings. President Johnson nullified Sherman's Field Order 15, which had created the Sherman lands. In addition, when the president began pardoning former Confederates and restoring their property rights, General Howard was forced to abandon his own land disbursement strategy and actually had to evict many freedmen from lands ceded to them under the earlier Sherman plan.[7] One former slave lamented, "We were friends on the march, brothers on the battlefield, but in the peaceful pursuit of life it seems we are strangers."[8]

The Freedmen's Bureau encouraged freedmen to stay home and perform "faithfully" in the plantation fields, a practice that has been criticized by some historians for being paternalistic and for unduly encouraging ex-slaves to return to work for former slave masters as plantation wage laborers. Tens of thousands of wage contracts were written and enforced by the bureau; General Howard estimated that at least 50,000 such contracts existed in each Southern state.[9] Many of these contracts reproduced slave-like conditions, however, and the bureau became involved in enforcing local vagrancy codes against those who chose not to sign such contracts. Absences from work could subject the freedman to a fine; quitting one's job could be ruled a breach of contract and land the violator in jail.

Despite the bureau's efforts, a good many former slaves resisted working under such conditions. In particular, many black women chose to remain at home rather than be subjected to physical and sexual exploitation in the fields.[10] The Freedmen's Bureau accompanied its promotion of wage contracts with a requirement that the corporal punishment of plantation workers come to an end. Bureau officials frequently arrested plantation overseers for violating this mandate. Where necessary, a dual legal system was created to try such cases, empowering local commissioners to adjudicate the charges when civilian courts refused to do so.

Although they were attacked as "carpetbaggers,"[11] some bureau commissioners got themselves elected to local office. With the passage of congressional Reconstruction in 1867 and the extension of black suffrage, the commissioners utilized organizations such as the Union Leagues to mobilize political support. Bureau officials, for example, became some of the first Republicans to hold office in Alabama, and Assistant Commissioner Robert Scott became South Carolina's first Republican governor.

This latter turn of events helped spell the end of the bureau. Given the emergence of Reconstruction governments throughout much of the South, there was less need for the vigilance of the Freedmen's Bureau. In addition, there were continuing allegations of inefficiency and corruption in a welfare program that carried a relatively high price tag.[12] Consequently, most of the bureau's operations had ceased by 1868. Its educational division survived for four more years, as did its efforts to attain bounties owed to black veterans. Nonetheless, all such activities wound to a close by June 30, 1872.[13]

THE LAW

This act established the Freedmen's Bureau[14] and set forth specifics regarding the management and operation of that agency. Pursuant to the act, the bureau was charged with the responsibility of providing former slaves and displaced Southern whites with relief assistance and resettlement. Specifically, the act provided for food, clothing, and fuel. It also permitted abandoned land to be offered to refugees and freed slaves on a rental basis with an option to purchase the land under certain conditions.

13. The Freedmen's Bureau Act

CHAP. XC.

An Act to establish a Bureau for the Relief of Freedmen and Refugees.

Be it enacted . . . That there is hereby established in the War Department, to continue during the present war of rebellion, and for one year thereafter, a bureau of refugees, freedmen, and abandoned lands, to which shall be committed, as hereinafter provided, the supervision and management of all abandoned lands, and the control of all subjects relating to refugees and freedmen from rebel states, or from any district of the country within the territory embraced in the operations of the army, under such rules and regulations as may be prescribed by the head of the bureau and approved by the President. . . .

SEC. 2. And be it further enacted, That the Secretary of War may direct such issues of provisions, clothing, and fuel, as he may deem needful for the immediate and temporary shelter and supply of destitute and suffering refugees and freedmen and their wives and children, under such rules and regulations as he may direct. . . .

SEC. 4. And be it further enacted, That the commissioner, under the direction of the President, shall have authority to set apart, for the use of loyal refugees and freedmen, such tracts of land within the insurrectionary states as shall have been abandoned, or to which the United States shall have acquired title by confiscation or sale, or otherwise, and to every male citizen, whether refugee or freedman, as aforesaid, there shall be assigned not more than forty acres of such land, and the person to whom it was so assigned shall be protected in the use and enjoyment of the land for the term of three years. . . .

APPROVED, March 3, 1865.

NOTES

1. Veto message of President Andrew Johnson, The Freedmen Bureau's Act, February 19, 1866, as reprinted in Amilcar Shabazz, ed., *The Forty Acres Documents* (Baton Rouge: House of Songhay, 1994), p. 84.

2. For example, see George R. Bentley, *A History of the Freedmen's Bureau* (Philadelphia: University of Pennsylvania Press, 1955), p. 181.

3. See Paul Skeels Peirce, *The Freedmen's Bureau: A Chapter of the History of the Reconstruction* (New York: Haskell House Publishers, 1971), pp. 82–83; John Hope Franklin and Alfred A. Moss, Jr., *From Slavery to Freedom: A History of African Americans* (New York: Knopf, 1994), pp. 230–231.

4. Other prominent African American colleges founded with the help of the Freedmen's Bureau include Hampton Institute, St. Augustine College, Atlanta University, Fisk University, Storer College, and Biddle Memorial Institute (later known as Johnson C. Smith University).

5. See Franklin and Moss, *From Slavery to Freedom*, p. 229.

6. Quoted in John Mack Faragher et al., *Out of Many* (Upper Saddle River, N.J.: Prentice-Hall, 2000), p. 495.

7. Also see William McFeely, *Yankee Stepfather: General O.O. Howard and the Freedmen* (New York: Norton, 1968).

8. Quoted in Faragher, *Out of Many*, p. 495.

9. See Hanes Walton, Jr. and Robert C. Smith, *American Politics and the African American Quest for Universal Freedom* (New York: Longman, 2000), p. 239.

10. See David Goldfield et al., *The American Journey* (Upper Saddle River, N.J.: Prentice-Hall, 1998), p. 535.

11. This derisive term was used to describe the unwanted aliens from the North who were caricatured as arriving with no more than the belongings they could carry in their carpet-fabric suitcases, suggesting little long-term commitment to the area.

12. See Walton and Smith, *American Politics*, p. 239.

13. For more on the Freedmen's Bureau, see Bentley, *A History of the Freedmen's Bureau*; Paul Cimbala, *Under the Guardianship of the Nation: The Freedmen's Bureau and the Reconstruction of Georgia, 1865–1870* (Athens: University of Georgia Press, 1997).

14. *Statutes at Large of the United States* (Washington, D.C.: GPO), vol. 13, pp. 507–509.

14

Thirteenth Amendment to the United States Constitution

1865

The thirteenth constitutional amendment ended slavery as a legal institution in the United States.

HISTORICAL CONTEXT

For the Emancipation Proclamation to lead to emancipation, it would have to be codified so that its force would survive after the Reconstruction armies had departed. There were lingering doubts about the federal government's constitutional authority to require states to prohibit practices such as slavery or to forbid private individuals from engaging in them. The strongest way to "obliterate the last lingering vestiges of the slave system," as Representative James Wilson (Rep., La.) stated during the congressional debate on the Thirteenth Amendment, was to write it into the United States Constitution alongside the nation's other enduring principles.[1] In the words of Abraham Lincoln, this would allow the nation to "return to the fountain of whose waters spring close by the blood of the Revolution."[2]

As could have been expected, the debate would be heated once the United States Congress took up the constitutional amendment in 1864 and 1865. That contention only increased when some proponents attempted not only to end slavery, but end "the necessary incidents of slavery," including extending full rights to the newly freed slaves.

Those supporting an amendment to end slavery argued that it was "time to stamp universal freedom on our national Constitution," because slavery, "[an] insatiable enemy of all that is lovely, desirable, just, and sacred," posed "incessant, unrelenting aggressive warfare upon the principles . . . for which the Constitution was ordained" and "trampled on the most sacred rights of the citizen." It was "disgraceful to civilization and destructive of free Government."[3]

In opposition, Representative Fernando Wood (Dem., N.Y.) argued against making "social interests subjects of governmental action" and against such a "tyrannical destruction of individual property." He also suggested that slavery might well be "the best possible condition to insure the happiness of the negro race."[4] Representative William Kelly (Rep., Pa.) worried about suddenly releasing millions of former slaves "without preparation or education for freedom, without property or the means whereby to live, and without the guidance, restraint and protection of the superior intelligence and forethought of their masters."[5] Meanwhile, most other opposition centered around fighting the usurpation of states' rights by the federal government.

Ironically enough, an earlier version of the Thirteenth Amendment, known as the Corwin Amendment, had been passed by Congress, signed by Abraham Lincoln, and sent to the states for ratification in March 1861, only one month before the South seceded. It would have prohibited Congress from interfering with slavery anywhere it existed. That proposed amendment lapsed during the Civil War, however, as it was clear that the Union was not going to be preserved by such a legislative guarantee.[6]

Abraham Lincoln's Proclamation of Amnesty and Reconstruction was signed on December 8, 1863, as the Civil War drew to a close. When Congress returned to the subject of a constitutional amendment concerning slavery in the spring of 1864, the language ultimately chosen was very similar to that found in the Northwest Ordinance. This time, however, it applied to the entire United States, both all governments and all individuals. It outlawed slavery or the involuntary servitude of any person in the United States without the due process of law. This included a federal ban on peonage as well, meaning compulsory service to pay off a debt. Its enforcement clause allowed Congress to enact penalties for noncomplying individuals or states.

The United States Senate adopted the new amendment rather expeditiously, approving it by a vote of 38–6 in April 1864. This easily met the constitutional requirement of a two-thirds majority. By June, it also had passed in the House, but the 93–65 margin was not large enough. Opposition in the House focused on fears of alienating loyal border states and the growth of federal power over the states.

Passing such an amendment became a central plank in the Republican Party's 1864 platform, and the Republicans gained ground in that fall's congressional elections. After President Lincoln was reelected that year as well, he lent the full weight of his political clout to the effort. By the end of January 1865, the amendment had finally achieved the necessary two-thirds majority in the House of Representatives, and it was submitted to the states. Shorn of more sweeping language like Senator Charles Sumner's "all persons are equal before the law," it still contained Sumner's enforcement clause, allowing Congress to "enforce this article by appropriate legislation."

Support of three-fourths of the state legislatures was required to ratify any constitutional amendment; thus, ratification of the Thirteenth Amendment would require the support of eight of the former Confederate states. As such support was a condition of their readmission into the Union, however, former Confederate states were essentially compelled to ratify the Thirteenth Amendment, as well as the Fourteenth and Fifteenth Amendments to come. Consequently, a sufficient number of "reconstituted" Southern governments did endorse it. Only the states of Texas and Mississippi refused. In the end, twenty-seven states supported ratification, including eight reconstituted Southern states. Final ratification occurred in December 1865, just eight months after Robert E. Lee had surrendered to end the Civil War. Interestingly, the state of Mississippi finally ended its holdout over a century later, formally ratifying the amendment in 1995.[7]

The Thirteenth Amendment did not, however, explicitly extend equal rights to emancipated slaves, and subsequent United States Supreme Courts would not extend its meaning to include equal rights to "public accommodations and conveyances."[8] Those extensions would be left to the ensuing Fourteenth and Fifteenth Amendments. In addition, one could still contractually obligate oneself to another, and the government could still demand service in the armed forces or on juries.

THE LAW

The Thirteenth Amendment prohibited slavery, except as punishment for a crime, in the United States and all places subject to the jurisdiction or authority of the United States. In addition, Congress was granted the authority to enforce the amendment through legislation.

14. Thirteenth Amendment

Section 1. Neither slavery nor involuntary servitude, except as a punishment for crime whereof the party shall have been duly convicted, shall exist within the United States, or any place subject to their jurisdiction.

Section 2. Congress shall have power to enforce this article by appropriate legislation.

NOTES

1. Bernard Schwartz, ed., *Statutory History of the United States: Civil Rights* (New York: Chelsea House, 1970), pt. 1 p. 23.

2. Ibid., p. 20.

3. Representative James Wilson (Rep., Ia.) in his introductory speech, United States House of Representatives, March 19, 1864, quoted in ibid., pp. 25–42.

4. Ibid., pp. 42–48.

5. Ibid., p. 50.

6. For example, see Mark Brandon, "The Original Thirteenth Amendment and the Limits to Formal Constitutional Change," in *Responding to Imperfection: The Theory and Practice of Constitutional Amendment*, ed. Sanford Levinson (Princeton, N.J.: Princeton University Press, 1995).

7. For a more detailed discussion, see George H. Hoemann, *What God Hath Wrought* (New York: Garland Publishers, 1987); Elizabeth Schleichert, *The 13th Amendment* (Hillside, N.J.: Enslow Publishers, 1998).

8. For a listing of the various federal court decisions spelling out these interpretations, see Edward S. Corwin, *The Constitution and What It Means Today* (Princeton, N.J.: Princeton University Press, 1978), pp. 455–460.

15

Civil Rights Act

1866

This Civil Rights Act of 1866 attacked Southern black codes by guaranteeing blacks equal protection under the law, essentially overturning the Supreme Court's Dred Scott decision of 1857.

HISTORICAL CONTEXT

The Civil Rights Act of 1866 was first proposed by Senator Lyman Trumball (Rep., Ill.), chairman of the Senate Judiciary Committee, in order to "provide [for] the real freedom of . . . former slaves." If passed, it would require states equally to protect all persons within their jurisdictions. In so doing, it would undo the United States Supreme Court's Dred Scott decision.[1] More specifically, it was designed to protect freedmen against discrimination by prohibiting such race-specific laws as the black codes.

Black codes, which were employed differently in the various Southern states, included such provisions as criminalizing failure of servant duties, denying blacks the right to own property or carry firearms, mandating that blacks carry permission passes if they traveled beyond certain boundaries, and requiring that blacks under the age of eighteen be "apprentices" of their former slave masters if they had been orphaned or if the child's parents lacked the financial means to support him or her.[2]

The Civil Rights Act was quickly passed by Republican majorities in both houses of Congress on March 13, 1866, but it was subsequently vetoed by President Andrew Johnson. Johnson, as well as most of the Southern delegation in Congress, believe that such laws amounted to an unconstitutional federal government usurpation of sovereign states' rights. Nevertheless, within two weeks, President Johnson's veto had been overridden by the requisite two-thirds majorities in both the House and the Senate. The Civil Rights Act of 1866 gave blacks "full and equal benefit of all laws and proceedings . . . as is enjoyed by white citizens."

Trumball and other proponents claimed constitutional authority for such a sweeping restriction on states' rights by arguing among other things that the act was being issued in order to lend meaning to the Thirteenth Amendment, utilizing its enforcement clause.[3] According to Senator Trumball, if a state violates one's liberty, it is the same as imposing a "badge of servitude," which Congress is expressly empowered to prohibit in the implementation clause of the Thirteenth Amendment.

Opponents, including Radical Republicans, thought the bill did not go far enough. Some wanted to see suffrage included as a fundamental civil right. Others wanted clear provisions for land acquisition and homesteading for freedmen. Others were dismayed that federal troops would not be dispatched continually to monitor the implementation of these rights at the state and local levels.

Also opposed was Representative John Bingham (Rep., Ohio), who later played a pivotal role in the passage of the Fourteenth Amendment, which he felt was the far more constitutionally appropriate way to extend this type of protection. Questions of this particular act's constitutionality were made moot by the ultimate passage of the Fourteenth Amendment, which incorporated the fundamental principle of equal protection directly into constitutional law.

Meanwhile, turmoil followed passage of the Civil Rights Act of 1866. For one thing, this was the first time a presidential veto of a major piece of legislation had been overridden. It also remained unclear whether state or federal courts had the primary jurisdiction for adjudicating such civil rights. On top of that, many continued to agree with Representative Bingham that the Thirteenth Amendment's enforcement clause did not authorize this type of civil rights extension. Consequently, development of the Fourteenth Amendment began almost immediately.

THE LAW

The first section of the Civil Rights Act of 1866[4] contains the provisions related to equal rights. This section specifically grants national citizenship to all people born in the United States, except certain Native Americans. It also delineates the rights of all citizens to make contracts, institute and participate in lawsuits, hold and transfer property, and enjoy the full and equal benefit of all laws and proceedings.

The remaining sections of the act contain enforcement provisions. These sections directly authorize district attorneys, marshals, and other officials to prosecute violators in federal court. Further, they allow for fining or imprisoning those convicted of violating the act. Included in the enforcement provisions is a section authorizing the president of the United States to use military force to uphold the act.

15. Civil Rights Act of 1866

Be it enacted . . . That all persons born in the United States and not subject to any foreign power, excluding Indians not taxed, are hereby declared to be citizens of the United States; and such citizens, of every race and color, without regard to any previous condition of slavery or involuntary servitude, except as a punishment for crime whereof the party shall have been, duly convicted, shall have the same right, in every State and Territory in the United States, to make and enforce contracts, to sue, be parties, and give evidence, to inherit, purchase, lease, sell, hold, and convey real and personal property, and to full and equal benefit of all laws and proceedings for the security of person and property, as is enjoyed by white citizens, and shall be subject to like punishment, pains, and penalties, and to none other, any law, statute, ordinance, regulation, or custom, to the contrary not withstanding.

NOTES

1. *Dred Scott v. Sandford*, 19 How. 393 (1857).

2. For example, see Donald Nieman, *Promises to Keep* (New York: Oxford University Press, 1991), pp. 60–61; C. Vann Woodward, *The Strange Career of Jim Crow* (New York: Oxford University Press, 1966), pp. 23–24.

3. For example, see John Cox and La Wanda Cox, *Politics, Principles, and Prejudices, 1865–1866* (New York: Free Press, 1963).

4. *Statutes at Large of the United States* (Washington, D.C.: GPO), vol. 14, pp. 27–30.

16

Reconstruction Act

1867

The Reconstruction Act provided a mechanism by which the former Confederate States could reconstitute their governments in order to be readmitted into the Union.

HISTORICAL CONTEXT

The period of Southern Reconstruction is generally dated from 1863 to 1877. It began when President Abraham Lincoln and his fellow Republicans in Congress first discussed reinstituting the seceding states. It concluded when the last of the Union soldiers finally left the South.

Lincoln argued for a relatively rapid and simple repatriation. His position was essentially that the Confederate states remained states under the United States Constitution, and only those individuals engaged in the rebellion were to be punished, including disenfranchisement. The rebels themselves could then be presidentially pardoned once they had demonstrated sufficient allegiance to the United States and all its laws, including the prohibition of slavery. If even 10 percent of the state's white males met these requirements, that Southern state would be allowed to return to full self-governance as long as it abolished slavery.[1]

The Radical Republicans in Congress pressed for a considerably more extreme process, including confiscating and redistributing large plantation holdings. Led by Charles Sumner (Rep., Mass.) and Benjamin Wade (Rep., Ohio) in the Senate and Henry Davis (Rep., Md.) and Thaddeus Stevens (Rep., Pa.) in the House, they took the position that rebelling states had forfeited all rights, and thus now lacked any constitutional standing whatsoever. Consequently, it was entirely up to Congress to determine how the states would be reconstituted.[2]

When Arkansas and Louisiana met President Lincoln's requirements and sent representatives to Congress, the Radical Republicans mustered enough votes to refuse to seat them. Meanwhile, the Wade-Davis Bill required the states to grant equal protection under their laws and for half of the state's white males to take a loyalty oath. President Lincoln exercised his pocket veto of that bill, opting not to sign it after Congress had already adjourned.

In between stood much of the congressional Republican Party. Their collective position was generally that the Southern states remained constitutional entities. Those states had, however, forfeited their constitutional rights by rebelling. Therefore, it was up to Congress to determine how and when those rights would be restored.[3]

With the assassination of President Lincoln, the matter of Southern reconstruction fell to President Andrew Johnson. Johnson was a Southerner, born in North Carolina and raised primarily in Tennessee. He was a lifelong populist Democrat, but he had also been the only Southern senator to remain in Washington after the Confederacy seceded. He had been selected as vice president in part to try to appease Southern moderates and shorten the war. In terms of reconstruction, he initially denounced all Confederates as "traitors" who "ought to be hanged."[4] Yet, he rather quickly took a position very similar to that of his predecessor.

President Johnson began implementing his views by extending Lincoln's clemency policy while Congress was not in session. Any Confederate with property valued at less than $20,000 was to have his rights reinstituted without even having to take a loyalty oath. The underlying assumption was that the lower classes of the South had been misled by the plantation elite. Johnson also proceeded to pardon many other former Confederates, approving roughly 90 percent of all such applications.[5] He then appointed provisional governors for each Confederate state and instructed them to restore local rule as soon as the respective state abolished slavery, repudiated the Confederacy's debts, and ratified the Thirteenth Amendment abolishing slavery.

Acting quickly, virtually all of the former confederate states complied. Each abolished slavery. Most repudiated the Confederate debt. All but Mississippi and Texas ratified the Thirteenth Amendment. With that, on April 6, 1866, the president declared the rebellion to be legally over and the Union to have been restored.[6]

It was not long before black codes began to proliferate in these newly constituted states. These laws treated blacks as second-class citizens, unable to vote and restricted in terms of movement, public accommodations, speech, property ownership, and other such liberties. There was no equal protection under state law, and the Fourteenth Amendment to the United States Constitution had yet to be become the law of the land.

Meanwhile, Congress had been pursuing its own approach. The radicals had managed to write their far more punitive beliefs into law in the Reconstruction Bill of 1864. President Lincoln had refused to sign it, however, and the Congress was not in session to override his veto. To further complicate matters, Southern states proceeded to elect more than seventy Confederate officeholders to Congress.[7] When Congress reconvened in December 1865, the Northern-dominated majority rather quickly voted to exclude all Southern members, extended the Freedmen's Bureau, and passed the Civil Rights Act of 1866. When President Johnson vetoed the latter two bills, Congress overrode him on both matters.

While these events were occurring, a special Joint Committee on Reconstruction reported on the conditions in the South, describing a state of near anarchy and detailing the discrimination and hardships faced by the region's African Americans. The full Congress then voted that the president's newly constituted Southern states were illegal, as only Congress had the authority to reconstitute them. Thereafter, bolstered by Republican gains in the 1866 fall elections, Congress passed its own Reconstruction Act.

President Johnson's readmission of provisional governments was invalidated. The rebel states were then placed under military rule, and military districts were established to provide governance, including the administration of voter registration. Tennessee was the exception, as it had ratified the Fourteenth Amendment shortly after it emerged from Congress in the summer of 1866. Consequently, Tennessee's readmission stood. In the remainder of the former Confederacy, many whites became disenfranchised as a result of new loyalty oaths. These former states also were compelled to grant black suffrage and ratify the Fourteenth Amendment in order to be readmitted into the Union.

President Johnson vetoed the legislation, claiming it was both an unconstitutional usurpation of power by the federal government and unfair to those states that had already reorganized. Neverthe-less, solid Republican majorities, produced by the 1866 elections, allowed Congress to override his veto quickly. The 1867 Reconstruction Act became the law of the land.

As a primary precondition to readmission, the act required former Confederate states to guarantee suffrage to all males over twenty-one years of age, regardless of "race, color, or previous condition." Thus, former slaves were to be guaranteed the right to vote. Many "disloyal" whites remained disenfranchised, however, unable or unwilling to meet the requirements of the prescribed loyalty oath.

Union Leagues organized the newly enfranchised blacks who were guided by Northern army officers and actually constituted a majority of the eligible voters in South Carolina, Mississippi, and Louisiana. They also included a handful of Northerners, derisively labeled carpetbaggers, and some renegade local whites, most of them poor small farmers, sarcastically referred to as scalawags.[8] Together they formed the Republican Party of the reconstructed South. This new electorate called constitutional conventions, elected convention delegates, drafted new state constitutions, and ratified these new constitutions at the ballot box. Only Mississippi defeated its newly drafted constitution.

These reconstructed state constitutions generally exceeded the mandates of the Reconstruction Act. Besides meeting the law's basic requisites, most committed their states to public education, expanded public services, and abolished property requirements to vote and hold office. Some ended imprisonment for indebtedness, and several even eliminated racial distinctions in the possession or inheritance of property. By the summer of 1868, eight additional states were sufficiently "reconstructed" and joined Tennessee in becoming reinstated into the Union. Only Texas, Mississippi, and Virginia remained outside the group by this period.

THE LAW

The Reconstruction Act of 1867[9] created five "military districts" to govern the states of the old Confederacy. The president was given the authority to assign army officials to command each district. The act set forth the powers and duties of the commanders. It also included provisions for forming new state governments and for adopting state constitutions that specifically included the Fourteenth Amendment.

Later in 1867, Congress passed a supplement to the Reconstruction Act. This supplement reiterated the original act's declaration that the existing governments in the rebel states were not legal. It further detailed the powers of the commanders of each district and contained numerous specific provisions regarding the implementation of reconstruction. The final provision allowed for a quite liberal interpretation of the entire act.

Finally, in 1868, an amendment to the Reconstruction Act and its supplement was passed regarding voting procedures in the districts.

16a. Reconstruction Act

CHAP. CLIII.

An Act to provide for the more efficient Government of the Rebel States.

Whereas no legal State governments or adequate protection for life or property now exists in the rebel States of Virginia, North Carolina, South Carolina, Georgia, Mississippi, Alabama, Louisiana, Florida, Texas, and Arkansas; and whereas it is necessary that peace and good order should be enforced in said States until loyal and republican State governments can be legally established: Therefore,

Be it enacted . . . That said rebel States shall be divided into military districts and made subject to the military authority of the United States as hereinafter prescribed. . . .

APPROVED, March 2, 1867.

16b. An Act Supplementary to the Reconstruction Act of 1867

CHAP. XXX.

An Act supplementary to an Act entitled "An Act to provide for the more efficient Government of the Rebel States" passed on the second day of March, eighteen hundred and sixty-seven, and the Act supplementary thereto, passed on the twenty-third day of March, eighteen hundred and sixty-seven.

Be it enacted . . . That it is hereby declared to have been the true intent and meaning of the act of the second day of March, one thousand eight hundred and sixty-seven, entitled "An act to provide for the more efficient government of the rebel States," and of the act supplementary thereto, passed on the twenty-third day of March, in the year one thousand eight hundred and sixty-seven, that the governments then existing in the rebel States of Virginia, North Carolina, South Carolina, Georgia, Mississippi, Alabama, Louisiana, Florida, Texas, and Arkansas were not legal State governments; and that thereafter said governments, if continued, were to be continued subject in all respects to the military commanders of the respective districts, and to the paramount authority of Congress. . . .

SEC. 11. And be it further enacted, That all the provisions of this act and of the acts to which this is supplementary shall be construed liberally, to the end that all the intents thereof may be fully and perfectly carried out.

APPROVED, July 19, 1867.

16c. Amendment to the Reconstruction Act of 1867

CHAP. XXV

An Act to amend the Act passed March twenty-third, eighteen hundred and sixty-seven, entitled "An act supplementary to 'An Act to provide for the more efficient Government of the Rebel States,' passed March second, eighteen hundred and sixty-seven, and to facilitate their Restoration."

Be it enacted . . . That hereafter any election authorized by the [Supplementary Reconstruction Act] . . . shall be decided by a majority of the votes actually cast; and at the election in which the question of the adoption or rejection of any constitution is submitted, any person duly registered in the State may vote in the election district where he offers to vote when he has resided therein for ten days next preceding such election, upon presentation of this certificate of registration, his affidavit, or other satisfactory evidence, under such regulations as the district commanders may prescribe. . . .

APPROVED, March 11, 1868.

NOTES

1. For example, see Lincoln's Proclamation of Amnesty and Reconstruction (December 1863). Also see Eric Foner, *Reconstruction: America's Unfinished Revolution,*

1863–1877 (New York: Harper and Row, 1988); David Donald, *Lincoln* (New York: Simon and Schuster, 1995), pp. 582–83.

2. For a good summary, see John Mack Faragher et al., *Out of Many* (Upper Saddle River, N.J.: Prentice-Hall, 2000), pp. 487–488.

3. For a more detailed discussion of these contrasting positions, see, for example, Avery O. Craven, *Reconstruction: The Ending of the Civil War* (New York: Holt, Rinehart and Winston, 1969); Rembert W. Patrick, *The Reconstruction of the Nation* (New York: Oxford University Press, 1967).

4. Quoted in Paul Johnson, *A History of the American People* (New York: HarperCollins, 1997), p. 500.

5. Faragher, *Out of Many*, p. 487.

6. For example, see James E. Sefton, *Andrew Johnson and the Uses of Constitutional Power* (New York: Addison-Wesley, 1980).

7. They sent fifty-eight members of the Confederate Congress, a vice president, four generals, five colonels, and six cabinet officers to the United States Congress. See John Hope Franklin and Alfred A. Moss, Jr., *From Slavery to Freedom: A History of African Americans* (New York: Knopf, 1994), pp. 225–226.

8. The term "carpetbagger" referred to the cloth satchel in which these Northern transplants were alleged to be carrying all their worldly belongings as they settled in the South. "Scalawag" conveyed the image of a lazy and mischievous person, derived from the Scalloway area of Scotland known for its scraggly livestock. See David Goldfield et al., *The American Journey* (Upper Saddle River, N.J.: Prentice-Hall, 1998), pp. 544–545.

9. *United States Statutes at Large* (Washington, D.C.: GPO), vol. 14, pp. 428–429; vol. 15, pp. 14–16, 41.

17

Fourteenth Amendment to the United States Constitution

1868

Among other things, this constitutional amendment required states to provide equal protection under their laws.

HISTORICAL CONTEXT

Following the Civil War, the first Reconstruction Congress held its initial meeting on December 4, 1865. At that very first session, a Joint Committee on Reconstruction was formed. In scarcely more than a month, that committee began consideration of a Fourteenth Amendment to the United States Constitution. The major concern came to be providing legal protection for newly freed slaves residing in less than friendly Southern states. Black codes, which made blacks second-class citizens under state law, restricted their rights and tied them to near slave-like working conditions.

The Civil Rights Act of 1866, passed over President Andrew Johnson's veto, was designed to protect the freedmen by guaranteeing among other things that former slaves were to enjoy the "full and equal benefit of all laws . . . as enjoyed by white citizens." Congress found its authority to pass such a law in its power to enforce the Thirteenth Amendment, which ended slavery. Opponents challenged its constitutionality, however, claiming that Congress lacked the authority to limit state governments in such a manner. In point of fact, the United States Supreme Court had explicitly read the United States Constitution's first ten amendments, the Bill of Rights, to apply only to the federal government. Consequently, such liberties were protected against federal intrusion, but state governments remained free to respect only those rights they so chose to respect.[1]

In order to head off a protracted constitutional battle over Congress's authority in this realm, the Republican-dominated first Reconstruction Congress finally passed the Fourteenth Amendment in June of 1866 and then submitted it to the states. If ratified, the amendment would nullify the infamous Dred Scott decision by granting full citizenship to all those born or naturalized in the United States.[2] Far more sweepingly, it would require states to provide due process and equal protection under their laws, as well as respect all federal privileges and immunities. The amendment essentially redefined U.S. federalism in a very significant way. It placed the federal government in the ultimate position of guaranteeing individual rights to life, liberty, and property, and it authorized Congress to pass the laws necessary to enforce such rights.

Ratification proceeded slowly, however, as many states feared further erosion of state power in the face of an expanding federal government. Delaware, Kentucky, and Maryland, for example, rejected it outright; California chose not to act at all; and New Jersey, Ohio, and Oregon passed and then rescinded their support. Nonetheless, the required three-fourths of the states was finally achieved in large part because the Southern states were forced to ratify the amendment as a condition of their reinstatement into the Union.[3]

Once enacted, the Southern states attempted to evade the Fourteenth Amendment by passing a series of laws such as grandfather clauses, which precluded a man from voting unless he could pass highly subjective literacy tests or meet poll tax requirements unless his grandparents had been registered voters. Although the law appeared to apply neutrally to everyone, it had the effect of eliminating virtually all black voters.[4]

Although it generated more litigation than virtually any other amendment, the Fourteenth Amendment was slow to be used to strike state laws and practices that discriminated against African Americans. The due process clause did allow a few blacks to have convictions overturned because their juries had been limited to whites.[5] Nevertheless, it would be decades before it was read broadly enough by federal judges to force states to provide many basic legal protections for their black residents.[6] Much more commonly, the United States Supreme Court interpreted the Fourteenth Amendment in a way that protected the property rights of corporations against state regulation in an era of full-scale industrial revolution.[7]

As one federal judge summarized these views at the time, "It should be remembered that of the three fundamental principles which underlie government, and for which government exists, the protection of life, liberty, and property, the chief of these is property."[8] That would all begin to change, however, in 1925 when the United States Supreme Court began to extend the reach of the Fourteenth Amendment.[9]

Simple in text, the amendment became more complicated as it was applied. Focusing primarily on Section One, there are three basic elements, all of which are complementary and each of which has come to overlap the other in actual interpretation. Given the centrality of the Fourteenth Amendment to so much of the civil rights law that was to follow, these three key clauses and their subsequent general interpretations are reviewed below.

The "privileges or immunities" clause was ultimately interpreted to imply that national citizenship is to be primary and state citizenship secondary. This means we are all first and foremost citizens of the United States. Because of that, state governments were not to interfere with the rights or privileges guaranteed by federal law to anyone born here or having gone through the proper steps to become a naturalized United States citizen.

For example, a federal law could guarantee that a prospective home buyer be allowed to buy any home he or she could afford to buy regardless of the buyer's race. This would then require that a seller sell to the person making the best offer, even if the seller would rather sell only to a white person. Assuming the federal law was constitutional, a state could not pass a contrary law allowing the seller to discriminate on such a basis. In that case, the state would be interfering with a right guaranteed to the buyer by federal law, and such a contrary law would be unconstitutional.

One major point of controversy, however, was whether states would be required to protect unwritten fundamental rights or just those rights expressly provided for in federal law. For example, were states required to protect a fundamental right to privacy and tranquility against mob violence in the absence of any federal law to that effect? Or, to put it another way, could the federal courts use the "privileges and immunities" clause to intervene and require states to prosecute lynch mobs, or would they have to wait for Congress to pass an antilynching law?

Given that Southern congresspersons continued to be successful at fending off further extensions of federal power, such as antilynching laws, the courts' initial narrow reading of this passage cost many Southern blacks years of judicial protection against mob violence. Essentially the federal courts read the "privileges or immunities" clause to mean only that states could not discriminate against citizens of other states in favor of their own residents.[10]

The second basic element of the Fourteenth Amendment was the "due process" clause. Neither states nor their localities were to take away anyone's life, liberty, or property without first providing "due process of law." In other words, they were not to act in an arbitrary manner.[11] Rather, they were to follow a standard and a reasonable process before any such fundamental rights could be taken from someone—even if that "person" was not a citizen of the United States.

This passage also came to facilitate a legal process known as selective incorporation. Throughout the nineteenth century, the court held that the federal Bill of Rights (the first ten amendments to the United States Constitution) did not limit the legal prerogatives of the states,[12] but this interpretation changed in the twentieth century. Because the state regulations in effect restricted people's liberty, the Fourteenth Amendment's due process clause came to protect a whole host of federally guaranteed liberties against state interference. Put another way, the due process clause of the Fourteenth Amendment required states and their localities to guarantee select federal liberties provided for in the Bill of Rights. A state, for example, would not be allowed to regulate protest marches more extensively than the First Amendment to the United States Constitution was being interpreted to allow.

It has not always been easy to distinguish between "due process" and "equal protection." The grandfather clause example noted above suggests two potential interpretations of due process of law. The more narrow reading only guarantees procedural due process, meaning that everyone is subject to the very same legal procedures. To that extent, the grandfather clause seems to meet that criterion. Yet, the effect was altogether different. Because of the historical context, the grandparents of former slaves were quite unlikely to have been registered voters. Even though the law appears to treat everyone fairly, it does so only in a historical vacuum.

The grandfather clause was ultimately struck down as an unreasonable interference with the Fifteenth Amendment's right to vote (see Chapter 18),[13] but the federal courts later came to recognize the related principle of substantive due process. Examining a law under such a standard, the court looked to see not only that the law was fair, providing the same procedures for everyone involved, but also that the content of the law was reasonable. Did its goals and means make sense, particularly if it was going to affect peoples' fundamental rights?[14] An award of punitive damages, for example, in an amount 500 times the actual damages, may well be determined in a procedurally acceptable manner. Nevertheless, it could still be "grossly excessive" and thus a violation of substantive due process.[15]

The last of the basic elements is the "equal protection" clause itself. States were to make and enforce laws in a manner that equally protected each person in the state, once again including noncitizens. In many ways, this seems implied in the due process clause. The United States Supreme Court recognized that overlap when it stated that "discrimination may be so unjustifiable as to be violative of due process."[16]

The problem is that virtually all laws treat people differently in terms of who will benefit and who will pay. The key dilemma, then, is to determine when such governmental discrimination violates the equal protection clause of the United States Constitution. In order to help decide this, the federal courts gradually concluded that laws that discriminate against certain suspect classes of people would be held to the strictest legal review.

Suspect classes have been defined by the court as groups

> saddled with such disabilities, or subjected to such a history of purposeful unequal treatment, or relegated to such a position of political powerlessness as to command extraordinary protection from the majoritarian political process [meaning certain minorities will need special protection in a political process in which the majority rules].[17]

African Americans were explicitly defined as such a group.

The courts did not insist that such groups could never be treated differently, but only that such differential treatment would have to be justified under what is known as a "strict scrutiny test."[18] To pass that test, governmental discrimination on the basis of a classification such as race would require a "compelling state interest" and no more usage than was necessary to accomplish those legitimate ends.

In the case of affirmative action (giving members of designated groups certain advantages because those groups have been discriminated against in the past), the court might allow the fact that one is black to be a positive criterion in a state medical school's admission formula under certain circumstances. The school, for instance, might well have to show a compelling need for more black students, either because of a clear history of past discrimination or because the state desperately needed more black graduates in order to have enough individuals willing to practice medicine in predominantly black neighborhoods. In addition, it might be necessary to show that other less suspect methods were unlikely to work, that race would be only one of several selection criteria, and that it would be used only until the compelling need was met.[19]

Just how are the courts to determine whether discrimination is occurring in the first place, thus setting off the strict scrutiny process? If such differentiation is written directly into the law, or if an administrator is found to be making such distinctions (both known as discriminatory intent), this is obvious. But, similar to the logic of substantive due process is a legal concept called "disparate impact." A job requirement, for example, could be found racially discriminatory and thus unconstitutional, not because it was applied differently for black applicants, but because it led to a racially uneven result. In such cases, the employer could be required to justify usage of that particular criterion as being a necessary requirement for the job.[20]

Thus, a law could be applied equally to everyone, yet still have constitutionally unacceptable results. A seniority system, for example, might work procedurally in the same way for all employees. Those who had worked there the longest would be the last to be fired, but, if its impact was to require that members of a formerly excluded group, by definition the most recently hired, were always the first ones fired, the seniority system might have an unconstitutional discriminatory effect, particularly if that formerly excluded group was from a suspect class and had been excluded illegally for years.

The amendment explicitly applies only to the actions of "states," meaning state and local governments, but as the federal courts came to interpret it, state action would be read to include private actions even remotely connected to government. As an example, the United States Supreme Court found that the equal protection clause applied to a private restaurant refusing to serve black patrons because that restaurant sat on publicly owned land, and public land was not to be leased in a manner inconsistent with the Fourteenth Amendment.[21] In point of fact, for the two decades following the first such extension in 1948,[22] the United States Supreme Court, on the grounds that no state action was present, never once denied relief to those found to be suffering from racial discrimination.[23] Beginning in 1970, however, a more conservative court began to rein in such extensions. In 1972, for instance, the justices ruled that a private club was not involved in "state action" when it refused to serve blacks, even though it held a state liquor license.[24]

Finally, as implied in the previous two examples, forcible separation of the races would come to be seen as a violation of the equal protection clause even if equal facilities were available. As recently as 1896, the United States Supreme Court allowed governments legally to segregate by race as long as they provided "separate but equal" facilities.[25] Beginning with the momentous *Brown v. Board of Education* decision in 1954, it was ruled that "separate but equal was inherently unequal."[26] Segregated public schools, no matter how equal, were still constitutionally unacceptable. Consequently, the equal protection clause also came to require considerable desegregation.[27]

THE LAW

The Fourteenth Amendment comprises five sections. Section One prohibits state governments from passing or enforcing laws that interfere with the privileges of its citizens. It also prohibits state governments from denying anyone life, liberty, or property without due process of law, as the federal government had been prohibited from doing by the Fifth Amendment. It also guaranteed all persons, regardless of color, equal protection under the laws.

Section Two directs the states to count each person as a whole person for purposes of determining the number of representatives for each state. This section provides penalties for states failing to do so.

The political rights of former Confederates to hold office are limited by Section Three.

Section Four addresses the disposition of Confederate debt and prohibits "any claim for the loss or emancipation of any slave."

Finally, Section Five grants Congress the power to enforce the provisions of the amendment.

17. Fourteenth Amendment

Sec. 1. All persons born or naturalized in the United States, and subject to the jurisdiction thereof, are citizens of the United States and of the State wherein they reside. No State shall make or enforce any law which shall abridge the privileges or immunities of citizens of the United States; nor shall any State deprive any person of life, liberty, or property, without due process of law; nor deny to any person within its jurisdiction the equal protection of the laws.

Sec. 2. Representatives shall be apportioned among the several States according to their respective numbers, counting the whole number of persons in each State, excluding Indians not taxed. But when the right to vote at any election for the choice of electors for President and Vice President of the United States, Representatives in Congress, the Executive and Judicial officers of a State, or the members of the Legislature thereof, is denied to any of the male inhabitants of such State, being twenty-one years of age, and citizens of the United States, or in any way abridged, except for participation in rebellion, or other crime, the basis of representation therein shall be reduced in the proportion which the number of such male citizens shall bear to the whole number of male citizens twenty-one years of age in such State.

Sec 3. No person shall be a Senator or Representative in Congress, or elector of the President and Vice President, or hold any office, civil or military, under the United States, or under any State, who, having previously taken an oath, as a member of Congress, or as an officer of the United States, or as a member of any State legislature, or as an executive or judicial officer of any State, to support the Constitution of the United States, shall have engaged in insurrection or rebellion against the same, or given aid or comfort the enemies thereof. But Congress may, by a vote of two thirds of each House, remove such disability.

Sec. 4. The validity of the public debt of the United States, authorized by law, including debts incurred for payment of pensions and bounties for services in suppressing insurrection or rebellion, shall not be questioned. But neither the United States nor any State shall assume or pay any debt or obligation incurred in aid of insurrection or rebellion against the United States, or any claim for the loss of emancipation of any slave; but all such debts, obligations and claims shall be held illegal and void.

Sec. 5. The Congress shall have power to enforce, by appropriate legislation, the provisions of this article.

NOTES

1. See *Baltimore v. Barron,* 7 Pet. 243 (1833).
2. *Dred Scott v. Sandford,* 19 How. 393 (1857).
3. For example, see Horace Flack, *The Adoption of the 14th Amendment* (New York: AMS Press, 1999).
4. For example, see William E. Nelson, *The 14th Amendment* (Cambridge, Mass.: Harvard University Press, 1995); Hermine H. Meyer, *The History and Meaning of the 14th Amendment* (New York: Vintage Press, 1977).
5. See *Strauder v. West Virginia,* 100 U.S. 303 (1880); *Ex parte Virginia,* 100 U.S. 313 (1880); *Neal v. Delaware,* 103 U.S. 370 (1880).
6. For example, see the "Slaughterhouse Cases" of 1873, 83 U.S. 36, and the "Civil Rights Cases" of 1883, 109 U.S. 3.
7. For example, see *Lochner v. New York,* 198 U.S. 45 (1905).
8. *Children's Hospital v. Adkins,* 284 Fed. 613, 622 D.C. Cir. (1922).
9. For example, see *Gitlow v. New York,* 268 U.S. 652 (1925); *West Coast Hotel v. Parrish,* 300 U.S. 379 (1937); *National Labor Relations Board v. Jones and Laughlin Steel Corporation,* 301 U.S. 1 (1937).
   As for race specific extensions, see *Gaines v. Canada,* 305 U.S. 337 (1938); *Sweatt v. Painter,* 339 U.S. 629 (1950); *Loving v. Virginia,* 388 U.S. 1 (1967).
10. The more general principle was set out in a series of rulings that have come to be called the "Slaughterhouse Cases." For an example that deals more specifically with lynching, see *United States v. Wheeler,* 254 U.S. 281 (1920).
11. For example, see the discussion in *Dixon v. Love,* 431 U.S. 105 (1977).
12. For example, see *Barron v. the Mayor and City Council of Baltimore,* 32 U.S. 243 (1833).
13. *Guinn v. United States,* 238 U.S. 347 (1915).
14. For one of the earliest articulations of this contemporary version of "substantive due process," see the dissent of Justice John Harlan II in *Poe v. Ullman,* 367 U.S. 497 (1961). More recently, see Justice David Souter's concurrence in *Washington v. Glucksberg,* 521 U.S. 702 (1997).
15. *BMW of North America v. Gore,* 517 U.S. 559 (1996).
16. *Bolling v. Sharpe,* 347 U.S. 497, 499 (1954).
17. *San Antonio Independent School District v. Rodriquez,* 411 U.S. 1, 28 (1973).
18. This same test is applied when a fundamental right is being infringed upon by government; for example, the right to vote.
19. For example, see *De Funis v. Odegaard,* 416 U.S. 312 (1974); *Alevy v. Downstate Medical Center,* 348, N.E. 2nd 537 (1976); *Bakke v. Regents of the University of California,* 438 U.S. 265 (1978).
20. *Griggs v. Duke Power Company,* 401 U.S. 424 (1971); reversed in *Wards Cove Packing, Inc. v. Antonio,* 490 U.S. 642 (1989); but then reinstated in the 1991 Civil Rights Act (see Chapter 33).
21. *Burton v. Willimington Parking Authority,* 365 U.S. 715 (1961).
22. *Shelley v. Kramer,* 334 U.S. 1 (1948).
23. David O'Brien, *Constitutional Law and Politics: Civil Rights and Civil Liberties* (New York: Norton, 1997), p. 1225.
24. *Moose Lodge No. 107 v. Irvis,* 407 U.S. 163 (1972).
25. *Plessy v. Ferguson,* 163 U.S. 537 (1896).

26. *Brown v. Board of Education of Topeka, Kansas,* 347 U.S. 483 (1954).

27. For a more general discussion, see Michael Kent Curtis, *No State Shall Abridge: The Fourteenth Amendment and the Bill of Rights* (Durham, N.C.: Duke University Press 1990).

18

Fifteenth Amendment to the United States Constitution

1870

This constitutional amendment prohibits voting discrimination on the basis of race, color, or previous condition of servitude.

HISTORICAL CONTEXT

This was the third and final Civil War amendment. In the debate surrounding its predecessor, the Fourteenth Amendment, there was considerable disagreement over whether the conferring of citizenship included a federally guaranteed right to vote. In fact, after opposing the inclusion of the term "political rights" within the sweep of Fourteenth Amendment protections, the opponents of the Fourteenth argued that it would still require states to extend political rights to all persons despite the absence of any express provision to that effect. They then used the fear of such federal intrusion in what previously had been a state prerogative in order to rally opposition to the Fourteenth Amendment.

In a representative democracy, however, the right to vote is clearly an essential component of full citizenship. In addition, if one belongs to a group that traditionally has been discriminated against, such a right is even more important in pressing government to address such discrimination. When several states, including most Northern states, continued to restrict suffrage on racial grounds following passage of the Fourteenth Amendment, explicitly guaranteeing such a right appeared to be absolutely essential. The Fifteenth Amendment settled the issue, at least formally.

Like the Fourteenth Amendment before it, the Fifteenth was

spawned by Congress's Joint Committee on Reconstruction. Yet, it was not formally introduced into Congress until the congressional judiciary committees reported out bills in January 1869. The House version contained a right to "vote and hold office," but this was ultimately reduced to a "right to vote." Legally speaking, however, the amendment did not technically confer a right to vote. Instead, what it did do was forbid voting discrimination "by the United States or by any state" on the basis of "race, color, or previous condition of servitude."

Proponents included such Radical Republicans as Representative James Blaine (Rep., Maine) who called for a reduction in congressional representation for any state caught discriminating on the basis of race or color, as required by Section 2 of the Fourteenth Amendment. Supporters also included political partisans who hoped such an amendment would add a sizable number of black voters to the Republican ranks, as well as pragmatists who believed it would protect suffrage extensions from repeal by subsequent congresses.

These proponents were heartened when Congress overrode President Andrew Johnson's vetoes of a law providing for black suffrage in Washington, D.C., and another conditioning Nebraska's statehood on black enfranchisement. In addition, the Republican-dominated Congress voted to require black suffrage in the federal territories, and Southern states would be forced to extend the vote to blacks in order to be readmitted into the union.

Meanwhile, congressional opposition to the Fifteenth Amendment came from several directions. Most prominent were those who argued that the federalization of this right amounted to a usurpation of what had traditionally been a state function. There were also radicals who argued that even the constitutional amendment process did not extend to such a politically sacred matter. Meanwhile, at the other end of the spectrum were such liberals as Representative John Bingham (Rep., Ohio) and Senator Willard Warner (Rep., Ala.) who contended that the amendment did not go far enough, in that it focused on former slaves rather than guaranteeing the right to all males. These opponents preferred to allow discrimination only on the basis of "sex, age, residence, and crime."

During the congressional deliberation, several amendments to this constitutional amendment were proposed. Ironically, the Senate passed one that would have guaranteed the right to vote against discrimination on the basis of education. They feared the prospect of subjective educational tests in the South. The House did not concur, however, and that provision fell away, opening the door for decades of literacy tests. In the end, the version included here passed by three-to-one margins in both houses of Congress, although there were several abstentions.

The Fifteenth Amendment to the United States Constitution was finally ratified by three-fourths of the states on February 3, 1870. The support of at least eight states from the former Confederacy had been needed to secure ratification. Such ratification by Southern states had been a requirement for readmission to the union, and the process was overseen by occupying federal troops where necessary, as was the case this time in the state of Georgia. Virginia, Texas, and Mississippi had to be prodded as well. As it turned out, those Southern votes proved necessary when New York attempted to rescind, and California, Delaware, Kentucky, Maryland, Oregon, and Tennessee failed to ratify.[1]

The Fifteenth Amendment took effect on March 30, 1870; nevertheless, in the former Confederacy, mere passage was not enough to guarantee that African Americans would have the same right to vote as whites. Instead, it almost immediately gave rise to a number of obstructive tactics. Employers threatened to fire blacks who tried to register, and night riders terrorized them after the sun went down.[2] In addition, government evasions proliferated following the Supreme Court's 1876 ruling that the Fifteenth Amendment prohibited race-based discrimination, but it did not preclude states from discriminating on other bases.[3] Subsequent evasions of the Fifteenth Amendment included poll taxes, literacy tests, white-only primary elections, grandfather clauses (see Chapter 17), and physical intimidation. When Radical Reconstruction ended and the federal troops were withdrawn in the late 1870s, many states of the former Confederacy proceeded to undo the protective provisions in their state constitutions that had been established during the Northern occupation.

It would take decades before such practices were struck down by the United States Supreme Court[4]; outlawed by constitutional amendment, for example, the Twenty-fourth Amendment passed in 1964; or reigned in by acts of Congress, for example, the 1870 Enforcement Act, the 1957 and 1964 Civil Rights Acts, and the 1965 Voting Rights Act.

THE LAW

The Fifteenth Amendment prohibits the denial of any United States citizen's right to vote on the basis of that person's race, color, or prior status as a slave. Furthermore, it grants Congress the authority to pass any laws necessary to enforce the amendment.

18. Fifteenth Amendment

Section 1. The right of citizens of the United States to vote shall not be denied or abridged by the United States or by any State on account of race, color, or previous condition of servitude.

Section 2. The Congress shall have power to enforce this article by appropriate legislation.

NOTES

1. For example, see John M. Mathews, *Legislative and Judicial History of the 15th Amendment* (Baltimore: Johns Hopkins Press, 1909).

2. For example, see Susan Banfield, *The 15th Amendment* (Berkeley Heights, N.J.: Enslow Publishers, 1998).

3. *United States v. Reese*, 92 U.S. 214 (1876).

4. For example, see *Nixon V. Herndon*, 273 U.S. 536 (1927); *Nixon v. Condon*, 286 U.S. 73 (1932); *Smith v. Allwright*, 321 U.S. 649 (1944), which strike down white primaries. For a fuller listing of the various federal court decisions spelling out these interpretations, see Edward S. Corwin, *The Constitution and What It Means Today* (Princeton, N.J.: Princeton University Press, 1978), pp. 532–39.

19

Enforcement Act

1870

The Enforcement Act established federal sanctions for interfering with another person's civil rights, especially a black's right to vote. It also allowed for federal election supervisors to oversee registration and voting procedures.

HISTORICAL CONTEXT

In 1868 a wave of murders and assaults was launched including assassinations designed to keep Negroes from the polls. The States themselves were helpless, despite the resort by some of them to extreme measures such as making it legal to hunt down and shoot any disguised man. . . . Within Congress pressures mounted . . . for drastic measures.[1]

Representative John Bingham (Rep., Ohio), one of the primary sponsors of the Fourteenth Amendment, introduced the first of the Enforcement Acts in the spring of 1870. He argued that there was a need "to enforce the legal right of citizens of the United States to vote in the several States of this Union . . . [especially where such rights have been] defiantly denied."[2] His bill, passed by the House without debate, made it a crime for state election officials to discriminate on the basis of race.

By contrast, there was a full debate in the United States Senate. Senators such as William Stewart (Rep., Nev.) worried that the House bill was not strong enough. These senators wanted sanctions to protect against private interference with the right to vote as well.

Discriminatory "state action" could be governed under the enforcement clauses of both the Fourteenth and Fifteenth Amendments. That was clear. But, they also argued that the definition of "state action" should go beyond overt state laws and routine state practices. It should be broad enough to encompass both state acts of commission and omission. Thus, the federal government's punitive authority was regarded as extending to the acts of private individuals the states had failed to prevent.

Senator Matthew Carpenter (Rep., Wis.) declared,

> if we design to go beyond merely punishing specific violations of the law, and to carry out and enforce the principle of this amendment to the Constitution, and give effect to the votes of colored persons offered at the polls, then we should have some such provision as is contained in the Senate bill.[3]

Opponents worried that Congress was embarking on a costly venture that would require considerable money and manpower to implement. Some also questioned the motives of its supporters, seeing this as little more than a ruse to bolster the strength of the national Republican Party by increasing the ranks of black supporters in the South. To make matters worse, all of this was to be enforced by the heavy hand of a federal military presence. Representative Charles Eldredge (Dem., Wis.) referred to it as establishing an "empire of despotism . . . under the sword."[4] It also was viewed as an approach that would once again extend federal power in an unconstitutional manner in as much as states had a constitutionally guaranteed right to police their own elections. In addition, nowhere in the United States Constitution was there federal authority to punish the discriminatory actions of private individuals.

Nonetheless, despite such concerns, Congress passed the Civil Rights Act of 1870 only two months after the final ratification of the Fifteenth Amendment. In Section 16, it reiterated the Fourteenth Amendment's guarantee of equal protection under the law. More specifically, however, it criminalized both public and private violations of voting rights set out in the Fifteenth Amendment, including conspiracies to violate those rights. The president of the United States was authorized to use armed forces if necessary to enforce this law.[5]

In February 1871, Representative John Churchill (Rep., N.Y.) introduced an amendment to the 1870 Enforcement Act, designed to add an enforcement mechanism. The amendment, which came to be known as the Force Act of 1871, allowed residents of any town larger than 20,000 to petition the nearest federal circuit court to provide federalized election supervisors to oversee and enforce registration and voting procedures.

So anxious and confident was the congressional Republican majority, they scheduled only one day each for House and Senate debates. The primary substantive contention of the Democratic minority, once again, was that such federal intrusions were unconstitutional, unnecessary, and designed primarily for partisan political advantage. According to Representative Eldredge, these newest devices would "bind the several States hand and foot, and deliver them over to the Federal Government subjugated and helpless . . . the crowning act of centralization and consolidation."[6] Nevertheless, numerous Democratic amendments were subsequently defeated, including ones that merely sought to correct misprintings. Within two weeks of the first floor debate, the Force Act had been approved.

Various sections of the 1870 Enforcement Act were ultimately declared unconstitutional. Sections three and four, for example, were regarded as creating a federal "right to vote," when all the Fifteenth Amendment actually did was to forbid voting discrimination on the basis of race.[7] The court also held that the act included more offenses than were punishable under the Fifteenth Amendment.[8] Nevertheless, a central premise—that the federal government could punish individuals for private acts that interfered with legitimate federal rights—was subsequently upheld.[9] In addition, the United States Supreme Court upheld the federal government's authority to use federal officials to enforce these rights.[10]

Politics, on the other hand, would prove to be a much weightier impediment to these efforts. At the end of the highly contentious 1876 elections, the Republicans had to commit to the Compromise of 1877 in order to break an impasse over contested voting results in South Carolina and Louisiana.[11] When Republican Rutherford B. Hayes was finally declared the president, he and Congress soon put an end to Southern reconstruction by withdrawing federal troops. Soon the South returned to Democratic control, and, through a variety of legal manueverings and physical intimidation, black suffrage all but ceased to exist.

Before the century wound to a close, a Democratic-dominated Congress, coupled with a Democratic president, passed the Repeal

Act of 1894, repealing all laws providing for federal monitors of state elections, as well as the more general federal protection of the right to vote. Shortly thereafter, the Amnesty Act of 1898 granted a final amnesty to all of the former Confederate states.

THE LAW

The Civil Rights Act of 1870[12] guaranteed equal protection under state law and established federal criminal sanctions for interfering with another's civil rights, especially a black's right to vote.

Specifically, the act declared that "race, color or previous condition of servitude" could not be used as a basis for interfering with a citizen's right to vote. It outlawed the unequal application of any voting prerequisite on account of "race, color, or previous condition of servitude" and set forth penalties for noncompliance. It outlawed the use of "force, bribery, threats, [and] intimidation . . . [to] hinder, delay, prevent, or obstruct" any eligible person from registering to vote or voting, and it imposed penalties for violation. The act also contained provisions prohibiting various types of voting fraud and prohibiting any attempt to prevent the winner of an election from taking office.

The Civil Rights Act of 1870 specifically protected the rights secured by the Fifteenth Amendment and prohibited acts intended to prevent the exercise of those rights. It made it unlawful for citizens to conspire to prevent other citizens from exercising any United States Constitutional right or privilege, and it clearly guaranteed that all persons were to have the same rights in every state as were enjoyed by white persons.

In addition, it set forth details relevant to prosecuting violators. Included in its provisions were penalties for obstructing any prosecution under the act and for rescuing or harboring those charged with violation of this law. The act also made it lawful for the president to use military force if necessary to uphold the provisions of the law.

The act was amended a year later, revising the penalties imposed under the original Enforcement Act. It added a provision that allowed residents of towns larger than 20,000 to petition the nearest federal circuit court to provide election supervisors and special deputy federal marshals to oversee registration and voting procedures. The amendment also provided a procedure for the appointment of a chief supervisor of elections.

19a. Civil Rights Act of 1870

CHAP. CXIV.

An Act to enforce the Right of Citizens of the United States to vote in the several States of this Union, and for other Purposes.

Be it enacted . . . That all citizens of the United States who are or shall be otherwise qualified by law to vote at any election by the people in any State, Territory, district, county, city, parish, township, school district, municipality, or other territorial subdivision, shall be entitled and allowed to vote at all such elections, without distinction of race, color, or previous condition of servitude; any constitution, law, custom, usage, or regulation of any State or Territory, or by or under its authority, to the contrary notwithstanding.

SEC. 2. And be it further enacted, That if by or under the authority of the constitution or laws of any State, or the laws of any Territory, any act is or shall be required to be done as a prerequisite or qualification for voting, and by such constitution or laws persons or officers are or shall be charged with the performance of duties in furnishing to citizens an opportunity to perform such prerequisite, or to become qualified to vote, it shall be the duty of every such person and officer to give to all citizens of the United States the same and equal opportunity to perform such prerequisite, and to become qualified to vote without distinction of race, color, or previous condition of servitude. . . .

SEC. 4. And be it further enacted, That if any person, by force, bribery, threats, intimidation, or other-unlawful means, shall hinder, delay, prevent, or obstruct, or shall combine and confederate with others to hinder, delay, prevent, or obstruct, any citizen from doing any act required to be done to qualify him to vote or from voting at any election as aforesaid, such person shall for every such offence forfeit and pay the sum of five hundred dollars . . . and shall also for every such offence be guilty of a misdemeanor, and shall, on conviction thereof, be fined not less than five hundred dollars, or be imprisoned not less than one month and not more than one year, or both, at the discretion of the court.

SEC. 5. And be it further enacted, That if any person shall prevent, hinder, control, or intimidate, or shall attempt to prevent, hinder, control, or intimidate, any person from exercising the right of suffrage, to whom the right of suffrage is secured or guaranteed by the fifteenth amendment to the Constitution of the United States, by means of bribery, threats, or threats of depriving such person of employment or occupation, or of ejecting such person from rented house, lands, or other property, or by threats of refusing to renew leases or contracts for labor, or by threats of violence to himself or family, such person so offending shall be deemed guilty of a misdemeanor, and shall, on conviction thereof be fined not less than five hundred dollars, or be imprisoned not less than one month and not more than one year, or both, at the discretion of the court.

SEC. 6. And be it further enacted, That if two or more persons shall band or conspire together, or go in disguise upon the public highway, or upon the premises of another, with intent to violate any provision of this act, or to injure, oppress, threaten, or intimidate any citizen with intent to prevent or hinder his free exercise and enjoyment of any right or privilege granted or secured to him by the Constitution or laws of the United States, or because of his having exercised the same, such persons shall be held guilty of felony, and, on conviction thereof, shall be fined or imprisoned, or both, at the discretion of the court. . . .

SEC. 16. And be it further enacted, That all persons within the jurisdiction of the United States shall have the same right in every State and Territory in the United States to make and enforce contracts, to sue, be parties, give evidence, and to the full and equal benefit of all laws and proceedings for the security of person and property as is enjoyed by white citizens, and shall be subject to like punishment, pains, penalties, taxes, licenses, and exactions of every kind, and none other, any law, statute, ordinance, regulation, or custom to the contrary notwithstanding. [All persons were to have the same rights in all states and territories as white citizens possessed.] No tax or charge shall be imposed or enforced by any State upon any person immigrating thereto from a foreign country which is not equally imposed and enforced upon every person immigrating to such State from any other foreign country; and any law of any State in conflict with this provision is hereby declared null and void. . . . [No special taxes could be imposed on immigrants.]

SEC. 18. And be it further enacted, That the act to protect all persons in the United States in their civil rights, and furnish the means of their vindication, passed April nine, eighteen hundred and sixty-six, is hereby enacted; and sections sixteen and seventeen hereof shall be enforced according to the provisions of [the] act. . . .

SEC. 23. And be it further enacted, That whenever any person shall be defeated or deprived of his election to any office, except elector of President or Vice-President, representative or delegate in Congress, or member of a State legislature, by reason of the denial to any citizen or citizens who shall offer to vote; of the right to vote, on account of race, color, or previous condition of servitude, his right to hold and enjoy such office, and the emoluments [benefits] thereof, shall not be impaired by such denial. . . .

APPROVED, May 31, 1870.

19b. Amendment to the Civil Rights Act of 1870

CHAP. XCIX.

Act to amend an Act approved May thirty-one, eighteen hundred and seventy, entitled "An Act to enforce the Rights of Citizens of the United States to vote in the several States of this Union, and for other Purposes."

Be it enacted . . . That section twenty of the "Act to enforce the rights of citizens of the United States to vote in the several States of this Union, and for other purposes," approved May thirty-one, eighteen hundred and seventy, shall be, and hereby is, amended so as to read as follows: . . .

SEC. 2. And be it further enacted, That whenever in any city or town having upward of twenty thousand inhabitants, there shall be two citizens thereof who, prior to any registration of voters for an election for representative or delegate in the Congress of the United States, or prior to any election at which a representative or delegate in Congress is to be voted for, shall make known, in writing, to the judge of the circuit court of the United States for the circuit wherein such city or town shall be, their desire to have [the] registration, or [the] election, or both, guarded and scrutinized, it shall be the duty of the . . . judge of the circuit court, within not less than ten days prior to [the] registration, if one there be, or, if no registration be required, within not less than ten days prior to [the] election, to open the . . . circuit court at the most convenient point in [the] circuit. And the . . . court, when so opened by [the] judge, shall proceed to appoint and commission, from day to day and from time to time, and under the hand of the . . . circuit judge, and under the seal of [the] court, for each election district or voting precinct in each and every such city or town as shall, in the manner herein prescribed, have applied therefor, and to revoke, change, or renew [the] appointment from time to time, two citizens, residents of [the] city or town, who shall be of different political parties, and able to read and write the English language, and who shall be known and designated as supervisors of election. And the . . . circuit court, when opened by the . . . circuit judge . . . shall . . . up to and including the day following the day of election, be always open for the transaction of business under this act, and the powers and jurisdiction hereby granted and conferred shall be exercised as well in vacation as in term time; and a judge sitting at chambers shall have the same powers and jurisdiction, including the power of keeping order and of punishing any contempt of his authority, as when sitting in court. . . .

SEC. 8. And be it further enacted, That whenever an election at which representatives or delegates in Congress are to be chosen shall be held in any city or town of twenty thousand inhabitants or upward, the marshall of the United States for the district in which [the] city or town is situated shall have power, and it shall be his duty, on the application, in writing, of at least two citizens residing in any such city or town, to appoint special deputy marshals. . . .

SEC. 13. And be it further enacted, That it shall be the duty of each circuit court of the United States in and for each judicial circuit, upon the recommendation in writing of the judge thereof, to name and appoint, on or before the first day of May, in the year eighteen hundred and seventy-one, and thereafter as vacancies may from any cause arise, from among the circuit court commissioners in and for each judicial district in each of [the] judicial circuits, one of such officers, who shall be known for the duties required of him under this act as the chief supervisor of elections of the judicial district in and for which he shall be a commissioner, and shall, so long as faithful and capable, discharge the duties in this act imposed. . . .

APPROVED, February 28, 1871.

NOTES

1. From the majority opinion of the United States Supreme Court in *United States v. Price*, 383 U.S. 787 (1966), pp. 803–804.

2. Bernard Schwartz, ed., *Statutory History of the United States: Civil Rights*, Part 1 (New York: Chelsea House, 1970), p. 443.

3. Ibid., p. 462.

4. Ibid., p. 530.

5. For example, see William Watson Davis, "The Federal Enforcement Act," in *Studies in Southern History and Politics*, ed. William Archibald Dunning (New York: Columbia University Press, 1914).

6. Ibid., p. 559.

7. *United States v. Reese*, 92 U.S. 542 (1876). As other examples, see the challenge to Section 5 in *James v. Bowman*, 190 U.S. 127 (1903) and the challenge to Section 16 in *Hodges v. U.S.*, 203 U.S. 1 (1906).

8. *United States v. Cruikshank*, 92 U.S. 542 (1876).

9. *Ex Parte Yarborough*, 110 U.S. 651 (1884).

10. For example, see *Ex Parte Siebold*, 100 U.S. 371 (1880); *South Carolina v. Katzenbach*, 383 U.S. 301 (1966).

11. For example, see C. Vann Woodward, *Reunion and Reaction: The Compromise of 1877 and the End of Reconstruction* (Garden City, N.Y.: Doubleday, 1956).

12. *Statutes at Large of the United States* (Washington, D.C.: GPO), vol. 16, pp. 140–46, 433–40.

20

Klan Act

1871

The Ku Klux Klan Act established federal criminal sanctions and enforcement mechanisms to be used against those who denied others equal protection under the law.

HISTORICAL CONTEXT

Although several reactionary white organizations began operating in the postwar South, the best known of these was the Knights of the Ku Klux Klan.[1] This group, which first appeared in 1866, apparently was founded in Tennessee by six Confederate veterans, including General John B. Gordon and General William Bedford Forrest who probably was the organization's first grand wizard.

The Klan viewed its activities as an effort to restore law and order to the war-ravaged South and to protect Southern culture from the social and political "pollution" of blacks, Jews, Catholics, and many other racial, ethnic, and religious minorities. Less overtly, it was intent on restricting black voting and officeholding, defeating the Republican Party, and ending Reconstruction. At times the Klan engaged in carefully targeted terrorist activities against members of all of these enemy groups. Such terrorism included intimidation, ostracism, cross burnings, vandalism, physical assault, and even murder.[2]

The prosecution of illegal Klan activities initially fell to the U.S. Army, then occupying the South, which, however, was reluctant to override local law enforcement and local courts in peacetime. Consequently, much of the Klan's terror went legally undeterred.

Given that much of the Klan's activity was directed at undermining Republican-dominated Southern state governments, Republican governors utilized their state militias to fight the Klan. Only Arkansas, however, had much success. Meanwhile, in states such as Tennessee, North Carolina, and Georgia, Klan activity helped undercut the Republicans and allow Democratic candidates to be elected.[3]

As Representative William Stoughton (Rep., Mich.) declared,

> When thousands of murders and outrages have been committed in the southern States and not a single offender brought to justice, when the State courts are notoriously powerless to protect life, person, and property, and when violence and lawlessness are universally prevalent, the denial of equal protection of the law is too clear to admit of question or controversy.[4]

Representative Benjamin Butler (Rep., Mass.) then asked rhetorically, "If the Federal Government cannot pass laws to protect the rights, liberty, and lives of citizens of the United States in the States, why were those fundamental rights put in the Constitution?"[5]

When the Enforcement Acts of 1870 and 1871 failed to halt the violence and intimidation directed particularly at blacks who were attempting to register and vote, Congress responded once again. Confronted with a relatively steady barrage of complaints from Southern Republicans, the United States Senate formed an investigative committee in the spring of 1871. In particular, the committee was to review the violence that recently had been occurring in North Carolina. The committee filed its report on March 10; in response, President Ulysses S. Grant urged Congress to enact an antiterrorism law in order to address "A condition of affairs . . . in some of the states of the Union rendering life and property insecure."[6] By mid-April, Congress had passed the Ku Klux Klan Act, designed more effectively to enforce the civil rights guaranteed by the Fourteenth Amendment.

The Klan Act of 1871 criminalized violations of the Fourteenth Amendment's equal protection clause, declaring further that combined acts of unlawful harassment and terrorism committed by the Klan amounted to a rebellion against the government of the United States. Thus, in areas where this was occurring, the president was authorized to use military force; if necessary, the president could suspend the writ of habeas corpus[7] and proclaim martial law. In a

subsection commonly referred to today as "Section 1983," the act
also allowed federal civil suits to be brought against those violating,
or conspiring to violate, the civil rights of others.

In many ways, this amounted to a reenactment and strengthening
of the Civil Rights Act of 1866. This time, however, there was more
arguable constitutional authority for such federal action, given the
enforcement clauses of the Fourteenth and Fifteenth Amendments.
Opponents, however, again stressed that those amendments were
designed to constrain overt state actions, not the offenses committed by private individuals that may or may not have come about as
the result of state inaction. They also railed against the sweeping
powers this bill handed to the president.

President Grant, a former military general, hesitated to employ
military forces explicitly for this purpose. Instead, the Secret Service
was used to infiltrate the Klan and gather evidence for subsequent
prosecution. Following lengthy investigations, reports revealed considerable white involvement in Klan activities. In states such as
South Carolina, for instance, nearly two-thirds of the white population appears to have participated in Klan activities to some degree. In light of such facts, President Grant ordered the Klan to
disband and to surrender their arms and disguises.

When the Klan persisted, mass arrests and indictments followed,
beginning in the fall of 1871 and continuing throughout much of
1872. Some Klan leaders subsequently were punished under these
provisions. President Grant sent federal troops to nine South Carolina counties, for instance, in order to round up Klan members.
In South Carolina alone, nearly 100 individuals were convicted and
fined in one year.[8] Attorney General Amos T. Ackerman prosecuted
hundreds of Klansmen in North Carolina and Mississippi. Yet, the
federal courts were soon swamped; in the end, few Klansmen were
actually prosecuted, convicted, and punished. Selective pardons became common, and most charges had been dropped by 1875.

Despite only a limited number of actual convictions, the first Klan
diminished considerably in size and activity following these federal
efforts. This helped the Republican Party hold most of the South
in the 1872 elections, thanks in large part to significant black support.

Nonetheless, a second wave of Klan-type activity soon followed.
This time it would be much more overt, in part because allegations
of incompetence and corruption were weakening Northern support
for many Southern Republican regimes.[9] One of the very most vi-

olent episodes occurred in Colfax, Louisiana, in 1873 when a white mob massacred scores of blacks who had fought for three weeks to retain their elected control of that city. In 1874 President Grant used federal military force for the last time in the South when the White League attempted to unseat an elected Republican government in Louisiana. Grant refused the call of the state of Mississippi the following year, even though a series of violent attacks were aimed at suppressing the black vote in that state. Once federal troops were withdrawn altogether in 1877, Klan activity became even more successful in intimidating blacks from exercising their right to register and vote, a right that was soon to disappear altogether.[10]

The United States Supreme Court dealt the Klan Act its biggest blow when it declared several provisions were unconstitutional. In particular, it ruled that the federal government could no longer prosecute private individuals for such activity, although states and their employees could still be compelled to comply.[11]

THE LAW

The Civil Rights Act of 1871, better known as the Klan Act,[12] created several mechanisms for the more effective enforcement of the rights of citizens, especially black citizens, to obtain the equal protection of the law guaranteed by the Fourteenth Amendment.

The Klan Act provided that any person depriving another of rights secured by the Constitution could be required to pay damages to the party injured. Likewise, any party who knew of impending wrongs could also be required to pay damages if they took no action to prevent the wrong.

The act made it unlawful to use disguises to deny people their civil rights. Conspiracies to overthrow the government, hinder laws, or seize United States property also were prohibited.

In addition, the Klan Act prohibited interference with persons holding office or with parties, witnesses, or jurors appearing, testifying, or serving in court. Specifically, the act provided that it was unlawful to conspire to interfere with the "due course of justice."

Finally, it set forth penalties for violation of its provisions and granted the president the authority to use troops and even to suspend the writ of habeas corpus if necessary in order to suppress violence.

20. Civil Rights Act of 1871

CHAP. XXII

An Act to enforce the Provisions of the Fourteenth Amendment to the Constitution of the United States, and for other Purposes.

Be it enacted . . . That any person who, under color of any law, statute, ordinance, regulation, custom, or usage of any State, shall subject, or cause to be subjected, any person within the jurisdiction of the United States to the deprivation of any rights, privileges, or immunities secured by the Constitution of the United States, shall, any such law, statute, ordinance, regulation, custom, or usage of the State to the contrary notwithstanding, be liable to the party injured in any action at law, suit in equity, or other proper proceeding for redress . . . with and subject to the same rights of appeal, review upon error, and other remedies provided in like cases in such courts, under the provisions of the act of the ninth of April, eighteen hundred and sixty-six, entitled "An act to protect all persons in the United States in their civil rights, and to furnish the means of their vindication" . . .

SEC. 2. That if two or more persons within any State or Territory of the United States shall conspire together to overthrow . . . the government of the United States, or to levy war against the United States, or to oppose by force the authority of the government of the United States, or by force, intimidation, or threat to prevent, hinder, or delay the execution of any law of the United States, or by force to seize, take, or possess any property of the United States contrary to the authority thereof, or by force, intimidation, or threat to prevent any person from accepting or holding any office or trust or place of confidence under the United States, or from discharging the duties any thereof, or by force, intimidation, or threat to induce any officer of the United States to leave any State, district, or place where his duties as such officer might lawfully be performed, or to injure him in his person or property on account of his lawful discharge of the duties of his office, or to injure his person while engaged in the lawful discharge of the duties of his office, or to injure his property so as to molest, interrupt, hinder, or impede him in the discharge of his official duty, or by force, intimidation, or threat to deter any party or witness in any court of the United States from attending such court, or from testifying in any matter pending in such court fully, freely, and truthfully, or to injure any such party or witness in his person or property on account of his having so attended or testified, or by force, intimidation, or threat to influence the verdict, presentment, or indictment, of any juror or grand juror in any court of the United States, or to injure such juror in his person or property on account of any verdict, presentment, or indictment lawfully assented to by him, or on account of his being or having been such juror, or shall conspire together, or go in disguise upon the public highway or upon the premises of another for the purpose, either directly or indirectly, of depriving any person or any class of persons of the equal protection of the laws, or of equal privileges or immunities under the laws, or for the purpose of preventing or hindering the constituted authorities of any State from giving or securing to all persons within such State the equal protection of the laws, or shall conspire together for the purpose of in any manner impeding, hindering, obstructing, or defeating the due course of justice in any State or Territory, with intent to deny to any citizen of the United States the due and equal protection of the laws, or to injure any person or his property for lawfully enforcing the right of any person or class of persons to the equal protection of the laws, or by force, intimidation, or threat to prevent any citizen of the United States lawfully entitled to vote from giving his support or advocacy in a lawful manner towards or in favor of the election of any lawfully qualified person as an elector of President or Vice-President of the United States, or as a member of the Congress of the United States, or to injure any such citizen in his person or property on account of such support or advocacy, each and every person so offending shall be deemed guilty of a high crime, and, upon conviction thereof in any district or circuit court of the United States or district or supreme court of any Territory of the United States having jurisdiction of similar offenses, shall be punished. . . . And if any one or more persons engaged in any such conspiracy shall do, or cause to be done, any act in furtherance of the object of such conspiracy, whereby any person shall be injured in his person or property, or deprived of having and exercising any right or privilege of a citizen of the United States, the person so injured or deprived of such rights and privileges may have and maintain an action for the recovery of damages occasioned by such injury or deprivation of rights and privileges against any one or more of the persons engaged in such conspiracy. . . . [Conspirators injuring others are liable for damages.]

SEC. 3. That in all cases where insurrection, domestic violence, unlawful combinations, or conspiracies in any State shall so obstruct or hinder the execution of the laws thereof, and of the United States, as to deprive any portion or class of the people of such State of any of the rights, privileges, or immunities, or protection, named in the Constitution and secured by this act, and the constituted authorities of such State shall either be unable to protect, or shall, from any cause, fail in or refuse protection of the people in such rights, such facts shall be deemed a denial by such State of the equal protection of the laws to which they are entitled under the Constitution of the United States; and . . . it shall be lawful for the President, and it shall be his duty to take such measures, by the employment of the militia or the land and naval forces of the United States, or of either, or by other means, as he may deem necessary for the suppression of such insurrection, domestic violence, or combinations. . . . [The President may use military force to suppress violence.]

SEC. 4. That whenever in any State or part of a State the unlawful combinations named in the preceding section of this act shall be organized and Armed, and so numerous and powerful as to be able, by violence, to either overthrow or set at defiance the constituted authorities of such State, and of the United States within such State, or when the constituted authorities are in complicity with, or shall connive at the unlawful purposes of, such powerful and armed combinations; and whenever, by reason of either or all of the causes aforesaid, the conviction of such offenders and the preservation of the public safety shall become in such district impracticable, in every such case such combinations shall be deemed a rebellion against the government of the United States, and during the continuance of such rebellion, and within the limits of the district which shall be so under the sway thereof, such limits to be prescribed by proclamation, it shall be lawful for the President of the United States, when in his judgment the public safety shall require it, to suspend the privileges of the writ of habeas corpus, to the end that such rebellion may be overthrown. . . . [If necessary, the President may suspend the right to be brought promptly before a judge to learn of the cause of one's detention and to be released if there is not adequate legal cause for the person to be held.]

SEC. 6. That any person or persons, having knowledge that any of the wrongs conspired to be done and mentioned in the second section of this act are about to be committed, and having power to prevent or aid in preventing the same, shall neglect or refuse so to do, and such wrongful act shall be committed, such person or persons shall be liable to the person injured, or his legal representatives, for all damages caused by any such wrongful act which such first-named person or persons by reasonable diligence could have prevented; and such damages may be recovered in an action on the case in the proper circuit court of the United States, and any number of persons guilty of such wrongful neglect or refusal may be joined as defendants in such action. . . .

APPROVED, April 20, 1871.

NOTES

1. Other such organizations included groups called the Jayhawkers, the Regulators, the Black Horse Calvary, the Knights of the White Camelia, the Constitutional Union Guards, the Pale Faces, the White Brotherhood, the Council on Safety, and the 1876 Association. There were also numerous local organizations such as the White League of Louisiana, the White Line of Mississippi, and the Rifle Clubs of South Carolina.

2. For example, see Ben Haas, *KKK* (New York: Regency Books, 1963); Charles Waller Tyler, *The KKK* (Freeport, N.Y.: Books for Libraries Press, 1972).

3. See Robert Divine et al., *America: Past and Present* (New York: Longman, 1999), p. 502.

4. Bernard Schwartz, ed., *Statutory History of the United States: Civil Rights*, Part 1 (New York: Chelsea House, 1970), p. 606.

5. Ibid., p. 613.

6. Ibid., p. 591.

7. This right guarantees that anyone placed under arrest may request to be brought promptly before a judge to learn of the cause for detention and to be released if there is not adequate legal cause for the person to be held.

8. John Hope Franklin and Alfred A. Moss, Jr., *From Slavery to Freedom: A History of African Americans* (New York: Knopf, 1994), p. 250.

9. See Divine, *America: Past and Present*, p. 503.

10. For example, see Franklin and Moss, *From Slavery to Freedom*, pp. 251–53. Also see Nancy MacLean, *Behind the Mask of Chivalry: The Making of the Second Ku Klux Klan* (New York: Oxford University Press, 1994).

11. See *United States v. Harris*, 106 U.S. 629 (1882); *Baldwin v. Franks*, 120 U.S. 678 (1887); *United States v. Reese*, 92 U.S. 214 (1876); *United States v. Cruikshank*, 92 U.S. 542 (1876).

12. *Statutes at Large of the United States* (Washington, D.C.: GPO), vol. 17, pp. 13–15.

21

Civil Rights Act

1875

The Civil Rights Act of 1875 outlawed racial segregation in public accommodations, and it prohibited the exclusion of blacks from jury duty.

HISTORICAL CONTEXT

Although the Klan Act of 1871 constrained some of the worst of the terrorist intimidation, the South continued to resist implementing the Fourteenth Amendment's guarantee of equal protection under the law. For all of the reasons noted previously, African Americans were being treated differently, most noticeably in the region's black codes. Blacks were being denied equal access to most private amenities as well.

In the face of such resistance, Congress introduced yet another sweeping Civil Rights bill. This legislation went beyond the acts of 1866, 1870, and 1871 to require revolutionary levels of desegregation. Exceeding the rights guaranteed by most local reconstruction governments, this was the first national civil rights bill to forbid racial segregation in juries and in various public amenities. Originally proposed in 1870 by Senator Charles Sumner (Rep., Mass.), this particular bill finally passed in 1875 and was the last of the Reconstruction-era laws.

Senator Sumner's initial proposal would have prohibited racial discrimination in all public accommodations, transportation, and schools. Specifically, it guaranteed "full and equal enjoyment" in all hotels, theaters, churches, railroad cars, steamboats, schools, and cemeteries that were licensed by either the state or the federal government. Besides criminal sanctions for the violators, those whose rights were violated stood to gain as much as $500 in compensation. That particular version never made it out of committee, however, and it would be two years before Sumner could steer even a modified variant through the Senate. The bill then stalled in the House, at which point it ran headlong into the 1874 elections.

Up to this point, besides the more general continuing concern about federal usurpation of legitimate states' rights, some of the most intense debate had surrounded the issue of school integration. Was the equal protection clause of the Fourteenth Amendment met when the races were kept separate by law, but equal facilities were provided for both races? And, if not, what would be the educational impact on black and white children alike if some Southern states simply closed their public schools rather than submit to desegregation?

Passage became even more complicated with the Democratic gains in 1874. A full 90 of the bill's original 160 Republican supporters in the House were defeated in those national elections. Representatives James Blaine (Rep., Maine) and James Garfield (Rep., Ohio) then introduced a compromise that excluded schools and cemeteries but retained a provision guaranteeing blacks the right to sit on juries. The amended legislation was finally passed and then signed by President Ulysses S. Grant. Senator Sumner did not live long enough to see his years of effort finally come to fruition.

The timing of the final passage could not have been much worse. By the time the ink had dried, the federal government had lost much of its zeal for reconstruction. President Grant had already indicated a reticence to utilize military might to enforce such rights, and the Compromise of 1877 would mean even less enthusiasm on the part of presidents such as Rutherford B. Hayes, James Garfield, and Chester Arthur. African Americans were about to be left pretty much to their own local devices. Historian Raymond Arensault has referred to the act as "a symbolic relic of a fading reform impulse."[1]

Given that no special enforcement mechanisms were built into the act, aggrieved African Americans were required to bring lawsuits to the federal courts themselves. Such actions often involved significant personal and financial costs. Although one Texas judge actually fined a Galveston theater $500 for failing to admit a black patron, most federal judges either read the law narrowly or ruled it to be unconstitutional.[2]

The act's death knell was struck by eight justices of the United States Supreme Court, all appointed by Republican presidents. In a series of 1883 decisions, consolidated by the high court for the purposes of clarity, the Thirteenth and Fourteenth Amendments were once again seen as limited to "state," not "private," action. Only the states, not Congress, would be permitted to redress "a private wrong, or a crime of the individual." Consequently, a host of convictions were overturned, as most of the law's provisions were struck.[3]

It is interesting to note that key positions taken by the Court rather closely parallel the more general arguments raised during the congressional debates on the legislation. Justice Joseph Bradley commented,

> It would be running the slavery argument into the ground to make it apply to every act of discrimination which a person may see fit to make as to the guest he will entertain, or as to the people he will admit into his coach or cab, or admit to his concert or theater. . . . The denial of equal accommodations . . . imposes no badge of slavery.[4]

In addition, there was concern, not about sufficiently protecting blacks, but about showing them favoritism, making them a "special favorite of the laws." Justice Bradley went on to argue,

> When a man has emerged from slavery, and by the aid of beneficent legislation has shaken off the inseparable concomitants of that state, there must be some stage in the progress of his elevation when he takes the rank of a mere citizen, and ceases to be the special favorite of the laws, and when his rights as a citizen, or a man, are to be protected in the ordinary modes by which other men's rights are protected.[5]

The lone dissenter, Justice John Marshall Harlan, countered that racial discrimination in state-licensed facilities did raise Thirteenth and Fourteenth Amendment issues, especially given Congress's clear constitutional authority to regulate commerce. Nonetheless, it would take Title II of the Civil Rights Act of 1964 (see Chapter 33) to breathe new life into Harlan's views and the legal principles laid to rest by this Court. Historian James McPherson regards the Civil Rights Act of 1875 as a legal "bridge" between the language of the

Fourteenth Amendment and the Civil Rights Act of 1964, which would finally begin to give that language effective meaning in the lives of African Americans, especially in the American South.[6]

Meanwhile, the South responded with renewed vigor, emboldened by the post-Reconstruction decisions of the United States Supreme Court. African Americans would find it even more difficult to gain access to hotels, restaurants, and theaters. Not only was there no remedy for privately enforced segregation, but, within two years, most of these states had laws that mandated separate schools. Then, as the states discarded their Reconstruction-era constitutions and adopted new ones, the "color line" was written ever more indelibly into state law.

THE LAW

The Civil Rights Act of 1875[7] provided for "equal enjoyment" of public amenities for "citizens of every race and color, regardless of any previous condition of servitude." The act provided penalties for violation of its provisions, including payment of damages to the aggrieved party and institution of criminal proceedings against the wrongdoer. It also contained a provision penalizing district attorneys for failure to prosecute actions arising from violations of this act. Finally, the act prohibited the exclusion of citizens from jury duty based on their race or prior position as a slave.

21. Civil Rights Act of 1875

CHAP. 114.

An act to protect all citizens in their civil and legal rights.

Whereas, it is essential to just government that we recognize the equality of all men before the law, and hold that it is the duty of government in its dealings with the people to mete out [provide] equal and exact justice to all, of whatever nativity, race, color, or persuasion, religions or political; and it being the appropriate object of legislation to enact great fundamental principles in to law: Therefore,

Be it enacted . . . That all persons within the jurisdiction of the United States shall be entitled to the full and equal enjoyment of the accommodations, advantages, facilities, and privileges of inns, public conveyances on land or water, theaters, and other places of public amusement; subject only to the conditions and limitations established by law, and applicable alike to citizens of every race and color, regardless of any previous condition of servitude.

SEC. 2. That any person who shall violate the foregoing section . . . shall, for every such offense, forfeit and pay the sum of five hundred dollars to the person aggrieved thereby, to be recovered in an action of debt, with full costs; and shall also, for every such offense, be deemed guilty of a misdemeanor, and, upon conviction thereof, shall be fined not less than five hundred nor more than one thousand dollars, or shall be imprisoned not less than thirty days nor more than one year. . . .

APPROVED, March 1, 1875.

NOTES

1. Raymond Arensault, "Civil Rights Act of 1875," in *Encyclopedia of Minorities in American Politics: African Americans and Asian Americans*, ed. Jeffrey Schultz et al. (Westport, CT: Oryx Press, 2000), vol. 1, p. 143.

2. See David Goldfield et al., *The American Journey* (Upper Saddle River, N.J.: Prentice-Hall, 1998), p. 551.

3. *Civil Rights Cases*, 109 U.S. 3 (1883).

4. Ibid.

5. Ibid.

6. For more on the history of the 1875 Civil Rights Act, see John Hope Franklin, "The Enforcement of the Civil Rights Act of 1875," in *Race and History: Selected Essays, 1938–1988*, ed. John Hope Franklin (Baton Rouge: Louisiana State University Press, 1989); James McPherson, "Abolitionists and the Civil Rights Act of 1875," *Journal of American History* 52 (1965): 493–510; Bertram Wyatt-Brown, "The Civil Rights Act of 1875," *Western Political Quarterly* 18 (1965): 763–775.

7. *United States Statutes at Large* (Washington, D.C.: GPO) vol. 18, pp. 335–37.

III

CIVIL RIGHTS ERA

Not a single significant piece of civil rights legislation made it through the United States Congress between 1875 and 1957. Congress, for example, could not overcome its regional divisions to pass a federal anti-lynching bill, even though more than 4,700 black lynchings occurred between 1882 and 1948.[1] Such an absence of congressional response ultimately prompted several presidents to act in lieu of congressionally passed laws. From 1941 until 1957, presidents proceeded with antidiscrimination and desegregation efforts by virtue of their authority to issue executive orders.

EXECUTIVE ORDERS

With the Great Depression driving national unemployment rates to nearly 25 percent and food riots occurring in the streets, something had to be done. In response, President Franklin D. Roosevelt initiated the New Deal. Beyond pressing for the establishment of a social welfare state, he offered little that directly addressed the discrimination and violence plaguing blacks in both the North and the South at the time.

Virtually nothing was forthcoming until blacks began to rebel with violence in such cities as New York and Detroit. A. Phillip Randolph a civil rights activist and head of the Brotherhood of Sleeping Car Porters labor union, threatened to lead a massive march on Washington just as U.S. involvement was beginning in World War II. Roosevelt responded by appointing a number of blacks to advisory positions in various federal departments, who made up what came to be called his Negro Cabinet. He also issued Executive Order 8802 (22) prohibiting racial discrimination in defense-related industries and in government. Then, as an enforcement vehicle, he created the Fair Employment Practices Commission to investigate discrimination in industries servicing the federal government. However, the commission had no authority to punish the companies when such discrimination was encountered, and it was reluctant to cancel government contracts with discriminating companies in the middle of a war effort. Therefore, besides embarrassing a few such firms into compliance, job discrimination continued.

Harry S Truman was the first president openly to advocate full equal rights for African Americans. With Executive Order 9908 (23), he established the President's Committee on Civil Rights to investigate the status of civil rights in the United States. Executive Order 9980 (24) promised blacks fair treatment in federal employment and established a Fair Employment Board to monitor and enforce it. He also issued Executive Order 9981 (25), which finally desegregated the military.

Dwight D. Eisenhower never formally announced his support of the 1954 *Brown v. Board of Education* decision, yet his Executive Order 10730 (26) authorized use of the National Guard to assist in the desegregation of schools in Little Rock, Arkansas. Five years later, John F. Kennedy's Executive Order 11053 (30) authorized the use of federal troops to restore order after riots occurred at the University of Mississippi. Meanwhile, Kennedy also issued Executive Order 10925 (29) creating the President's Equal Employment Opportunity Committee [EEOC] and Executive Order 11063 (31) prohibiting discrimination in housing either loaned or directly financed by the federal government. Shortly thereafter, Lyndon B. Johnson's Executive Order 11246 (35) prohibited discrimination by federal contractors and required them to take positive steps to hire and promote qualified minorities and women.

ACTS OF CONGRESS

As social unrest rocked the nation throughout much of the period between 1930 and 1968, some direct aid and protection finally began to emerge from Washington in response to black demands. Domestic crises once again would provide the catalyst necessary to overcome the inherent stasis of the legislative process.

New Deal legislation in the 1930s was designed to address many of the violent and nonviolent biracial demands arising out of the Great Depression. Emergency relief was provided. Social welfare programs, such as Aid to Families with Dependent Children (AFDC), were created. Unemployment compensation was established, as was a minimum wage and a forty-hour workweek. Collective bargaining was protected. A variety of federal jobs were created to put unemployed people back to work. Child labor was prohibited. In addition, the Social Security System was initiated.

Following World War II, violent and nonviolent protest gathered momentum. This time, however, the rebels were predominantly African Americans demanding the enforcement of the rights they had gained nearly a century earlier by Constitutional amendment, and there was a groundswell of popular support stirred by the televising of violence heaped on peaceful civil rights demonstrators.[2] In addition, the NAACP came into its own as an extremely effective lobbying force, and Congress ultimately found ways to respond.

The Civil Rights Act of 1957 (27) was the first major piece of civil rights legislation to find its way through Congress since 1875. Among other things, it established a nonpartisan Civil Rights Commission to monitor civil rights progress. It was followed by the Civil Rights Act of 1960 (28), which empowered federal referees to facilitate voting, and the twenty-fourth Amendment (32) was ratified barring poll taxes.

Then came three civil rights landmarks. The Civil Rights Act of 1964 (33) directly involved the federal government in the enforcement of an extensive list of civil rights, including voting, public accommodations, public facilities, federally assisted programs, education, and employment. The Voting Rights Act of 1965 (34) prohibited literacy tests and comparable vote-impeding devices, as well as provided federal examiners to conduct registration and observe voting as needed. The Fair Housing Act of 1968 (36) barred racial discrimination in the advertising, sale, rental, or financing of most housing units.

No major civil rights legislation would be forthcoming after 1968. As a matter of fact, the real battles would be over efforts to reduce black gains from the previous era. There were, for example, serious efforts to pass antibusing legislation and to reduce the federal courts' jurisdiction over school desegregation and affirmative action. A second fair housing bill was defeated in 1981, and the renewal of the Voting Rights Act of 1965 faced some stiff opposition. The resulting reality led Ronald Reagan's conservative EEOC chairman Clarence Thomas to lament that "there are greater penalties for breaking into a mailbox than there are for violating someone's basic civil rights."[3]

Nevertheless, the Voting Rights Act was ultimately renewed; additional enforcement provisions were amended to the Fair Housing Act; and both the 1988 and 1991 Civil Rights Acts combined to nullify the negative effects of a handful of narrow U.S. Supreme Court interpretations of the 1964 act.

NOTES

1. For example, see Robert Zangrando, *The NAACP Crusade Against Lynching 1909–1950* (Philadelphia: Temple University Press, 1980).

2. For example, see David Garrow, *Protest at Selma* (New Haven, Conn.: Yale University Press, 1978), chap. 7.

3. Interview in Jeffrey Elliot, ed., *Black Voices in American Politics* (Orlando, Fla.: Harcourt Brace Jovanovich, 1986), p. 150.

22

Executive Order 8802

1941

President Franklin D. Roosevelt's Executive Order 8802 created a Committee on Fair Employment Practices, empowered to investigate racial discrimination in defense industry employment or related vocational training programs.

HISTORICAL CONTEXT

As the United States began gearing up for World War II, the employment hopes of African Americans began to rise. Yet, blacks continued to face the same kinds of employment discrimination in the defense industry that they faced elsewhere. Aircraft factories, for example, restricted them to "janitors and other similar capacities."[1] Meanwhile, the government's own training programs discriminated on the basis of race.[2]

In 1940 several branches of the federal government responded with admonitions of various types. The United States Office of Education declared that there should be no racial discrimination in defense training programs. The National Defense Advisory Committee advised defense plants not to discriminate. President Roosevelt expressed similar views in a message to Congress. The Office of Production Management even created a black employment and training division in order to increase the number of blacks hired in the defense industry. Nevertheless, very little changed.

Congress soon found itself being lobbied aggressively by the National Association for the Advancement of Colored People (NAACP). The NAACP wanted Congress to guarantee equal job opportunities for blacks in the nation's defense industries. In January 1941, the NAACP sent letters to President Roosevelt and his War and Navy Departments.[3]

In February 1941, Senators John Barbour (Rep., N.J.), Prentiss Brown (Dem., Mich.), Robert Wagner (Dem., N.Y.), and Arthur Capper (Rep., Kans.) introduced a resolution calling for an investigation into the treatment of African Americans in the defense field. That resolution, however, met with little enthusiasm in the United States Senate. Consequently, it never even made it onto the Senate floor for either a debate or a vote.

About this same time, A. Phillip Randolph, president of the Brotherhood of Sleeping Car Porters, decided to turn up the heat. Randolph used the union's newspaper, the *Messenger*, to call for nationwide mass demonstrations in order to dramatize defense industry discrimination. He organized thousands of people to conduct a protest march on Washington, D.C., on July 1 in order to draw further attention to racial discrimination in such employment practices. The timing of the threatened march was carefully calculated: the world was recoiling from Nazi racism, and the United States was trying to rally national unity for an impending war effort.[4]

Throughout the first few weeks of June, many of the nation's premier leaders attempted to convince Randolph to call off the march. He was approached by both Franklin and Eleanor Roosevelt, Mayor Fiorello LaGuardia of New York, Secretary of War Henry Stimson, Secretary of the Navy William Knox, and several others. When Randolph continued to hold firm, President Roosevelt finally persuaded him to cancel the march in return for an executive order "with teeth in it." The order would bar discrimination in both government and in defense industry employment.[5]

On June 25, just three days after the Nazis invaded the Soviet Union, President Roosevelt issued Executive Order 8802. It prohibited racial discrimination in employment and vocational training programs in defense-related industries. As an enforcement vehicle, it created the Fair Employment Practices Commission (FEPC) within the Office of Production Management in order to investigate discrimination in industries servicing the federal government.

The commission, which included members of the public, management, and labor, held hearings in large cities across the country. Evidence of discrimination soon began to surface. Nevertheless, the FEPC had only a small staff, a very limited budget, and no authority to punish the companies where such discrimination was encountered. It also appeared reluctant to propose canceling government contracts with discriminating companies in the middle of a war effort.

Despite its limitations, the FEPC was opposed by a variety of groups from its inception. Conservative Republicans and Southern Democrats opposed it in Congress, and business interests and some trade unions lobbied against it. By the summer of 1942, just when the commission's public hearings were beginning to attract national attention, President Roosevelt placed it under the War Manpower Commission, further removing it from White House control. The following January, when the commission postponed its scheduled hearings into discrimination occurring in the nation's railroads, a number of black leaders launched a nationwide drive to "Save the FEPC."[6]

The Fair Employment Practices Commission functioned throughout the course of World War II. Given all of its limitations, the FEPC was able to act only on roughly one-third of the 8,000 complaints it received.[7] Other than embarrassing some firms into compliance, pervasive job discrimination continued, especially in the private sector.

It has been estimated that nearly 2 million African Americans had found at least some type of work in defense industries by war's end; another 200,000 entered the federal civil service. It is hard to delineate how much of that was a result of the efforts of the FEPC as opposed to simple economics, a shortage of white workers, and the fact that more than one million black workers had entered the ranks of organized labor.[8]

The commission's efforts, limited as they were, lost virtually all momentum rather quickly after the war. The last official act of the FEPC was to urge Congress to make it a permanent, independent agency. That effort died at the hands of a Southern filibuster in January and February of 1946. Subsequent legislative efforts to revive the proposal proved equally unsuccessful.[9]

THE LAW

In issuing Executive Order 8802,[10] President Roosevelt articulated that it was the policy of the United States to encourage "full participation in the national defense program by all citizens . . . regardless of race, creed, color or national origin." He did acknowledge, however, that there was evidence of discrimination in the defense industry. President Roosevelt issued this order to address that discrimination.

The order required departments and agencies of the U.S. government to take action to ensure that there was no discrimination in regard to race, creed, color, or national origin in the administration of vocational and training programs related to defense production.

To further ensure that the U.S. goal of full participation of all citizens was met, the order mandated that all contracts with the government contain a provision that the contractor would not discriminate on the basis of race, creed, color, or national origin.

Finally, the executive order created a Committee on Fair Employment Practices, empowered to receive and investigate complaints of discrimination. The order directed the committee to determine whether discrimination was occurring in violation of the provisions of the order and to take steps to redress the wrongs. Specifically, the order granted the committee the authority to make recommendations to the departments and agencies of the government and to the president regarding measures that could be taken to carry out the provisions of the order.

22. Executive Order 8802

Reaffirming Policy of Full Participation in the Defense Program by All Persons, Regardless of Race, Creed, Color, or National Origin, and Directing Certain Action In Furtherance of Said Policy

WHEREAS it is the policy of the United States to encourage full participation in the national defense program by all citizens of the United States, regardless of race, creed, color, or national origin, in the firm belief that the democratic way of life within the Nation can be defended successfully only with the help and support of all groups within its borders; and

WHEREAS there is evidence that available and needed workers have been barred from employment in industries engaged in defense production solely because of considerations of race, creed, color, or national origin, to the detriment of workers' morale and of national unity:

NOW, THEREFORE, by virtue of the authority vested in me by the Constitution and the statutes, and as a prerequisite to the successful conduct of our national defense production effort, I do hereby reaffirm the policy of the United States that there shall be no discrimination in the employment of workers in defense industries or government because of race, creed, color, or national origin, and I do hereby declare that it is the duty of employers and of labor organizations in furtherance of said policy and of this order, to provide for the full and equitable participation of all workers in defense industries, without discrimination because of race, creed, color, or national origin;

And it is hereby ordered as follows:

1. All departments and agencies of the Government of the United States concerned with vocational and training programs for defense production shall take special measures appropriate to assure that such programs are administered without discrimination because of race, creed, color, or national origin;

2. All contracting agencies of the Government of the United States shall include all defense contracts hereafter negotiated by them a provision obligating the contractor not to discriminate against any worker because of race, creed, color, or national origin;

3. There is established in the Office of Production Management a Committee on Fair Employment Practice, which shall consist of a chairman and four other members to be appointed by the President. The Chairman and members of the Committee shall serve as such without compensation but shall be entitled to actual and necessary transportation, subsistence and other expenses incidental to performance of their duties. The Committee shall receive and investigate complaints of discrimination in violation of the provisions of this order and shall take appropriate steps to redress grievances which it finds to be valid. The Committee shall also recommend to the several departments and agencies of the Government of the United States and to the President all measures which may be deemed by it necessary or proper to effectuate the provisions of this order.

FRANKLIN D. ROOSEVELT

THE WHITE HOUSE,

June 25, 1941.

NOTES

1. See Louis Coleridge Kesselman, *The Social Politics of FEPC: A Study in Reform Pressure Movements* (Chapel Hill: University of North Carolina Press, 1948), p. 7.

2. For example, see Charles H. Thompson, "The American Negro and the National Defense," *Journal of Negro Education* 9 (October 1940): 547–52; E. Franklin Frazier, *The Negro in the United States* (New York: Macmillan, 1957), pp. 599–606; Robert C. Weaver, "Racial Employment Trends in National Defense," *Phylon* 2 (Fourth Quarter, 1941): 337–58.

3. See John Hope Franklin and Alfred A. Moss, Jr., *From Slavery to Freedom: A History of African Americans* (New York: Knopf, 1994), p. 436.

4. For example, see Herbert Garfinkel, *When Negroes March: The March on Washington Movement in the Organizational Politics for FEPC* (New York: Atheneum, 1969).

5. See Franklin and Moss, *From Slavery to Freedom*, p. 437.

6. See Garfinkel, *When Negroes March*, pp. 103–8.

7. See Robert Divine et al., *America: Past and Present* (New York: Longman, 1999), p. 854.

8. See John Mack Faragher et al., *Out of Many* (Upper Saddle River, N.J.: Prentice-Hall, 2000), p. 851.

9. See Garfinkel, *When Negroes March*, chap. 6; Louis Ruchames, *Race, Jobs, and Politics: The Story of FEPC* (New York: Columbia University Press, 1953).

10. *Federal Register* (Washington D.C.: GPO), vol. 7, p. 3109.

23

Executive Order 9808

1946

President Harry S Truman's Executive Order 9808 established the President's Committee on Civil Rights to investigate the status of civil rights in the United States.

HISTORICAL CONTEXT

Several lynchings and other forms of racial unrest followed World War II. In 1946, for example, there were six reported lynchings and other acts of racial violence in Southern cities. A crowd in Mississippi, for example, horsewhipped a black veteran who was attempting to register to vote; a black man was lynched in Georgia when he attempted to cast his ballot.[1]

When these reports rolled in, President Truman expressed his personal revulsion when he stated, "My very stomach turned over when I learned that Negro soldiers just back from overseas were being dumped out of Army trucks in Mississippi and beaten."[2] In the wake of these events, the president responded to a plea from NAACP Executive Secretary Walter White. He established the President's Committee on Civil Rights to investigate the status of civil rights in the United States at the time and to make recommendations.[3]

Constituted of a diverse group whose names were listed in the body of the executive order itself, the committee immediately launched into intensive research. On October 29, 1947, within a year after it had been established, the committee reported back to President Truman with their findings and a host of recommendations. They had found considerable evidence of ongoing racial discrimination, and they proposed addressing it in several ways. For example, they recommended adding a permanent civil rights division in the Justice Department, antilynching legislation, increased federal efforts to protect voting rights, and an end to racial segregation. They even proposed that a constitutional vehicle, such as the commerce clause, might be used legally to justify federal intervention.

In their report, entitled *To Secure These Rights*, the committee also set out moral, economic, and international reasons for acting at that moment to secure basic civil rights.[4] "There are times when the difference between what we preach about civil rights and what we practice is shockingly illustrated by individual outrages."[5] Examples included the disenfranchisement of blacks in the South and wartime segregation in the nation's armed forces. "All of us must endure the cynicism about democratic values which our failure breeds. The United States can no longer countenance these burdens on its common conscience, these inroads on its moral fiber."[6]

Economically, blacks and whites were hurt by such inefficiencies as the duplication bred by segregation, lost labor and markets, and the cost of additional social services to deal with the poverty resulting from discrimination. "What we have lost in money, production, invention, citizenship, and leadership as the price for damaged, thwarted personalities—these are beyond estimate. The United States can no longer afford this heavy drain upon its human wealth, its national competence."[7]

Internationally, they argued that ongoing discrepancies in the application of civil rights in the United States undercut its ability to lead the world toward freedom and democracy. This also fueled the propaganda machines of our enemies abroad. "The United States is not so strong, the final triumph of the democratic ideal is not so inevitable that we can ignore what the world thinks of us or our record."[8]

President Truman incorporated many of the committee's recommendations into a special message presented to Congress on February 2, 1948. According to the president,

> This Nation was founded by men and women who sought these shores that they might enjoy greater freedom and greater opportunity than they had known before. The founders of the United States proclaimed to the world the American belief that all men are created

equal, and that governments are instituted to secure the inalienable rights with which all men are endowed. . . . The Federal Government has a clear duty to see that Constitutional guarantees of individual liberties and of equal protection under the laws are not denied or abridged anywhere in our Union.[9]

Although he was later criticized by civil rights leaders for not crafting specific legislative proposals, the president did ask Congress to

1. Establish a permanent Commission on Civil Rights to review civil rights policies and practices at all levels, study problems, and make recommendations to the president at frequent intervals.

2. Establish a Joint Congressional Committee on Civil Rights "to make a continuing study of legislative matters relating to civil rights and . . . consider means of improving respect for and enforcement of those rights."[10]

3. Create a Civil Rights Division in the Department of Justice.

4. Provide federal protection against lynching. "So long as one person walks in fear of lynching, we shall not have achieved equal justice under the law."[11]

5. Protect more adequately the right to vote; for example, forbidding physical interference and poll taxes.

6. Outlaw discrimination in employment based on race, color, religion, or national origin, and reestablish a Fair Employment Practice Commission to prevent unfair discrimination in employment.

7. Prohibit discrimination in both public and private interstate transportation facilities.

Truman concluded by stating emphatically,

If we wish to inspire the peoples of the world whose freedom is in jeopardy, if we wish to restore hope to those who have already lost their civil liberties, if we wish to fulfill the promise that is ours, we must correct the remaining imperfections in our practice of democracy.[12]

Although all of these proposals eventually would be enacted to one degree or another, none was passed by Congress during Truman's tenure in the Oval Office. It appeared that the nation, and the Congress that represented it, were simply not yet ready to act as dramatically as the committee had recommended and the president had proposed.[13]

THE LAW

The preliminary paragraphs of Executive Order 9808[14] declare that the preservation of civil rights is essential to the functioning of the United States and that the actions of individuals taking the law into their own hands undermine the nation's democracy. It is on these premises that Truman ordered a temporary Civil Rights Commission be established. The names of the members of the committee were set forth in the order. The committee was directed to assess whether current law enforcement practices could be improved to protect the civil rights of U.S. residents.

The order directed departments and agencies of the federal government to cooperate with the committee. It specifically directed the departments and agencies to provide information to the committee and make documents available for the committee's review.

The committee was ordered to make a written report of its recommendations to the president. Once the report was made, the order declared that the committee was dissolved.

23. Executive Order 9808

ESTABLISHING THE PRESIDENT'S COMMITTEE ON CIVIL RIGHTS

WHEREAS the preservation of civil rights guaranteed by the Constitution is essential to domestic tranquility, national security, the general welfare, and the continued existence of our free institutions; and

WHEREAS the actions of individuals who take the law into their own hands and inflict summary punishment and wreak personal vengeance is subversive of our democratic system of law enforcement and public criminal justice, and gravely threatens our form of government; and

WHEREAS it is essential that all possible steps be taken to safeguard our civil rights:

NOW, THEREFORE, by virtue of the authority vested in me as President of the United States by the Constitution and the statutes of the United States, it is hereby ordered as follows:

1. There is hereby created a committee to be known as the President's Committee on Civil Rights, which shall be composed of the following-named members, who shall serve without compensation:

Mr. C.E. Wilson, chairman; Mrs. Sadie T. Alexander, Mr. James B. Carey, Mr. John S. Dickey, Mr. Morris L. Ernst, Rabbi Roland B. Gittelsohn, Dr. Frank P. Graham, The Most Reverend Francis J. Haas, Mr. Charles Luckman, Mr. Francis P. Matthews, Mr. Franklin D. Roosevelt, Jr., The Right Reverend Henry Knox Sherrill, Mr. Boris Shishkin, Mrs. M.E. Tilly, and Mr. Channing H. Tobias.

2. The Committee is authorized on behalf of the President to inquire into and to determine whether and in what respect current law enforcement measures and the authority and means possessed by the Federal, State, and local governments may be strengthened and improved to safeguard the civil rights of the people.

3. All executive departments and agencies of the Federal Government are authorized and directed to cooperate with the Committee in its work, and to furnish the Committee with such information on services of such persons as the Committee may require in the performance of its duties.

4. When requested by the Committee to do so, persons employed in any of the executive departments and agencies of the Federal Government shall testify before the Committee and shall make available for the use of the Committee such documents and other information as the Committee may require.

5. The Committee shall make a report of its studies to the President in writing, and shall in particular make recommendations with respect to the adoption or establishment, by legislation or otherwise, of more adequate and effective means and procedures for the protection of civil rights of the people of the United States.

6. Upon rendition of its report to the President, the Committee shall cease to exist, unless otherwise determined by further Executive Order.

HARRY S TRUMAN
THE WHITE HOUSE,
December 5, 1946.

NOTES

1. For example, see Robert Zangrando, *The NAACP Crusade Against Lynching, 1909–1950* (Philadelphia: Temple University Press, 1980).

2. Quoted in James Roark et al., *The American Promise* (Boston: Bedford Books, 1998), p. 1040.

3. For example, see Zangrando, *The NAACP Crusade Against Lynching*, chap. 8.

4. President's Committee on Civil Rights, *To Serve These Rights* (Washington, D.C.: GPO, 1947).

5. Quoted in Albert Blaustein and Robert Zangrando, *Civil Rights and the Black American* (New York: Washington Square Press, 1968), p. 376.

6. Ibid., p. 377.

7. Ibid., p. 378.

8. Ibid., p. 379.

9. Ibid., p. 380–81.

10. Ibid., p. 382.

11. Ibid.

12. Ibid., p. 384.

13. For example, see Zangrando, *The NAACP Crusade Against Lynching*.

14. *Federal Register* (Washington, D.C.: GPO), vol. 11, p. 14153.

24

Executive Order 9980

1948

President Harry S Truman's Executive Order 9980 guaranteed blacks fair treatment in federal employment and established a Fair Employment Board to monitor and enforce it.

HISTORICAL CONTEXT

When President Truman came to office as the result of the death of President Franklin D. Roosevelt in April 1945, he inherited both World War II and mounting racial and labor unrest at home. His Democratic Party, which had held solid congressional majorities since 1932, was dealt a stunning defeat in the 1946 midterm elections. Republicans captured clear majorities in both houses of Congress, and the president's approval rating sank to 32 percent.[1]

The subsequent two years were just as difficult. Truman got little cooperation from what he referred to as the "do nothing" Republican majorities in the Congress. Beyond that, his own party was in disarray as Southern Democrats began to defect. Generally referred to as the Dixiecrats, they were upset in part at the president's civil rights posture. Yet, even though the party's civil rights plank had caused the Democrats to split badly at their national nominating convention in the summer of 1948, Truman still handed down two significant civil rights orders, both on July 26, 1948.

The first of these executive orders required fair employment practices throughout the federal government: "[T]he principles on which our Government is based require a policy of fair employment throughout the Federal establishment, without discrimination because of race, color, religion, or national origin." The second, discussed in Chapter 25, began the process of desegregating the U.S. military.

President Roosevelt's Fair Employment Practices Commission, discussed in Chapter 22, was the federal government's first major attempt to end discrimination in federal employment. However, it had several inherent limitations. Because it did not have any sort of enforcement power, all it could do was investigate and report to the president. Also, it was limited to the defense industry. Finally, the fact that these investigations took place during time of war made it even less likely that an offending contractor would be punished by withdrawing a federal contract for a war-related product.

With Executive Order 9980, once again a president went on record as opposing discrimination in federal employment "because of race, color, religion, or national origin." But this time, the order was not limited to the defense industry; there was no longer a war in progress; and President Truman's Fair Employment Board would be attached to a well-established federal bureaucracy, the existing Civil Service Commission.

The Civil Service Commission had been in existence since the Pendleton Act of 1883. Its primary duties were to classify most federal jobs by category, set personnel policies, administer exams, rank applicants as a result of their scores on those exams, and then certify for the various government agencies which persons on the "eligible list" were available to be hired.

Attaching the fair employment machinery to such an agency would enable this commission to be more than just another investigatory body. The president was adding clout to the charge because the Civil Service Commission was the clearinghouse for most federal employment. Each federal department was then to add a fair employment officer, with the "full operating responsibility . . . for carrying out the fair employment policy." Disciplinary decisions made by the fair employment officers were thereafter reviewable by the Fair Employment Board, and that board was to report any noncompliance directly to the president.

President Truman's two executive orders were not the only civil rights endorsements made in the summer of 1948. When a relatively strong civil rights plank was adopted in that year's Democratic Party platform,[2] the Dixiecrats revolted. Led by Governor Strom Thurmond of South Carolina and Governor Fielding Wright of Mississippi, some three dozen Southern delegates walked out of the

Democratic Party's 1948 nominating convention.[3] Thurmond subsequently was nominated as the 1948 presidential candidate of the splinter State's Rights Party; he won four states and thirty-nine electoral votes.[4] The national Democratic Party never again held the "solid South" as part of its electoral coalition.

Meanwhile, even though public opinion polls showed only a bare majority of the nation favoring federal efforts to end job discrimination,[5] President Truman announced in his nomination acceptance speech that he would call Congress back into session on July 27 in order, among other things, to enact civil rights legislation. In addition, he became the first sitting president to address the NAACP's national convention.

Truman's Justice Department also filed legal briefs supporting various NAACP appeals to the United States Supreme Court. The Court upheld the legal position of the NAACP and the Justice Department in 1948 and struck down "restrictive covenants," which were contributing to housing discrimination by precluding homeowners from selling to African Americans.[6] Two years later, the justices ruled that the University of Oklahoma could not physically segregate its black students, and that the University of Texas Law School had not provided equal protection under the law when it established an inferior law school option for its African American students.[7]

THE LAW

President Truman recognized in Executive Order 9980[8] that the principles of the United States require a policy of fair employment within the federal government itself and that steps should be taken to ensure the carrying out of this policy.

The order specifically directed that employment decisions be based on qualifications and prohibited discrimination based on race, color, religion, or national origin. It placed responsibility for these fair employment actions on the leaders of the departments of the executive branch of government and directed each department head to appoint a fair employment officer.

The fair employment officers, serving at the direction of the department heads, were given full responsibility for carrying out the fair employment policy. Specifically, the fair employment officers were required to assess personnel actions of the department, receive complaints regarding alleged discriminatory personnel actions, appoint others to assist in receiving and investigating complaints of discrimination, and take any necessary corrective or disciplinary action. Findings of the fair employment officer were subject to appeal to the department head with further appeal to the Fair Employment Board of the Civil Service Commission.

The Fair Employment Board of the Civil Service Commission was established by the executive order. In addition to hearing appeals of decisions of the department heads, this board, consisting of no fewer than seven people, was directed to make rules and regulations, advise departments on issues related to fair employment, disseminate information on fair employment, and make reports and submit recommendations to the Civil Service Commission. The order directed departments to cooperate with the board by providing the information requested.

Finally, the order conferred on the Civil Service Commission, in conjunction with the board, the authority to make additional rules necessary to carry out the purposes of the executive order regarding fair employment in the federal government.

24. Executive Order 9980

REGULATIONS GOVERNING FAIR EMPLOYMENT PRACTICES WITHIN THE FEDERAL ESTABLISHMENT

WHEREAS the principles on which our Government is based require a policy of fair employment throughout the Federal establishment, without discrimination because of race, color, religion, or national origin; and

WHEREAS it is desirable and in the public interest that all steps be taken necessary to insure that this long-established policy shall be more effectively carried out:

NOW, THEREFORE, by virtue of the authority vested in me as President of the United States, by the Constitution and the laws of the United States, it is hereby ordered as follows:

1. All personnel actions taken by Federal appointing officers shall be based solely on merit and fitness; and such officers are authorized and directed to take appropriate steps to insure that In all such actions there shall be no discrimination because of race, color, religion, or national origin.

2. The head of each department in the executive branch of the Government shall be personally responsible for an effective program to insure

that fair employment policies are fully observed in all personnel actions within his department.

3. The head of each department shall designate an official thereof as Fair Employment Officer. Such Officer shall be given full operating responsibility, under the immediate supervision of the department head, for carrying out the fair employment policy herein stated. Notice of the appointment of such Officer shall be given to all officers and employees of the department. The Fair Employment Officer shall, among other things—

(a) Appraise the personnel actions of the department at regular intervals to determine their conformity to the fair-employment policy expressed in this order.

(b) Receive complaints or appeals concerning personnel actions taken in the department on grounds of alleged discrimination because of race, color, religion, or national origin.

(c) Appoint such central or regional deputies, committees, or hearing boards, from among the officers or employees of the department, as he may find necessary or desirable on a temporary or permanent basis to investigate, or to receive, complaints of discrimination.

(d) Take necessary corrective or disciplinary action. In consultation with, or on the basis of delegated authority from, the head of the department.

4. The findings or action of the Fair Employment Officer shall be subject to direct appeal to the head of the department. The decision of the head of the department on such appeal shall be subject to appeal to the Fair Employment Board of the Civil Service Commission, hereinafter provided for.

5. There shall be established in the Civil Service Commission a Fair Employment Board (hereinafter referred to as the Board) of not less than seven persons, the members of which shall be officers or employees of the Commission. The Board shall—

(a) Have authority to review decisions made by the head of any department which are appealed pursuant to the provisions of this order, or referred to the Board by the head of the department for advice, and to make recommendations to such head. In any instance in which the recommendation of the Board is not promptly and fully carried out the case shall be reported by the Board to the President, for such action as he finds necessary.

(b) Make rules and regulations, in consultation with the Civil Service Commission, deemed necessary to carry out the Board's duties and responsibilities under this order.

(c) Advise all departments on problems and policies relating to fair employment.

(d) Disseminate Information pertinent to fair-employment programs.

(e) Coordinate the fair-employment policies and procedures of the several departments.

(f) Make reports and submit recommendations to the Civil Service Commission for transmittal to the President from time to time, as may be necessary to the maintenance of the fair-employment program.

6. All departments are directed to furnish to the Board all information needed for the review of personnel actions or for the compilation of reports.

7. The term "department" as used herein shall refer to all departments and agencies of the executive branch of the Government, including the Civil Service Commission. The term "personnel action," as used herein, shall include failure to act. Persons failing of appointment who allege a grievance relating to discrimination shall be entitled to the remedies herein provided.

8. The means of relief provided by this order shall be supplemental to those provided by existing statutes, Executive orders, and regulations. The Civil Service Commission shall have authority, in consultation with the Board, to make such additional regulations, and to amend existing regulations, in such manner as may be found necessary or desirable to carry out the purposes of this order.

HARRY S TRUMAN
THE WHITE HOUSE,
July 26, 1948.

NOTES

1. James Roark et al., *The American Promise* (Boston: Bedford Books, 1998), p. 1021.

2. Passed under the leadership of Senator Hubert Humphrey (Dem., Minn.), the Democratic platform plank read,

The Democratic Party is responsible for the great civil rights gains made in recent years in eliminating unfair and illegal discrimination based on race, creed, or color. The Democratic Party commits itself to continuing efforts to eradicate all racial, religious, and economic discrimination. We again state our belief that racial and religious minorities must have the right to live, the right to work, the right to vote, and full and equal protection of the laws on a basis of equality with all citizens as guaranteed by the Constitution. We highly recommend President Harry Truman for his courageous stand on the issue of civil rights. We call upon the Congress to support our President in guaranteeing these basic and fundamental rights: (1) the right of full and equal political participation, (2) the right of equal opportunity of employment, (3) the right of security of person, (4) and the right of equal treatment in the service and defense of our nation.

See *Congress and the Nation: 1945–1964* (Washington, D.C.: Congressional Quarterly Service, 1965), p. 1617.

3. Thirteen of Alabama's delegates and all of Mississippi's twenty-three delegates walked out of the convention following the adoption of the party's civil rights plank. For a detailed discussion of these events, see V.O. Key, "The Revolt of 1948," in *Southern Politics*, ed. V.O. Key (New York: Knopf, 1949), pp. 329–44.

4. Thurmond carried South Carolina, Alabama, Mississippi, and Louisiana. He also picked up one of Tennessee's twelve electoral votes.

5. Polling results quoted in Roark, *The American Promise*, p. 1041.

6. *Shelly v. Kramer*, 334 U.S. 1 (1948). In this context, a "restrictive covenant" was a clause written into the deed of a house that precluded owners from selling that house to members of specified minority groups.

7. *McLaurin v. Oklahoma State Regents*, 339 U.S. 637 (1950); *Sweat v. Painter*, 339 U.S. 629 (1950).

8. *Federal Register* (Washington, D.C.: GPO), vol. 13, pp. 4311–13.

25

Executive Order 9981

1948

President Harry S Truman's Executive Order 9981 guaranteed blacks "equality of treatment and opportunity" in the armed services and established a committee to investigate discriminatory practices and submit a report to the president with recommendations for improvement.

HISTORICAL CONTEXT

As the United States promoted freedom and democracy around the world during World War II and afterward in the Cold War era, its troops stationed abroad were segregated by skin color, undercutting the message.[1] In addition, black leaders and black war veterans were demanding an end to racial segregation in the U.S. military.

A. Philip Randolph, head of the Brotherhood of Sleeping Car Porters labor union, asked a 1948 Senate hearing, "How could any permanent Fair Employment Practices Commission dare to criticize job discrimination in private industry if the Federal Government itself were simultaneously discriminating against Negro youth in military installations all over the world?"[2]

Lester Granger, the executive secretary of the National Urban League, spoke for a group of black leaders who met with Secretary of Defense James Forrestal and representatives of the various military branches. Granger told the military hierarchy, "No one [in the group] wanted to continue in an advisory capacity on the basis of continued segregation in the armed services."[3]

Meanwhile, in March 1948, Randolph and others began organizing a civil disobedience campaign aimed at ending racial discrimination in the U.S. military. Randolph, despite being threatened with the possibility of a charge of treason, declared to a congressional committee, "I personally pledge myself to openly counsel, aid and abet youth, both white and Negro . . . in an organized refusal to register and be drafted."[4] In June, the NAACP announced the results of a poll indicating that 71 percent of draft-eligible black men sympathized with the antidraft campaign.[5] A month later, while urging young men in Harlem not to register, Randolph stated that he was prepared to "oppose a Jim Crow Army until I rot in jail."[6]

On July 26, the same day he issued Executive Order 9980 creating the Fair Employment Board, President Truman issued Executive Order 9981 guaranteeing blacks "equality of treatment and opportunity" in the armed services. At that point, Randolph and the other protest leaders called off their draft resistance campaign.[7]

The president then began implementing his desegregation policy on September 18 by creating the President's Committee on Equality of Treatment and Opportunity in the Armed Services. The seven-member committee was granted the authority to investigate discriminatory practices and make recommendations to the president. It was chaired by Charles Fahy, a former solicitor general of the United States, and it also included two prominent black leaders, Lester Granger of the National Urban League and John Sengstacke, publisher of the *Chicago Defender.*

The committee reported to President Truman and issued a report, *Freedom to Serve.* The report provides a detailed step-by-step blueprint for achieving military desegregation.[8] The secretary of defense then issued a desegregation directive in April 1949, directing that "there shall be equality of treatment and opportunity for all persons in the Armed Services without regard to race, color, religion, or national origin." First the U.S. Army, then the U.S. Navy and the U.S. Air Force, formally complied. Implementation progressed slowly, however, as the services battled internal resistance.

It finally took the practical realities involved in fighting the Korean War to integrate the nation's fighting forces. The Ninth United States Infantry Regiment was one of the first to integrate on the battlefield. The summer of 1951 saw the level of combat integration increase from 9 percent to 30 percent; and General Matthew Ridgeway soon had permission to integrate all the forces under his command in the entire Far East.[9]

THE LAW

Recognizing that the high standards of democracy were essential to the U.S. military, Executive Order 9981[10] declared that all persons in the armed services be treated equally without regard to race, color, religion, or national origin.

Furthermore, the order permanently established the President's Committee on Equality of Treatment and Opportunity. The seven committee members, appointed by the president, were charged with the responsibility of carrying out the executive order. The committee was specifically directed to review the rules, procedures, and practices of the military for evidence of discrimination, and to make recommendations to the president and the secretaries of all the military branches for eliminating discrimination in regard to "race, color, religion or national origin." Pursuant to the order, all executive departments and agencies of the federal government and all members of the armed services were directed to cooperate with the committee in their investigation.

25. Executive Order 9981

ESTABLISHING THE PRESIDENT'S COMMITTEE ON EQUALITY OF TREATMENT AND OPPORTUNITY IN THE ARMED SERVICES

WHEREAS it is essential that there be maintained in the armed services of the United States the highest standards of democracy, with equality of treatment and opportunity for all those who serve in our country's defense:

NOW, THEREFORE, by virtue of the authority vested in me as President of the United States, by the Constitution and the statutes of the United States, and as Commander in Chief of the armed services, it is hereby ordered as follows:

1. It is hereby declared to be the policy of the President that there shall be equality of treatment and opportunity for all persons in the armed services without regard to race, color, religion or national origin. This

policy shall be put into effect as rapidly as possible, having due regard to the time required to effectuate any necessary changes without impairing efficiency or morale.

2. There shall be created in the National Military Establishment an advisory committee to be known as the President's Committee on Equality of Treatment and Opportunity in the Armed Services, which shall be composed of seven members to be designated by the President.

3. The Committee is authorized on behalf of the President to examine the rules, procedures and practices of the armed services in order to determine in what respect such rules, procedures and practices may be altered or improved with a view to carrying out the policy of this order. The Committee shall confer and advise with the Secretary of Defense, the Secretary of the Army, the Secretary of the Navy, and the Secretary of the Air Force, and shall make such recommendations to the President and to said Secretaries as in the judgment of the Committee will effectuate the policy hereof.

4. All executive departments and agencies of the Federal Government are authorized and directed to cooperate with the Committee in its work, and to furnish the Committee such information or the services of such person as the Committee may require in the performance of its duties.

5. When requested by the Committee to do so, persons in the armed services or in any of the executive departments and agencies of the Federal Government shall testify before the Committee and shall make available for the use of the Committee such documents and other information as the Committee may require.

6. The Committee shall continue to exist until such time as the President shall terminate its existence by Executive order.

HARRY S TRUMAN
THE WHITE HOUSE,
July 26, 1948.

NOTES

1. For example, see Mary Dudziak, "Desegregation as a Cold War Imperative," *Stanford Law Review* 41 (1988): 1147–75.

2. U.S. Congress, Senate, *Universal Military Training*, Hearings before the Committee on Armed Services, 80th Cong., 2d sess. (Washington, D.C.: U.S. Government Printing Office, 1948), p. 686.

3. Quoted in Herbert Garfinkel, *When Negroes March* (New York: Atheneum, 1969), pp. 161–62.

4. *Congressional Record*, 80th Cong., 2d sess., April 12, 1948, 94, pt. 4: 4312–18. Also see the *New York Times*, April 1, 1948, p. 1.

5. Garfinkel, *When Negroes March*, p. 161.

6. Quoted in ibid.

7. For example, see Grant Reynolds, "A Triumph for Civil Disobedience," *Nation* 167 (August 28, 1948): 228.

8. *Freedom to Serve* (Washington, D.C.: GPO, 1950).

9. See John Hope Franklin and Alfred A. Moss, Jr., *From Slavery to Freedom: A History of African Americans* (New York: Knopf, 1994), p. 462; Donald R. McCoy and Richard R. Ruetten, *Quest and Response: Minority Rights and the Truman Administration* (Lawrence: University of Kansas Press, 1973).

10. *Federal Register* (Washington, D.C.: GPO), vol. 13, p. 4313.

26

Executive Order 10730

1957

President Dwight D. Eisenhower's Executive Order 10730 authorized use of the National Guard to assist in the desegregation of schools in Little Rock, Arkansas.

HISTORICAL CONTEXT

Since the passage of the Fourteenth Amendment in 1868 (see Chapter 17), states had been required to guarantee that their residents receive equal protection under state law. In response, several states established a host of "Jim Crow" laws, or laws requiring the physical separation of the races.[1] Was that practice constitutional? In 1896 the United States Supreme Court ruled that it was constitutional, as long as the state facilities and services provided were "separate but equal."[2] For decades thereafter, it was legally permissible for states to require students to attend racially segregated schools, so long as the black schools were even marginally comparable to the white schools.

More than a half century later, the U.S. Supreme Court issued a revolutionary 1954 decision, *Brown v. Board of Education*.[3] The Court ruled unanimously that racially segregated schools were unconstitutional no matter how much effort had been made to make the separate facilities equal. A year later, they ruled that segregated schools needed to proceed "with all deliberate speed" to desegregate.[4]

The Court's decisions were met with almost immediate hostility in much of the white South. All eleven states of the old Confederacy passed interposition, nullification, or protest resolutions. More than 100 Southern members of the United States Congress signed the Southern Manifesto on Integration, condemning the ruling as a distortion of the United States Constitution and pledging to fight it with every legal means available.[5]

Twenty-one states and the District of Columbia had legally segregated public schools at the time. Consequently, they were legally obliged to begin to desegregate those schools in light of the Court's decisions. Eleven of the twenty-two jurisdictions complied in relatively short order. Eleven states, however, noticeably evaded and delayed. Three of them—Tennessee, North Carolina, and Texas— had changed their state laws by 1957, which left only eight states that did not appear to be proceeding to desegregate with "all deliberate speed": Arkansas, Alabama, Florida, Georgia, Louisiana, Mississippi, South Carolina, and Virginia.

In Arkansas, the Little Rock School District had complied with local federal court orders and had developed a comprehensive yet gradual desegregation plan by May 1955. Under that plan, nine black children were to enter previously all-white Central High School in the fall of 1957. Nevertheless, the school system ignored three separate court orders requiring the implementation to be expedited, and mobs lined up in front of Central High threatening violence if necessary to prevent integration. After two black reporters were beaten, Governor Orval Faubus, facing a tough reelection campaign, responded to the escalating violence. He ordered 270 National Guardsmen physically to prohibit the entry of black students into the high school.

President Eisenhower had openly expressed serious reservations about the Court's Brown decision. In March 1956, he had chosen not to respond when the University of Alabama violated a federal court order and refused to admit its first black student. He then waited nearly three weeks before responding in Little Rock. Governor Faubus had finally agreed to allow the students to enter, but his withdrawal of the National Guard left the nine students to face the angry mobs on their own.

As the nation watched images of ugly confrontations on the television news each evening, the pressure mounted on President Eisenhower. On September 23, 1957, the president ordered unruly mobs to disperse and cease their efforts to block the path of the black students attempting to enter Little Rock's Central High. When they reappeared the following day, Eisenhower responded by issuing Executive Order 10730 authorizing the use of federal troops to enforce the federal court orders. This was the first federal military intervention in the South since Reconstruction ended in 1877.

In his address to the nation on September 24, the president spoke of both his sadness and his resolve in moving to execute the orders of the federal district court in Little Rock against the "obstruction of justice" perpetrated by "demagogic extremists" and "disorderly mobs." Such extreme action was to be temporary and was dictated by the failure of local police to contain the situation themselves. To do otherwise, according to the president, was to invite "anarchy."[6]

As Eisenhower put it, "This challenge must be met and with such measures as will preserve to the people as a whole their lawfully protected rights in a climate permitting free and fair exercise." He added that

> at a time when we face grave situations abroad because of the hatred that Communism bears toward a system of government based on human rights, it would be difficult to exaggerate the harm that is being done to the prestige and influence, and indeed to the safety, of our nation and the world.[7]

The president then put the Arkansas National Guard under federal control and added 1,000 paratroopers from the 101st Airborne Division stationed in Little Rock. These federal soldiers stood armed with fixed bayonets on the steps of Central High School. They were to protect the nine students from angry crowds while those students went to and from the school.

In an attempt to defuse the crisis, the school board tried further to delay implementation of the federal desegregation order. The United States Supreme Court, however, returned for a special September term in order to hear the case. They subsequently ruled unanimously that the school's desegregation must move forward as previously ordered, declaring that it is "emphatically the province and duty of the judicial department to say what the law is." For further emphasis, they even took the unprecedented step of individually signing the decision.[8]

Escorted by paratroopers, the nine black students began regular attendance at Central High School. By November, the crisis had abated, and the troops were withdrawn.

This would far from resolve the issue of school desegregation, however. Some Southern cities closed their public schools rather than see them integrated. The following two years, for instance, Governor Faubus closed Little Rock public high schools to "prevent violence and disorder." Other cities used devices such as expending tax dollars to assist in the development of white-only private schools. When President John F. Kennedy took the oath of office in January 1961, only 6.4 percent of all black students in the South were attending integrated schools.[9]

THE LAW

The introductory provisions of Executive Order 10730[10] set forth the context in which President Eisenhower issued the order. Specifically, the president declared that the executive order was being issued because his previous proclamation commanding the citizens of Arkansas to cease obstructing federal court orders was not obeyed. Consequently, in this executive order, the president directed the secretary of defense to use military force in Arkansas. The order authorized the secretary of defense to call National Guard and Air National Guard units into active service. In addition, the order authorized use of other armed forces of the United States as needed to enforce the standing federal court orders.

The order granted the secretary of defense considerable latitude. It authorized the secretary of defense to "take all appropriate steps" to remove obstructions of justice in Arkansas with regard to enrollment and attendance at Little Rock public schools.

26. Executive Order 10730

PROVIDING ASSISTANCE FOR THE REMOVAL OF AN OBSTRUCTION OF JUSTICE WITHIN THE STATE OF ARKANSAS

WHEREAS on September 23, 1957, I issued Proclamation No. 3204 reading in part as follows:

WHEREAS certain persons in the state of Arkansas, individually and in unlawful assemblages, combinations, and conspiracies, have wilfully obstructed the enforcement of orders of the United States Court for the Eastern District of Arkansas with respect to matters relating to enrollment and attendance at public schools, particularly at Central High School, located in Little Rock school district, Little Rock, Arkansas: and

WHEREAS such wilful obstruction of justice hinders the execution of the laws of the state and of the United States, and makes it impracticable to enforce such laws by the ordinary course of judicial proceeding; and

WHEREAS such obstruction of justice constitutes a denial of the equal protection of the laws secured by the Constitution of the United States and impedes the course of justice under those laws;

NOW THEREFORE, I, Dwight D. Eisenhower, President of the United States, under and by virtue of the authority vested in me by the Constitution and the statutes of the United States, including Chapter 15 of Title 10 of the United States Code, particularly Sections 332, 333, and 334 thereof, do command all persons engaged in such obstruction of justice to cease and desist therefrom, and to disperse forthwith; and

Whereas the command contained in that proclamation has not been obeyed and wilful obstruction of enforcement of said court orders still exists and threatens to continue:

Now, therefore, by virtue of the authority vested in me by the Constitution and statutes of the United States, including Chapter 15 of Title 10, particularly Sections 332, 333, and 334 thereof, and Section 301 of Tittle 3 of the United States Code, it is hereby ordered as follows:

Section 1. I hereby authorize and direct the Secretary of Defense to order into the active military service of the United States as he may deem appropriate to carry out the purposes of this order, any or all of the units of the National Guard of the United States and of the Air National Guard of the United States within the state of Arkansas to serve in the active military service of the United States for an indefinite period and until relieved by appropriate orders.

Section 2. The Secretary of Defense is authorized and directed to take all appropriate steps to enforce any orders of the United States District Court for the Eastern District of Arkansas for the removal of obstruction of justice in the state of Arkansas with respect to matters relating to enrollment and attendance at public schools in the Little Rock School District, Little Rock, Arkansas. To carry out the provisions of this section, the Secretary of Defense is authorized to use the units, and members thereof, ordered into the active military service of the Untied States pursuant to Section 1 of this order.

Section 3. In furtherance of the enforcement of the aforementioned orders of the United States District Court for the Eastern District of Arkansas, the Secretary of Defense is authorized to use such of the armed forces of the United States as he may deem necessary.

Section 4. The Secretary of Defense is authorized to delegate to the Secretary of the Army or the Secretary of the Air Force, or both, any of the authority conferred upon him by this order.

DWIGHT D. EISENHOWER
THE WHITE HOUSE,
September 24, 1957.

NOTES

1. According to historian C. Vann Woodward, the origin of the term "Jim Crow" seems to have been "lost in obscurity," but probably it is related to minstrel songs performed by whites in black face. Thomas D. Rice wrote a song and dance called "Jim Crow" in 1832, and the words had come to be used as an adjective by 1838. The term "Jim Crow law" first appeared in English dictionaries in 1904. See C. Vann Woodward, *The Strange Career of Jim Crow* (New York: Oxford University Press, 1966), p. 7.

2. *Plessy v. Ferguson*, 163 U.S. 537 (1896).

3. *Brown v. Board of Education of Topeka, Kansas*, 347 U.S. 483 (1954).

4. *Brown v. Board of Education of Topeka, Kansas*, 349 U.S. 294 (1955).

5. The Southern Manifesto on Integration reads,

We regard the decision of the Supreme Court in the school cases as a clear abuse of judicial power. It climaxes a trend in the federal judiciary undertaking to legislate . . . and to encroach upon the reserved rights of the states and the people.

The original Constitution does not mention education. Neither does the Fourteenth Amendment nor any amendment. . . . The Supreme Court of the United States, with no legal basis for such action, undertook to exercise their naked judicial power and substituted their personal political and social ideas for the established law of the land.

This unwarranted exercise of power by the court, contrary to the Constitution, is creating chaos and confusion in the states principally affected. It is destroying the amicable relations between the white and negro races that have been created through ninety years of patient effort by the good people of both races. It has planted hatred and suspicion where there has been heretofore friendship and understanding. . . .

We pledge ourselves to use all lawful means to bring about a reversal of this decision which are contrary to the Constitution and to prevent the use of force in its implementation.

6. Dwight D. Eisenhower, *Vital Speeches*, September 24, 1957 (Washington D.C.: GPO, 1957).

7. Ibid.

8. *Cooper v. Aaron*, 358 U.S. 1 (1958).

9. James Roark et al., *The American Promise* (Boston: Bedford Books, 1998), pp. 1088–92.

10. *Federal Register* (Washington, D.C.: GPO), vol. 22, p. 7628.

27

Civil Rights Act

1957

Among other things, the Civil Rights Act of 1957 established a non-partisan Civil Rights Commission to monitor civil rights progress.

HISTORICAL CONTEXT

After President Harry S Truman's 1948 civil rights proposals to Congress, the United States Senate, and House of Representatives once again began actively to consider civil rights legislation. Between 1953 and 1957, for instance, the House approved several such bills. Nevertheless, powerful Southern senators, well entrenched in key legislative positions, managed to keep such bills from being voted on in the United States Senate.

Meanwhile, resistance to desegregation efforts continued across the South. Racist violence persisted with the emergence of such groups as the White Citizens' Councils and the reemergence of lynchings. Martin Luther King, Jr., engaged in a massive bus boycott in Montgomery, Alabama, which began in December 1955. In January 1957, black ministers joined together in Montgomery to form the Southern Christian Leadership Conference to coordinate civil rights protests.

Amidst such turmoil, and under the tireless pressure of Clarence Mitchell, Jr., the director of the Washington bureau of the National Association for the Advancement of Colored People (NAACP), Congress began to intervene. In 1957 Congress passed the first national civil rights legislation since 1875. The passage marked the beginning of the modern civil rights legislative era, although certain provisions actually made the law just as much a triumph for opponents of national-level civil rights laws.

The bill originated in 1955, when Attorney General Herbert Brownell became increasingly concerned about rising antiblack violence in the South. In 1955, for example, two black civil rights workers were murdered in Mississippi while engaging in voter registration efforts. That same year, fourteen-year-old Emmit Till was lynched in Mississippi for remarks he allegedly made to a white girl. In 1956, in order to help stem further racial confrontations, Brownell presented Congress with what would eventually form the basis of the Civil Rights Act of 1957.

The original bill established a Civil Rights Commission to investigate violations of the Fourteenth and Fifteenth Amendments, to gather information, and to make reports and recommendations to the president. It strengthened some existing civil rights provisions in the United States Code. It upgraded the civil rights unit of the Justice Department to a full-fledged Civil Rights Division—an idea dating back to President Truman—and it made this division the nation's primary enforcement arm for civil rights based on race, color, religion, sex, national origin, and disability. The bill authorized the attorney general of the United States to seek injunctive relief if necessary to protect school desegregation and federal voting rights, and it protected against discrimination in employment, housing, public accommodations, and health services. This included possible criminal prosecution of judges. In addition, nondiscriminatory criteria were established for the selection of federal jurors.

The Eisenhower administration was divided on the bill. The president himself supported only two components: the creation of the Civil Rights Commission and the reorganization of the civil rights unit within the Justice Department. FBI Director J. Edgar Hoover warned about Communist influence in the civil rights movement, and there was political concern about losing Republican Party inroads being made among white Southerners.

Nevertheless, President Eisenhower and congressional Republicans were hoping to draw considerable support from the soon-to-be-enfranchised Southern black voters. The president finally relented and endorsed the bulk of the bill in the heat of the 1956 presidential campaign. The basic proposal was subsequently supported by Vice President Richard M. Nixon after he met with Martin Luther King, Jr., on June 13, 1957.

The bill passed the House in 1956, but it died in the Senate's Judiciary Committee, chaired by powerful Mississippi Senator James O. Eastland. Senator Sam Ervin (Dem., N.C.) reasserted the states' rights position when he later argued against "the strange thesis that the best way to promote the civil rights of some Americans is to rob other Americans of civil rights equally as precious and to reduce the supposedly sovereign States to meaningless zeros on the Nation's map . . . an insulting and insupportable indictment of a whole people."[1] Representative William Winstead (Dem., Miss.) labeled it "un-American fanaticism" and added that "it has intensified the feeling between the races in the South and has retarded adjustment that was taking place before it appeared on the scene."[2]

After being reelected, Eisenhower pressed hard on the voting-related passages, downplaying such hotter political issues as school desegregation. As argued during the Reconstruction era, the logic was that enfranchised black voters could then use their voting rights to pursue other such rights. Taking that approach, Eisenhower ultimately attracted the support of the powerful Senate majority leader, Lyndon B. Johnson (Dem., Texas).

Johnson, a Texan, had presidential ambitions, and he had never been an ardent segregationist. For example, he never did sign the Southern Manifesto (see Chapter 26), which condemned the U.S. Supreme Court's *Brown v. Board of Education* decision. As Senate majority leader, Johnson brokered a deal between Northern and Southern Democrats, partly by avoiding the school desegregation controversy.

In the process, however, key components of the bill were altered. In particular, the attorney general would no longer be explicitly authorized to seek federal court orders because Southern senators feared "government by injunction" across the South, especially in an attempt to enforce school desegregation. In addition, if a federal judge tried to hold someone in contempt of court for disobeying a federal court order to enforce this law, that person was entitled to a jury trial if a significant criminal penalty were involved. President Eisenhower had long supported the former change, but he disagreed with the latter. In particular, he balked at the prospect of all-white Southern juries trying voter infraction cases. Besides that, punishing individuals for contempt without a jury had been a well-established practice in the law.

Senator Richard Russell (Dem., Ga.) found some consolation in the final version: "[T]he fact that we were able to confine the Federal invasion of the South to the field of voting and keep the withering hand of the Federal Government out of our schools and social order is to me . . . the sweetest victory of my 25 years as a Senator."[3] Meanwhile, much of the black leadership opposed passage of the significantly weakened bill, and they urged the president to veto the legislation. Nonetheless, despite reservations, President Eisenhower signed the Civil Rights Act of 1957 into law.[4]

In the course of the congressional debate, black leaders Charles Gomillion and William Mitchell had come to Washington with considerable evidence of racial discrimination committed by Alabama's Macon County registrars. Following passage of the act, Senator Paul Douglas (Rep., Ill.) urged Mitchell "to continue to assemble the facts that will help make the case for the next forward steps."[5] Mitchell complied by compiling volumes of evidence and turning them over to the Justice Department, which ultimately led to one of the first federal lawsuits filed under the 1957 act.

The act required that federal officials demonstrate both that the blacks involved had been denied the right to vote solely on the basis of race and that a pattern of such racial discrimination existed. The biggest stumbling block, however, was that there were to be jury trials for most of the election officials accused of such voting rights violations. Given that such juries in the South were likely to be all white, the prospects that they would convict local white election officials were minimal. In the end, federal officials won only a handful of verdicts under this act.

Although this particular law had its clear limitations, the creation of the Civil Rights Commission came to be very significant. Presidents often ignored or rejected their recommendations[6]; nonetheless, the commission continued to gather volumes of information on civil rights abuses in the South and elsewhere. Such reports eventually helped build the case for stronger laws in the future, including the Civil Rights Acts of 1960 and 1964, the Voting Rights Act of 1965, and the Fair Housing Act of 1968.[7]

THE LAW

The Civil Rights Act[8] of 1957 established a Commission on Civil Rights and set forth its duties, powers, and rules of procedure.

The act provided that the six-member commission could hold hearings and subpoena witnesses to testify. The United States District Courts were granted authority to enforce the subpoenas. Witnesses called at commission hearings could be represented by their own counsel. The act further provided that the commission could hold executive sessions to hear sensitive testimony of some witnesses if the commission determined "that the evidence or testimony at any hearing may tend to defame, degrade, or incriminate any person." Testimony taken in executive session could not be released to the public.

The act charged the commission with the duty of investigating allegations of discrimination on the basis of color, race, religion, or national origin with respect to voting. The commission also was responsible for studying the status of equal protection under the Constitution and evaluating the laws and policies of the federal government with respect to equal protection. Federal agencies were directed to cooperate fully with the commission. The commission was to submit interim reports as well as a final report and recommendations not later than two years from the date of the act.

To carry out its duties, the commission was granted a full-time paid staff director and the power to appoint other paid personnel. Under the provisions of this act, the commission also had the power to form state advisory committees. In addition, the act directed that the money necessary to carry out the provisions of the act be appropriated.

This act expanded the 1870 Enforcement Act by adding provisions prohibiting interference with a person's right to vote by attempting to intimidate, threaten, or coerce. It provided for injunctive relief that would allow the court to issue an order forbidding a person from engaging in activities prohibited by the act. It also provided for actions of criminal contempt and for punishment of fines and imprisonment. Significantly, under the act, an accused was granted the right to a jury trial.

Finally, the act set forth the necessary qualifications for federal jurors. Any person twenty-one years or older who had lived within the judicial district for more than one year was entitled to serve unless that person had been convicted of certain crimes, was unable to communicate in English, or had infirmities that rendered him incapable of serving.

27. Civil Rights Act of 1957

Be it enacted . . .

SEC. 101. (a) There is created in the executive branch of the Government a Commission on Civil Rights (hereinafter called the "Commission").

(b) The Commission shall be composed of six members who shall be appointed by the President by and with the advice and consent of the Senate. Not more than three of the members shall at any one time be of the same political party. . . .

RULES OF PROCEDURE OF THE COMMISSION

SEC. 102. (a) The Chairman or one designated by him to act as Chairman at a hearing of the Commission shall announce in an opening statement the subject of the hearing.

(b) A copy of the Commission's rules shall be made available to the witness before the Commission.

(c) Witnesses at the hearings may be accompanied by their own counsel for the purpose of advising them concerning their constitutional rights.

(d) The Chairman or Acting Chairman may punish breaches of order and decorum and unprofessional ethics on the part of counsel, by censure and exclusion from the hearings.

(e) If the Commission determines that evidence or testimony at any hearing may tend to defame, degrade, or incriminate any person, it shall (1) receive such evidence or testimony in executive session; (2) afford such person an opportunity voluntarily to appear as a witness; and (3) receive and dispose of requests from such person to subpena additional witnesses. . . .

(g) No evidence or testimony taken in executive session may be released or used in public sessions without the consent of the Commission. Whoever releases or uses in public without the consent of the Commission evidence or testimony taken in executive session shall be fined not more than $1,000, or imprisoned for not more than one year. . . .

DUTIES OF THE COMMISSION

SEC. 104. (a) The Commission shall—

(1) investigate allegations in writing under oath or affirmation that certain citizens of the United States are being deprived of their right to vote and have that vote counted by reason of their color, race, religion, or

nation origin; which writing, under oath or affirmation, shall set forth the facts upon which such belief or beliefs are based;

(2) study and collect information concerning legal developments constituting a denial of equal protection of the laws under the Constitution; and

(3) appraise the laws and policies of the Federal Government with respect to equal protection of the laws under the Constitution.

(b) The Commission shall submit interim reports to the President and to the Congress at such times as either the Commission or the President shall deem desirable, and shall submit to the President and to the Congress a final and comprehensive report of its activities, findings, and recommendations not later than two years from the date of the enactment of this Act.

(c) Sixty days after the submission of its final report and recommendations the Commission shall cease to exist.

POWERS OF THE COMMISSION

SEC. 105. (a) There shall be a full-time staff director for the Commission who shall be appointed by the President by and with the advice and consent of the Senate and who shall receive compensation at a rate, to be fixed by the President, not in excess of $22,500 a year. The President shall consult with the Commission before submitting the nomination of any person for appointment to the position of staff director. Within the limitations of its appropriations, the Commission may appoint such other personnel as it deems advisable, in accordance with the civil service and classification laws, and may procure services . . . at rates for individuals not in excess of $50 per diem. . . .

(c) The Commission may constitute such advisory committees within States composed of citizens of that State and may consult with governors, attorneys general, and other representatives of State and local governments, and private organizations, as it deems advisable. . . .

(e) All Federal agencies shall cooperate fully with the Commission to the end that it may effectively carry out its functions and duties. . . .

(g) In case of. . . . refusal to obey a subpoena, any district court of the United States or the United States court of any Territory or possession, or the District Court of the United States for the District of Columbia, within the jurisdiction of which the inquiry is carried on or within the jurisdiction of which said person guilty of . . . refusal to obey is found or resides or transacts business, upon application by the Attorney General of the United States shall have jurisdiction to issue to such person an order requiring such person to appear before the Commission or a subcommittee thereof, there to produce evidence if so ordered, or there to give testimony touching the matter under investigation; and any failure to obey such order of the court may be punished by said court as a contempt thereof.

APPROPRIATIONS

SEC. 106. There is hereby authorized to be appropriated, out of any money in the Treasury not otherwise appropriated, so much as may be necessary to carry out the provisions of this Act. . . .

PART IV—To Provide Means of Further Securing and Protecting the Right to Vote

SEC. 131. Section 2004 of the Revised Statutes [Section 1971, title 42 of the United State Code], is amended as follows:

(a) Amend the catch line of said section to read, "Voting rights".

(b) Designate its present text with the subsection symbol "(a)".

(c) Add, immediately following the present text, four new subsections to read as follows:

(b) No person, whether acting under color of law or otherwise, shall intimidate, threaten, coerce, or attempt to intimidate, threaten, or coerce any other person for the purpose of interfering with the right of such other person to vote or to vote as he may choose, or of causing such other person to vote for, or not to vote for, any candidate for the office of President, Vice President, presidential elector, Member of the Senate, or Member of the House of Representatives, Delegates or Commissioners from the Territories or possessions, at any general, special, or primary election held solely or in part for the purpose of selecting or electing any such candidate.

(c) Whenever any person has engaged or there are reasonable grounds to believe that any person is about to engage in any act or practice which would deprive any other person of any right or privilege secured by subsection (a) or (b), the Attorney General may institute for the United States, or in the name of the United States, a civil action or other proper proceeding for preventive relief, including an application for a permanent or temporary injunction, restraining order, or other order. In any proceeding hereunder the United States shall be liable for costs the same as a private person. . . .

PART V—To Provide Trial by Jury for Proceedings to Punish Criminal Contempt of Court Growing Out of Civil Rights Cases and to Amend the Judicial Code Relating to Federal Jury Qualifications

SEC. 151. In all cases of criminal contempt arising under the provisions of this Act, the accused, upon conviction, shall be punished by fine or imprisonment or both: Provided however, That in case the accused is a natural person [human being] the fine to be paid shall not exceed the sum of $1,000, nor shall imprisonment exceed the term of six months: Provided further, That in any such proceeding for criminal contempt, at the discretion of the judge, the accused may be tried with or without a jury: Provided further, however, That in the event such proceeding for criminal contempt be tried before a judge without a jury and the sentence of the court upon conviction is a fine in excess of the sum of $300 or imprisonment in excess of forty-five days, the accused in said proceeding, upon demand therefor, shall be entitled to a trial de novo [a new trial] before a jury, which shall conform as near as may be to the practice in other criminal cases. . . .

SEC. 152. Section 1861, title 28, of the United States Code is hereby amended to read as follows:

§ 1861. Qualifications of Federal jurors.

"Any citizen of the United States who has attained the age of twenty-one years and who has resided for a period of one year within the judicial district, is competent to serve as a grand or petit juror unless—

(1) He has been convicted in a State or Federal court of record of a crime punishable by imprisonment for more than one year and his civil rights have not been restored by pardon or amnesty.

(2) He is unable to read, write, speak, and understand the English language.

(3) He is incapable, by reason of mental or physical infirmities, to render efficient jury service."

SEC. 161. This Act may be cited as the "Civil Rights Act of 1957".

APPROVED, September 9, 1957.

NOTES

1. Bernard Schwartz, ed., *Statutory History of the United States: Civil Rights*, Part 2 (New York: Chelsea House, 1970), p. 861.

2. Ibid., p. 881.

3. Ibid., p. 932.

4. For example, see Virginia Bernhard et al., *Firsthand America* (St. James, N.Y.: Brandywine Press, 1994), p. 859.

5. Steven Lawson, *Running for Freedom* (Philadelphia: Temple University Press, 1991), p. 62.

6. For example, see Theodore Hesburgh, "Integer Vitae: Independence of the United States Commission on Civil Rights," *Notre Dame Lawyer* (Spring 1971): pp. 445–460.

7. For a fuller discussion of these events, see Lawson, *Running for Freedom*; Taylor Branch, *Parting the Waters: America in the King Years, 1954–1963* (New York: Simon and Schuster, 1988).

8. *United States Statutes at Large* (Washington, D.C.: GPO), vol. 71, pp. 634–38.

28

Civil Rights Act

1960

Among other things, the Civil Rights Act of 1960 required keeping better voting records, empowered federal referees to facilitate voting, and created penalties for political violence committed across state lines.

HISTORICAL CONTEXT

The Civil Rights Act of 1957 was not proving very useful in helping African Americans overcome voting impediments in the South. There was simply little likelihood that anyone was ever going to be indicted and convicted of obstructing the right to vote. For the most part, discrimination by local registrars and voting officials, not to mention outright violence and intimidation, continued unabated.

Nevertheless, the successful Montgomery bus boycott and the formation of the Southern Christian Leadership Conference marked the beginning of a growing civil rights movement. After four North Carolina A&T University students waged a sit-in demonstration[1] at a segregated Woolworth lunch counter in Greensboro, it was not long before nonviolent protest proliferated across the South.[2] The peaceful protests, however, often met with violent responses on the part of counterdemonstrators and even the police. Images of this violence were televised across the country.[3]

As both political parties jockeyed to respond to this phenomenon during a presidential election year, Congress passed and President Dwight Eisenhower signed the Civil Rights Act of 1960. The act was limited to voting rights, however, avoiding more controversial civil rights issues such as school desegregation, fair housing, job discrimination, and access to public accommodations.

The groundwork had been laid by civil rights activists including William Mitchell, who had carefully documented the resistance of Southern voting registrars. Similar obstructions were detailed in a September 1959 report of the Civil Rights Commission. Such evidence led to the demand by liberals and the Civil Rights Commission for federal registrars to handle voting registration in the South.

President Eisenhower, however, favored a more moderate approach. He outlined his preferences in a special seven-point message, which he sent to Congress on February 5, 1959. The administration was willing to accept federal voting referees, as opposed to federal registrars. They would be empowered to settle disputes when called upon by federal judges hearing voting challenges under the Civil Rights Act of 1957.

Congressional debate on these voting rights issues began in the Senate. The Senate minority leader, Everett Dirksen (Rep., Ill.), was able to bypass the Senate Judiciary Committee chaired by James O. Eastland (Dem., Miss.) and to introduce the president's plan for a floor vote as an amendment to a minor piece of defense legislation. A Southern filibuster then halted action in the Senate. J. William Fulbright (Dem., Ark.) referred to "clear historical testimony against Federal intervention in and control of elections." He concluded that "it is high time our northern brothers cease to treat the South as a conquered territory and conquered people."[4]

On the House side, Emanuel Celler (Dem., N.Y.), chairman of the House Judiciary Committee, presided over the deliberations as the bill was taken up by the House Committee of the Whole. Amendments designed to expand the bill to civil rights issues beyond voting were quickly disallowed as not germane. Representative Robert Kastenmeier (Dem., Wis.) attempted to substitute the more liberal "federal voting registrars" alternative, and his motion was defeated. Chairman Celler had made it clear from the outset that he was willing to accept the president's more moderate version, and that version passed within two weeks of the bill's introduction.

With the legislation no longer containing federal registrars and proceeding under the forceful guidance of Majority Leader Lyndon B. Johnson (Dem., Tex.), the Senate filibuster ended, and the bill was passed fifteen days after it had been approved in the House. Johnson referred to it as "one of the Congress' finest hours"[5]; Minority Leader Dirksen described it as "the fulfillment of the American dream."[6] Senator Joseph Clark (Dem., Pa.) was less excited as he conceded defeat. Clark called the final bill a "pale ghost" and stated that "the eighteen implacable defenders of the way of life of the Old South are entitled to congratulations from those of us they have so disastrously defeated."[7]

In the end, Congress left voting registration to local registrars and appeals of their decisions to the far slower judicial process. The act's registration provisions became applicable when a federal lawsuit was brought under the Civil Rights Act of 1957. If a "pattern or practice of discrimination" could be demonstrated, federal judges were authorized to adjudicate voter registration disputes. If that process failed, the attorney general of the United States could appoint federal referees to resolve the disputes.

The Civil Rights Act of 1960 also expanded the authority of the Justice Department's Civil Rights Division. It raised the fines for obstructing court orders. It mandated that stricter voting records be kept and that they be kept for a period of twenty-two months. Anyone concealing or damaging voting records could be fined. It also made it a federal crime to use interstate commerce to threaten or carry out a bombing and added much stiffer penalties for people convicted of such violent acts. These latter provisions were an attempt to address interracial violence without unduly constraining the authority of state and local law enforcement officials.

One of the act's first successful applications occurred in Macon County, Georgia. Federal District Judge Frank Johnson reviewed the volumes of information compiled by William Mitchell and his Tuskegee Civic Association, in conjunction with the United States Justice Department. Johnson then found local registrars in violation of federal law and ordered them to cease discriminating as well as to speed up remedial actions to enroll qualified black voters. Black voter registration soon doubled in Macon County.[8]

Within two years, the attorney general had brought more than thirty cases to protect would-be black voters in Mississippi, Louisiana, Alabama, Tennessee, and Georgia. In Fayette and Haywood Counties in Tennessee, for example, the Justice Department managed to gain court injunctions against local whites who had engaged in economic reprisals against blacks who were attempting to vote.[9] Overall, however, few blacks were added to the voting ranks as a direct result of this legislation.[10] Thurgood Marshall lamented that "the Civil Rights Act of 1960 isn't worth the paper it was printed on."[11]

THE LAW

Amending previous sections of the United States Code, the Civil Rights Act of 1960[12] called for fines, imprisonment, or both of anyone who "by threats or force, willfully prevents, obstructs, impedes or interferes with or willfully attempts to prevent, obstruct, impede or interfere with, the due exercise of rights or the performance of duties under any order . . . of a court of the United States." The act, however, clearly stated that no attempt was being made to usurp the jurisdiction of any local authorities.

The act provided for fines, imprisonment, or both for anyone who took flight to avoid prosecution for "willfully attempting to or damaging or destroying by fire . . . any building, structure, facility, vehicle, dwelling, house, synagogue, church, religious center or educational institution, public or private" or to avoid testifying in a proceeding related to such offenses. Foreign or interstate transport of explosives with knowledge or intent that the explosives would be used to damage or destroy property protected by the act was also punishable by fines, imprisonment, or both, even the death penalty if circumstances warranted. False threats of an attempt to damage or destroy protected property also were punishable by fines, imprisonment, or both.

Pursuant to the act, election officers were directed to retain and preserve voting records. Failing to maintain these records or willfully destroying them would subject the wrongdoer to penalties. The attorney general was entitled to review the records maintained by election officials. The United States district courts were granted authority to compel production of any records demanded by the attorney general.

This act amended the Civil Rights Act of 1957 to permit courts to determine whether there was or is a "pattern or practice" of voting rights deprivation. Upon finding such a pattern or practice, courts were granted the power to issue orders declaring individuals qualified to vote. It also allowed the courts to appoint referees who were charged with the responsibility of resolving voting disputes.

28. The Civil Rights Act of 1960

Be it enacted . . . That this Act may be cited as the "Civil Rights Act of 1960".

TITLE I

Obstruction of Court Orders

SEC. 101. Chapter 73 of title 18, United States Code, is amended by adding at the end thereof a new section as follows:

ß1509. Obstruction of court orders

Whoever, by threats or force, willfully prevents, obstructs, impedes, or interferes with, or willfully attempts to prevent, obstruct, impede, or interfere with, the due exercise of rights or the performance of duties under any order, judgment, or decree of a court of the United States, shall be fined not more than $1,000 or imprisoned not more than one year, or both.

No injunctive or other civil relief against the conduct made criminal by this section shall be denied on the ground that such conduct is a crime. . . .

TITLE II

Flight to avoid prosecution for damaging or destroying any building or other real or personal property; and, illegal transportation, use or possession of explosives; and, threats or false information concerning attempts to damage or destroy real or personal property by fire or explosives.

SEC. 201. Chapter 49 of title 18, United States Code, is amended by adding at the end thereof a new section as follows:

ß1074. Flight to avoid prosecution for damaging or destroying any building or other real or personal property.

(a) Whoever moves or travels in interstate or foreign commerce with intent either (1) to avoid prosecution, or custody, or confinement after conviction, under the laws of the place from which he flees, for willfully attempting to or damaging or destroying by fire or explosive any building, structure, facility, vehicle, dwelling house, synagogue, church, religious center or educational institution, public or private, or (2) to avoid giving testimony in any criminal proceeding relating to any such offense shall be fined not more than $5,000 or imprisoned not more than five years, or both. . . .

SEC. 203. Chapter 39 of title 18 of the United States Code is amended by adding at the end thereof the following new section:

ß 837. Explosives; illegal use or possession; and, threats or false information concerning attempts to damage or destroy real or personal property by fire or explosives. . . .

(b) Whoever transports or aids and abets another in transporting in interstate or foreign commerce any explosive, with the knowledge or intent that it will be used to damage or destroy any building or other real or personal property for the purpose of interfering with its use for educational, religious, charitable, residential, business, or civic objectives or of intimidating any person pursuing such objectives, shall be subject to imprisonment for not more than one year, or a fine of not more than $1,000, or both; and if personal injury results shall be subject to imprisonment for not more than ten years or a fine of not more than $10,000, or both; and if death results shall be subject to imprisonment for any term of years or for life, but the court may impose the death penalty if the jury so recommends. . . .

(d) Whoever, through the use of the mail, telephone, telegraph, or other instrument of commerce, willfully imparts or conveys, or causes to be imparted or conveyed, any threat, or false information knowing the same to be false, concerning an attempt or alleged attempt being made, or to be made, to damage or destroy any building or other real or personal property for the purpose of interfering with its use for educational, religious, charitable, residential, business, or civic objectives, or of intimidating any person pursuing such objectives, shall be subject to imprisonment for not more than one year or a fine of not more than $ 1,000, or both.

(e) This section shall not be construed as indicating an intent on the part of Congress to occupy the field in which this section operates to the exclusion of a law of any State, Territory, Commonwealth, or possession of the United States, and no law of any State, Territory, Commonwealth, or possession of the United States which would be valid in the absence of the section shall be declared invalid, and no local authorities shall be deprived of any jurisdiction over any offense over which they would have jurisdiction in the absence of this section. . . .

TITLE III

Federal Election Records

SEC. 301. Every officer of election shall retain and preserve, for a period of twenty-two months from the date of any general, special, or primary election of which candidates for the office of President, Vice President, presidential elector, Member of the Senate, Member of the House of Representatives, or Resident Commissioner from the Commonwealth of Puerto Rico are voted for, all records and papers which come into his possession relating to any application, registration, payment of poll tax, or other act requisite to voting in such election, except that, when required by law, such records and papers may be delivered to another officer of election and except that, if a State or the Commonwealth of Puerto

Rico designates a custodian to retain and preserve these records and papers at a specified place, then such records and papers may be deposited with such custodian, and the duty to retain and preserve any record or paper so deposited shall devolve upon such custodian. Any officer of election or custodian who willfully fails to comply with this section shall be fined not more than $1,000 or imprisoned not more than one year, or both.

SEC. 302. Any person, whether or not an officer of election or custodian, who willfully steals, destroys, conceals, mutilates, or alters any record or paper required by section 301 to be retained and preserved shall be fined not more than $1,000 or imprisoned not more than one year, or both.

SEC. 303. Any record or paper required by section 301 to be retained and preserved shall, upon demand in writing by the Attorney General or his representative directed to the person having custody, possession, or control of such record or paper, be made available for inspection, reproduction, and copying at the principal office of such custodian by the Attorney General or his representative. This demand shall contain a statement of the basis and the purpose therefore. . . .

SEC. 305. The United States district court for the district in which a demand is made pursuant to section 303, or in which a record or paper so demanded is located, shall have jurisdiction by appropriate process to compel the production of such record or paper. . . .

TITLE VI

SEC. 601. That section 2004 of the Revised Statutes [section 1971, title 42 of the United States Code], section 131 of the Civil Rights Act of 1957 . . . is amended as follows:

(a) Add the following as subsection (e) and designate the present subsection (e) as subsection "(f)":

In any proceeding instituted pursuant to subsection (c) in the event the court finds that any person has been deprived on account of race or color of any right or privilege secured by subsection (a), the court shall upon request of the Attorney General and after each party has been given notice and the opportunity to be heard make a finding whether such deprivation was or is pursuant to a pattern or practice. If the court finds such pattern or practice, any person of such race or color resident within the affected area shall, for one year and thereafter until the court subsequently finds that such pattern or practice has ceased, be entitled, upon his application therefor, to an order declaring him qualified to vote, upon proof that at any election or elections (1) he is qualified under State law to vote, and (2) he has since such finding by the court been (a) deprived of or denied under color of law the opportunity to register to vote or otherwise to qualify to vote, or (b) found not qualified to vote by any person acting under color of law. . . .

The court may appoint one or more persons who are qualified voters in the judicial district, to be known as voting referees, who shall subscribe to the oath of office . . . to serve for such period as the court shall determine, to receive such applications and to take evidence and report to the court findings as to whether or not at any election or elections (1) any such applicant is qualified under State law to vote, and (2) he has since the finding by the court heretofore specified been (a) deprived of or denied under color of law the opportunity to register to vote or otherwise to qualify to vote, or (b) found not qualified to vote by any person acting under color of law. In a proceeding before a voting referee, the applicant shall be heard ex parte [without the other party present] at such times and places as the court shall direct. His statement under oath shall be prima facie evidence [presumed to be true] as to his age, residence, and his prior efforts to register or otherwise qualify to vote. Where proof of literacy or an understanding of other subjects is required by valid provisions of State law, the answer of the applicant, if written, shall be included in such report to the court; if oral, it shall be taken down stenographically and a transcription included in such report to the court.

Upon receipt of such report, the court shall cause the Attorney General to transmit a copy thereof to the State attorney general and to each party to such proceeding together with an order to show cause within ten days, or such shorter time as the court may fix, why an order of the court should not be entered in accordance with such report. Upon the expiration of such period, such order shall be entered unless prior to that time there has been filed with the court and served upon all parties a statement of exceptions to such report. Exceptions as to matters of fact shall be considered only if supported by a duly verified copy of a public record or by affidavit of persons having personal knowledge of such facts or by statements or matters contained in such report; those relating to matters of law shall be supported by an appropriate memorandum of law. The issues of fact and law raised by such exceptions shall be determined by the court or, if the due and speedy administration of justice requires, they may be referred to the voting referee to determine in accordance with procedures prescribed by the court. A hearing as to an issue of fact shall be held only in the event that the proof in support of the exception discloses the existence of a genuine issue of material fact. The applicant's literacy and understanding of other subjects shall be determined solely on the basis of answers included in the report of the voting referee.

The court, or at its direction the voting referee, shall issue to each applicant so declared qualified a certificate identifying the holder thereof as a person so qualified.

Any voting referee appointed by the court pursuant to this subsection shall to the extent not inconsistent herewith have all the powers conferred upon a [judge] by rule 53(c) of the Federal Rules of Civil Procedure. The compensation to be allowed to any persons appointed by the court pursuant to this subsection shall be fixed by the court and shall be payable by the United States.

Applications pursuant to this subsection shall be determined expeditiously. In the case of any application filed twenty or more days prior to an election which is undetermined by the time of such election, the court shall issue an order authorizing the applicant to vote provisionally: Provided, however, That such applicant shall be qualified to vote under State law. In the case of an application filed within twenty days prior to an election, the court, in its discretion, may make such an order. In either case the order shall make appropriate provision for the impounding of the applicant's ballot pending determination of the application. The court may take any other action, and may authorize such referee or such other person as it may designate to take any other action, appropriate or necessary to carry out the provisions of this subsection and to enforce its decrees. This subsection shall in no way be construed as a limitation upon the existing powers of the court. . . .

APPROVED May 6, 1960.

NOTES

1. In the sit-in demonstration, the students refused to leave the lunch counter before being served.

2. For example, see Miles Wolff, *Lunch at the Five and Ten: The Greensboro Sit-In* (New York: Stein and Day, 1970); William H. Chafe, *Civilities and Civil Rights: Greensboro, North Carolina, and the Black Struggle for Freedom* (New York: Oxford University Press, 1980); David Halberstam, *The Children* (New York: Ballantine, 1999).

3. For example, see Harvard Sitkoff, *The Struggle for Black Equality 1954–1980* (New York: Hill and Wang, 1981).

4. Bernard Schwartz, ed., *Statutory History of the United States: Civil Rights*, Part 2 (New York: Chelsea House, 1970), p. 999.

5. Ibid., p. 998.

6. Ibid., p. 1013.

7. Ibid., pp. 1005–6.

8. See Steven Lawson, *Running for Freedom* (Philadelphia: Temple University Press, 1991), pp. 63–64.

9. John Hope Franklin and Alfred A. Moss, Jr., *From Slavery to Freedom: A History of African Americans* (New York: Knopf, 1994), p. 498.

10. For example, see Daniel M. Berman, *A Bill Becomes Law: The Civil Rights Act of 1960* (New York: Macmillan, 1962).

11. Quoted in Schwartz, ed., *Statutory History of the United States: Civil Rights* p. 938.

12. *United States Statutes at Large* (Washington, D.C.: GPO), vol. 74, pp. 86–92.

29

Executive Order 10925

1961

President John F. Kennedy's Executive Order 10925 created the President's Equal Employment Opportunity Committee and first used the term "affirmative action."

HISTORICAL CONTEXT

On March 26, 1960, presidential candidate John F. Kennedy made a now famous phone call to Coretta Scott King. Kennedy pledged his support for the early release of her husband, Martin Luther King, Jr., from a jail in Birmingham, Alabama. In one of the closest elections in the nation's history, Kennedy's gains in the black community proved very advantageous. He won 70 percent of the black vote, which provided the margin of victory in states such as Illinois, Michigan, Texas, Pennsylvania, and South Carolina. His Republican opponent, Richard M. Nixon, later lamented that "this one unfortunate incident in the heat of the campaign seemed to dissipate much of the support I had among Negro voters."[1]

Once elected, President Kennedy faced pressure to reward the African American community for its support.[2] Confronted with a conservative coalition of Republicans and Southern Democrats in Congress, however, the president proceeded very cautiously on the legislative front. Civil rights was not one of the sixteen legislative priorities he sent to Congress just after his inauguration, nor was it one of his legislative priorities the following year.

Nevertheless, Kennedy did respond in other ways. He made several high-profile black appointments.[3] He was the first president openly to socialize with African Americans in the White House. His attorney general, Robert Kennedy, attempted to enforce federal court orders more aggressively than had been done in the Eisenhower years, focusing on voter registration but including school desegregation as well.[4] In addition, the president issued three noteworthy executive orders.

The first of these three orders addressed racial discrimination in federal employment, a problem that had persisted despite the executive orders of Democratic Presidents Franklin D. Roosevelt and Harry S Truman (see chapters 22 through 25). Much of this recalcitrance could be found among federal government contractors in the South, where little had been done to fight Jim Crow laws and practices.

Given the dominance of the Democratic Party in the South, the region had managed continually to reelect a number of the same senators and representatives. Southern Democrats, then, gradually became some of the most senior members of the United States Congress, and thus became chairpersons of key congressional committees. One of the advantages to such a position is the ability to steer major government contracts to firms in the chairperson's home state. Consequently, many of the nation's defense contractors, for example, could be found in the South. Two of the more prominent of these included a large Lockheed aircraft factory outside of Atlanta, Georgia, and the shipyards in Norfolk, Virginia.

During the 1960 presidential campaign, Kennedy had attacked the Eisenhower administration's "do-nothing" Committee on Government Contracts for not more effectively addressing the problem of racial discrimination practiced by governmental contractors. President Eisenhower had appointed that committee, and Vice President Nixon had served as its chairman.[5] After his election, Kennedy asked Vice President Lyndon B. Johnson and his staff to devise a more effective enforcement mechanism.[6]

On March 6, 1961, Kennedy issued Executive Order 10925, setting out a plan drafted to a large extent by Abe Fortas, a Memphis lawyer and longtime advisor to Lyndon Johnson whom Johnson later appointed to the United States Supreme Court. The order created the President's Equal Employment Opportunity Committee chaired by Vice President Johnson. Its primary role was to eliminate obstacles to government employment based on race, creed, color, or national origin.

The plan combined two existing but obscure equal employment

committees: one for government contracts and one for jobs within the federal government. It also marginally increased committee authority. Subcontractors and labor unions, for example, would now be monitored as well. In addition, the committee could initiate its own investigations, rather than wait for complaints; and it could terminate contracts if necessary.

Given the political climate at the time, more elaborate options had been rejected by Kennedy, Johnson, and the Johnson staff. They would not attempt to reinvigorate Roosevelt's Fair Employment Practices Committee (FEPC). They spurned any organizational alternatives that would require Congress to approve either enforcement authority or annual appropriations, neither of which Congress was likely to approve. They also opted not to attempt to regulate those hired via federal grants, fearing a backlash in Congress. In addition, having Johnson, a Texan, as the chairman allowed Southern congresspersons to rest a little easier.[7]

As far as size, it should be remembered that the committee was created and funded without going through Congress. Thus, it had to be funded out of existing departmental budgets. On paper, the committee functioned with a staff of only forty people and an official budget of roughly a half million dollars, smaller than the budget allocated to the federal Bureau of Coal Research.[8] In practice, however, much of the committee's work was done by other departments and agencies. Consequently, it was a larger, more expensive operation than it appeared at first glance.[9]

Despite the committee's limitations, the president still touted it. Kennedy asserted, "[T]hrough this vastly strengthened machinery I have dedicated my administration to the cause of equal opportunity in employment by the government or its contractors. . . . I have no doubt that the vigorous enforcement of this order will mean the end of such discrimination."[10]

In practice, the committee never did cancel a federal contract and it seldom delayed one. Nonetheless, most major governmental contractors used the president's committee to negotiate nondiscrimination agreements. If those agreements were not acceptable, the committee could refer the case to Robert Kennedy's Justice Department, which often then did extract an acceptable accord. The committee finally required more than 1,600 "corrective actions" after receiving complaints of discrimination.[11]

Executive Order 10925 may have become best known, however, for making the first formal reference to racial "affirmative action" in relation to federal employment.[12] It required federal contractors to take "positive measures" in their fight against racial discrimination in the workplace, and to promote information about employment opportunities among minority groups, especially blacks, who previously had been excluded from such jobs.

The President's Equal Employment Opportunity Committee began with a presidentially ordered survey of the federal government's hiring practices. It found that African Americans were badly underrepresented, especially in the higher ranks of governmental employment.[13] The committee then acted on its affirmative action mandate in the summer of 1961, directing federal agencies to reduce their "underutilization" of blacks and other minorities, and to report back on their progress in the areas of hiring and promotion. Within a year, African Americans constituted 13 percent of the federal government's civilian workforce, exceeding their percentage of the national population, which then was less than 12 percent.[14]

THE LAW

Asserting that discrimination in regard to race, creed, color, and national origin was unconstitutional and articulating an ideal of equal opportunity with regard to federal employment and government contracts, President Kennedy issued Executive Order 10925[15] establishing his Committee on Equal Employment Opportunity.

After formally establishing the committee, the first part of the order set forth the composition of the committee, which included the vice president of the United States as the chairman of the committee and the secretary of labor as the vice chairman. This part of the order also addressed administrative matters. It specifically granted the committee authority to adopt rules and regulations for its proceedings and to provide policies and procedures necessary for implementation of the executive order. It further directed the committee to consider reports regarding progress under the order and reports of its members. Finally, in this part of the order, the committee was charged with the responsibility of making reports to the president.

The second section dealt specifically with actions necessary to address discrimination in federal employment. This part of the order mandated that the committee investigate the employment practices of the federal government and make recommendations to further the policy of nondiscrimination in federal employment. All executive departments and agencies were ordered to conduct self-evaluations of current employment practices and make reports to the committee.

The final part of this order related to the obligations of government contractors and subcontractors. This section set forth a myriad of provisions required in government contracts. Specifically, contractors had to agree not to engage in discriminatory employment practices and notify labor unions with which they had agreements of their commitment to nondiscriminatory practices. In addition, contractors were required to agree to "take affirmative action [positive measures] to ensure that applicants are employed, and that employees are treated during employment, without regard to their race, creed, color, or national origin." Contractors were subject to review by the President's Committee on Equal Employment Opportunity and were required to cooperate fully with any investigations made by that committee. The order provided that a contract could be canceled and future contracts denied for noncompliance with the nondiscrimination clauses. Provisions were made for the committee to monitor compliance by contractors and subcontractors.

Under this third part, the order directed the committee to use "its best efforts" to obtain cooperation of labor unions in complying with the purposes of the order.

Finally, the third part of the order granted the committee the authority to adopt rules and regulations to aid in obtaining compliance with all parts of the order and issue sanctions and penalties for noncompliance. The order also held the contracting agencies of the government responsible for obtaining compliance with the order, in regard to both contracts entered into by the agency and employment practices of the agency. The committee was given latitude in investigating the employment practices of government contractors.

29. Executive Order 10925

ESTABLISHING THE PRESIDENT'S COMMITTEE ON EQUAL EMPLOYMENT OPPORTUNITY

WHEREAS discrimination because of race, creed, color, or national origin is contrary to the Constitutional principles and policies of the United States; and

WHEREAS it is the plain and positive obligation of the United States

Government to promote and ensure equal opportunity for all qualified persons, without regard to race, creed, color, or national origin, employed or seeking employment with the Federal Government and on government contracts; and

WHEREAS it is the policy of the executive branch of the Government to encourage by positive measures equal opportunity for all qualified persons within the Government; and

WHEREAS it is in the general interest and welfare of the United States to promote its economy, security, and national defense through the most efficient and effective utilization of all available manpower; and

WHEREAS a review and analysis of existing Executive orders, practices, and government agency procedures relating to government employment and compliance with existing non-discrimination contract provisions reveal an urgent need for expansion and strengthening of efforts to promote full equality of employment opportunity; and

WHEREAS a single governmental committee should be charged with responsibility for accomplishing these objectives:

NOW, THEREFORE, by virtue of the authority vested in me as President of the United States by the Constitution and statutes of the United States, it is ordered as follows:

PART I—ESTABLISHMENT OF THE PRESIDENT'S COMMITTEE ON EQUAL EMPLOYMENT OPPORTUNITY

SECTION 101. There is hereby established the President's Committee on Equal Employment Opportunity.

SEC. 102. The Committee shall be composed as follows:

(a) The Vice President of the United States, who is hereby designated Chairman of the Committee and who shall preside at meetings of the Committee.

(b) The Secretary of Labor, who is hereby designated Vice Chairman of the Committee and who shall act as Chairman in the absence of the Chairman. The Vice Chairman shall have general supervision and direction of the work of the Committee and of the execution and implementation of the policies and purposes of this order.

(c) The Chairman of the Atomic Energy Commission, the Secretary of Commerce, the Attorney General, the Secretary of Defense, the Secretaries of the Army, Navy and Air Force, the Administrator of General Services, the Chairman of the Civil Service Commission, and the Administrator of the National Aeronautics and Space Administration. Each such member may designate an alternate to represent him in his absence.

(d) Such other members as the President may from time to time appoint.

(e) An Executive Vice Chairman, designated by the President, who shall be ex officio [by virtue of his position] a member of the Committee. The Executive Vice Chairman shall assist the Chairman, the Vice Chairman and the Committee. Between meetings of the Committee he shall be primarily responsible for carrying out the functions of the Committee and may act for the Committee pursuant to its rules, delegations and other directives. Final action in individual cases or classes of cases may be taken and final orders may be entered on behalf of the Committee by the Executive Vice Chairman when the Committee so authorizes.

SEC. 103. The Committee shall meet upon the call of the Chairman and at such other times as may be provided by its rules and regulations. It shall (a) consider and adopt rules and regulations to govern its proceedings; (b) provide generally for the procedures and policies to implement this order; (c) consider reports as to progress under this order; (d) consider and act, where necessary or appropriate, upon matters which may be presented to it by any of its members; and (e) make such reports to the President as he may require or the Committee shall deem appropriate. Such reports shall be made at least once annually and shall include specific references to the actions taken and results achieved by each department and agency. The Chairman may appoint subcommittees to make special studies on a continuing basis.

PART II—NONDISCRIMINATION IN GOVERNMENT EMPLOYMENT

SECTION 201. The President's Committee on Equal Employment Opportunity established by this order is directed immediately to scrutinize and study employment practices of the Government of the United States, and to consider and recommend additional affirmative steps which should be taken by executive departments and agencies to realize more fully the national policy of nondiscrimination within the executive branch of the Government.

SEC. 202. All executive departments and agencies are directed to initiate forthwith studies of current government employment practices within their responsibility. . . . Reports and recommendations shall be submitted to the Executive Vice Chairman of the Committee no later than sixty days from the effective date of this order, and the Committee, after considering such reports and recommendations, shall report to the President on the current situation and recommend positive measures to accomplish the objectives of this order. . . .

PART III—OBLIGATIONS OF GOVERNMENT CONTRACTORS AND SUBCONTRACTORS

Subpart A—Contractors' Agreements

SECTION 301. Except in contracts exempted in accordance with section 303 of this order, all government contracting agencies shall include in every government contract hereafter entered into the following provisions:

In connection with the performance of work under this contract, the contractor agrees as follows:

(1) The contractor will not discriminate against any employee or applicant for employment because of race, creed, color, or national origin. The contractor will take affirmative action to ensure that applicants are employed, and that employees are treated during employment, without regard to their race, creed, color, or national orgin. Such action shall include, but not be limited to, the following: employment, upgrading, demotion or transfer; recruitment or recruitment advertising; layoff or termination; rates of pay or other forms of compensation; and selection for training, including apprenticeship. The contractor agrees to post in conspicuous places, available to employees and applicants for employment, notices to be provided by the contracting officer setting forth the provisions of this nondiscrimination clause.

(2) The contractor will, in all solicitations or advertisements for employees placed by or on behalf of the contractor, state that all qualified applicants will receive consideration for employment without regard to race, creed, color, or national origin.

(3) The contractor will send to each labor union or representative of workers with which he has a collective bargaining agreement or other contract or understanding, a notice, to be provided by the agency contracting officer, advising the said labor union or workers' representative of the contractor's commitments under this section, and shall post copies of the notice in conspicuous places available to employees and applicants for employment.

(4) The contractor will comply with all provisions of [this executive order], and of the rules, regulations, and relevant orders of the President's Committee on Equal Employment Opportunity created thereby.

(5) The contractor will furnish all information and reports required by [this executive order], and by the rules, regulations, and orders of the said Committee, or pursuant thereto, and will permit access to his books, records, and accounts by the contracting agency and the Committee for

purposes of investigation to ascertain compliance with such rules, regulations, and orders.

(6) In the event of the contractor's non-compliance with the nondiscrimination clauses of this contract or with any of the said rules, regulations, or orders, this contract may be canceled in whole or in part and the contractor may be declared ineligible for further government contracts in accordance with procedures authorized in [this executive order], and such other sanctions may be imposed and remedies invoked as provided in [this executive order], or by rule, regulation, or order of the President's Committee on Equal Employment Opportunity, or as otherwise provided by law. . . .

Subpart B—Labor Unions and Representatives of Workers

SEC. 304. The Committee shall use its best efforts, directly and through contracting agencies, contractors, state and local officials and public and private agencies, and all other available instrumentalities, to cause any labor union, recruiting agency or other representative of workers who is or may be engaged in work under Government contracts to cooperate with, and to comply in the implementation of, the purposes of this order. . . .

Subpart C—Powers and Duties of the President's Committee on Equal Employment Opportunity and of Contracting Agencies

SEC. 306. The Committee shall adopt such rules and regulations and issue such orders as it deems necessary and appropriate to achieve the purposes of this order, including the purposes of Part II hereof relating to discrimination in Government employment.

SEC. 307. Each contracting agency shall be primarily responsible for obtaining compliance with the rules, regulations, and orders of the Committee with respect to contracts entered into by such agency or its contractors, or affecting its own employment practices. All contracting agencies shall comply with the Committee's rules in discharging their primary responsibility for securing compliance with the provisions of contracts and otherwise with the terms of this Executive order and of the rules, regulations, and orders of the Committee pursuant hereto. They are directed to cooperate with the Committee, and to furnish the Committee such information and assistance as it may require in the performance of its functions under this order. They are further directed to appoint or designate, from among the agency's personnel compliance officers. It shall be the duty of such officers to seek compliance with the objectives of this order by conference, conciliation, mediation, or persuasion. . . .

SEC. 309. (a) The Committee may itself investigate the employment practices of any Government contractor or subcontractor, or initiate such investigation by the appropriate contracting agency or through the Secretary of Labor, to determine whether or not the contractual provisions specified in section 301 of this order have been violated. Such investigation shall be conducted in accordance with the procedures established by the Committee, and the investigating agency shall report to the Committee any action taken or recommended.

(b) The Committee may receive and cause to be investigated complaints by employees or prospective employees of a Government contractor or subcontractor which allege discrimination contrary to the contractual provisions specified in section 301 of this order. The appropriate contracting agency or the Secretary of Labor, as the case may be, shall report to the Committee what action has been taken or is recommended with regard to such complaints.

SEC. 310. (a) The Committee, or any agency or officer of the United States designated by rule, regulation, or order of the Committee, may hold such hearings, public or private, as the Committee may deem advisable for compliance, enforcement, or educational purposes.

(b) The Committee may hold, or cause to be held, hearings in accordance with subsection (a) of this section prior to imposing, ordering, or recommending the imposition of penalties and sanctions under this order, except that no order for debarment of any contractor from further government contracts shall be made without a hearing.

SEC. 311. The Committee shall encourage the furtherance of an educational program by employer, labor, civic, educational, religious, and other nongovernmental groups in order to eliminate or reduce the basic causes of discrimination in employment on the ground of race, creed, color, or national origin. . . .

JOHN F. KENNEDY
THE WHITE HOUSE,
March 6, 1961.

NOTES

1. Richard M. Nixon, *Six Crises* (New York: Doubleday, 1962), p. 391.
2. For example, see Carl M. Brauer, *John F. Kennedy and the Second Reconstruction* (New York: Columbia University Press, 1977), pp. 58–60.
3. Robert C. Weaver was named head of the Housing and Home Finance

Agency and later secretary of the Department of Housing and Urban Development, the first African American to hold a Cabinet-level position; Thurgood Marshall was appointed to the circuit court of appeals; Wade McCree, James Parsons, Marjorie Lawson, Joseph Waddy, and Spottswood Robinson all were appointed to the federal district bench; George L.P. Weaver became the assistant secretary of labor; Carl Rowan, the deputy assistant secretary of state; Clifton Wharton and Mercer Cook, ambassadors to Norway and Niger, respectively; and Merle McCurdy and Cecil Poole, United States attorneys.

4. John Mack Faragher et al., *Out of Many* (Upper Saddle River, N.J.: Prentice-Hall, 2000), p. 860.

5. For example, see Hugh Davis Graham, *The Civil Rights Era* (New York: Oxford University Press, 1990), pp. 16–19, 27–32.

6. Hugh Davis Graham, *Civil Rights and the Presidency* (New York: Oxford University Press, 1992), pp. 36–39.

7. Brauer, *John F. Kennedy*, pp. 80–81.

8. Ibid., pp. 38–43.

9. Ibid., p. 80.

10. "Statement of the President upon Signing Order Establishing the President's Committee on Equal Employment Opportunity," March 7, 1961, *Public Papers of the Presidents of the United States: John F. Kennedy, 1961* (Washington, D.C.: U.S. Government Printing Office, 1962), p. 150.

11. Ibid., pp. 43–45; Brauer, *John F. Kennedy*, pp. 81–84.

12. The term itself actually appeared first in the 1935 Wagner Act, where it referred to the positive obligation of the National Labor Relations Board to root out unfair labor practices. See Graham, *Civil Rights and the Presidency*, p. 39.

13. Brauer, *John F. Kennedy*, pp. 82–83.

14. Ibid., p. 44.

15. *Federal Register* (Washington, D.C.: GPO), vol. 26, pp. 1977–79.

30

Executive Order 11053

1962

President John F. Kennedy's Executive Order 11053 authorized the use of federal troops to restore order after riots occurred at the University of Mississippi in Oxford, Mississippi.

HISTORICAL CONTEXT

James Meredith, an Air Force veteran, was a student at all-black Jackson State College in Jackson, Mississippi. On January 21, 1961, the day after John Kennedy was inaugurated, Meredith wrote to the all-white University of Mississippi for an application. In the fall of 1961, he attempted to become the first African American to attend the University of Mississippi at Oxford. When the school resisted, Meredith took his case to federal court. Legal proceedings finally ended on September 10 when United States Supreme Court Justice Hugo Black issued a court order requiring that Meredith be admitted.[1]

Mississippi Governor Ross Barnett defied that court order. On September 13, he asserted to a Mississippi television audience that the state had the constitutional right to disobey federal laws it deemed to be unconstitutional. He asked state residents to help him resist this federal government policy of "racial genocide." Eleven days later, he issued a proclamation directing that "representatives of the federal government are to be summarily arrested and jailed" if they interfere with Mississippi officials. He also told

Attorney General Robert Kennedy, "[w]e have been part of the United States but I don't know whether we are [now] or not."[2]

Meanwhile, the United States Justice Department was working aggressively behind the scenes. Among other things, the department's staff was trying to persuade Mississippi business leaders of the potential economic consequences of a continued state-federal confrontation. In particular, they wanted them to pressure the university's board of trustees to comply with the federal court order and admit Meredith. The attorney general also established a direct line of communication with the governor.

On September 25, one day after a federal court of appeals had found the university's board of trustees in contempt of court, the governor physically stood in Meredith's path, blocking his entry into the school. When Barnett was then summoned to appear before the court of appeals on a contempt charge of his own, Lieutenant Governor Paul Johnson physically blocked Meredith's entry the following day.

Speaking to Attorney General Robert Kennedy, Barnett declared, "I won't agree to let that boy get to Ole Miss. I will never agree to that. I would rather spend my whole life in a penitentiary than do that. . . . Why don't you let the NAACP run their own affairs and quit cooperating with that crowd?"[3]

Barnett was held in contempt of court on Friday, September 28. The next day, he capitulated and agreed to allow Meredith to be registered on Monday, October 1. The governor, facing a federal prison sentence, was not anxious to be responsible for bloodshed. He also had been lobbied by prominent state business leaders.[4]

Facing the possibility of violence committed by mobs of angry whites, however, the attorney general asked Governor Barnett for assurances that James Meredith would be protected by Mississippi state police when he attempted to register on Monday. When the governor failed to provide those assurances, Robert Kennedy sent 320 federal marshals. The marshals entered the campus on Sunday and secured Meredith in a dormitory room.

President Kennedy spoke directly to the residents of Mississippi in a nationally televised address that evening. He outlined the series of events that had occurred, including the actions of a court of appeals composed entirely of Southerners. He encouraged calm and appealed to both the residents' reason and their patriotism. It was too late; the federal marshals were under siege.

Governor Barnett also made an emergency television address to call for nonviolence. Yet, the governor refused to guarantee police protection for James Meredith, and he also spoke defiantly of resisting the "oppressive power of the United States."

As the State Highway Patrol retreated, several thousand whites, many of whom were armed, attacked the federal marshals as well as fifty-five National Guardsmen sent in as reinforcements. The mob attacked officers and guardsmen with rocks, clubs, bottles, gasoline bombs, and firearms. The federal marshals, however, were ordered not to fire back and instead battled with tear gas and other nonlethal means. Before the night was over, two demonstrators were dead, and 375 people were injured, including 166 federal marshals and twelve guardsmen. Of the injured federal marshals, twenty-nine had gunshot wounds.[5]

President Kennedy responded by issuing Executive Order 11053, entitled "Providing Assistance for the Removal of Unlawful Obstructions of Justice in the State of Mississippi." It authorized the use of federal troops to restore order at the University of Mississippi. Kennedy then sent 5,000 U.S. Army troops to the campus, and order was finally restored.

Under the protection of federal marshals and the U.S. Army, James Meredith was registered on Monday morning and was escorted to his first classes, held on Tuesday, October 2. Some 300 federal law enforcement officers remained on the campus until Meredith graduated the following summer. His successful enrollment formally desegregated the University of Mississippi; nevertheless, as historian Carl Brauer noted, "[I]t would be several years before black students could matriculate at Ole Miss in a relatively uneventful way."[6]

THE LAW

In the preamble to Executive Order 11053,[7] President Kennedy asserted that the commands of his previous proclamation were not being followed, and he ordered that the obstruction of justice in Mississippi peaceably end. The president's order directed the secretary of defense to "take appropriate steps" to enforce court orders and remove obstructions of justice in Mississippi. The order specifically authorized the secretary of defense to use the armed forces of the United States and to call into active military service the Army

National Guard and Air National Guard of Mississippi to carry out the purposes of the order.

30. Executive Order 11053

PROVIDING ASSISTANCE FOR THE REMOVAL OF UNLAWFUL OBSTRUCTIONS OF JUSTICE IN THE STATE OF MISSISSIPPI

WHEREAS on September 30, 1962, I issued Proclamation No. 3497 reading in part as follows:

WHEREAS the Governor of the State of Mississippi and certain law enforcement officers and other officials of that State, and other persons, individually and in unlawful assemblies, combinations and conspiracies, have been and are willfully opposing and obstructing the enforcement of orders entered by the United States District Court for the Southern District of Mississippi and the United States Court of Appeals for the Fifth Circuit; and

WHEREAS such unlawful assemblies, combinations and conspiracies oppose and obstruct the execution of the laws of the United States, impede the course of justice under those laws and make it impracticable to enforce those laws in the State of Mississippi by the ordinary course of judicial proceedings; and

WHEREAS I have expressly called the attention of the Governor of Mississippi to the perilous situation that exists and to his duties in the premises, and have requested but have not received from him adequate assurances that the orders of the courts of the United States will be obeyed and that law and order will be maintained:

NOW, THEREFORE, I, John F. Kennedy, President of the United States, under and by virtue of the authority vested in me by the Constitution and laws of the United States . . . do command all persons engaged in such obstructions of justice to cease and desist therefrom and to disperse and retire peaceably forthwith; and

WHEREAS the commands contained in that proclamation have not been obeyed and obstruction of enforcement of those court orders still exists and threatens to continue:

NOW, THEREFORE, by virtue of the authority vested in me by the Constitution and laws of the United States . . . it is hereby ordered as follows:

SECTION 1. The Secretary of Defense is authorized and directed to take all appropriate steps to enforce all orders of the United States District

Court for the Southern District of Mississippi and the United States Court of Appeals for the Fifth Circuit and to remove all obstructions of justice in the State of Mississippi.

SEC. 2. In furtherance of the enforcement of the aforementioned orders of the United States District Court for the Southern District of Mississippi and the United States Court of Appeals for the Fifth Circuit, the Secretary of Defense is authorized to use such of the armed forces of the United States as he may deem necessary.

SEC. 3. I hereby authorize the Secretary of Defense to call into the active military service of the United States, as he may deem appropriate to carry out the purposes of this order, any or all of the units of the Army National Guard and of the Air National Guard of the State of Mississippi to serve in the active military service of the United States for an indefinite period and until relieved by appropriate orders. In carrying out the provisions of Section 1, the Secretary of Defense is authorized to use the units, and members thereof, ordered into the active military service of the United States pursuant to this section. . . .

JOHN F. KENNEDY
THE WHITE HOUSE,
September 30, 1962.

NOTES

1. For a more detailed discussion of this entire series of events, see Carl M. Brauer, *John F. Kennedy and the Second Reconstruction* (New York: Columbia University Press, 1977), chap. 7; James Meredith, *Three Years in Mississippi* (Bloomington: Indiana University Press, 1966).

2. Quoted in Brauer, *John F. Kennedy*, p. 185.

3. Quoted in Robert Divine et al., *America: Past and Present* (New York: Longman, 1999), p. 941.

4. For example, see Brauer, *John F. Kennedy*, pp. 189–193.

5. See C. Vann Woodward, *The Strange Career of Jim Crow* (New York: Oxford University Press, 1966), pp. 174–175.

6. Brauer, *John F. Kennedy*, p. 197.

7. *Federal Register* (Washington, D.C.: GPO), vol. 27, p. 9693.

31

Executive Order 11063

1962

President John F. Kennedy's Executive Order 11063 prohibited discrimination in housing either loaned or directly financed by the federal government.

HISTORICAL CONTEXT

During the 1960 presidential campaign, John Kennedy behaved very cautiously in his approach to civil rights issues, especially the extremely volatile issues of school and housing desegregation. He needed to appeal to black voters but, at the same time, he could not afford to alienate too many white Southerners. Early on, for example, he pledged that upon election he would end racial discrimination in the selling and rental of housing "by a stroke of the pen." Nevertheless, a more detailed campaign statement outlining an executive order to that effect was delayed as the result of pressure from Senators Richard Russell (Dem., Ga.) and John Sparkman (Dem., Ala.).[1]

After his election, Kennedy advisors, including Lawrence O'Brien and Kenneth O'Donnell, counseled delay.[2] Besides the same constitutional and administrative dilemmas that had long plagued government's attempts to regulate discriminatory private behavior, there also were very few political allies in the quest for housing desegregation. Even Northern Democrats balked. They preferred to attack the South's legally mandated segregation in accommodations such as hotels and restaurants. On the other hand, they did not appear to be ready to accept a nationwide ban on housing discrimination. Ironically, Southern Jim Crow laws were written to apply to virtually every area but housing, while de facto [actual] residential segregation was the one form of segregation that was accepted and well entrenched in the North.[3]

When the president's promised fair housing order was not forthcoming by a "stroke of the pen," protestors responded cynically. They sent him hundreds of fountain pens and bottles of ink just in case an absence of pen or ink was the reason behind the delay. Pickets began to appear in front of the White House. One of them was actually joined by Senator Jacob Javits (Rep., N.Y.), a longtime Kennedy ally.

President Kennedy finally responded in the summer of 1962. He asked subordinates to begin fashioning the long-awaited executive order. Months passed, however, as Kennedy continued to defer to those counseling caution, and he decided to postpone any announcement until after the 1962 congressional elections.[4]

The president also heeded words of caution in terms of the order's scope. Home builders feared any such order might reduce demand for new home construction. The Justice Department questioned the legality of extending the order retroactively or attempting to regulate the activities of either private banks or savings and loan associations. Meanwhile, several Northern Democrats quietly relayed the fears and prejudices of white homeowners.[5]

Finally, on November 20, at a press conference held on Thanksgiving Eve, President Kennedy issued Executive Order 11063. Skirting the larger question of private housing discrimination, the order was limited to discrimination in housing either loaned or directly financed by the federal government. In addition, it was not to be applied retroactively. It did, however, create a President's Committee on Equal Housing to monitor and coordinate department and agency enforcement efforts.

Public opposition to the order turned out to be minimal because it had "less scope and fewer teeth" than many had anticipated.[6] Several states already had similar policies in effect, and they had not experienced any massive migrations of blacks into predominantly white neighborhoods. According to historian Carl Brauer, "The blacks' fear of white hostility and their general inability to afford the high prices of suburban homes [already effectively] impeded their mobility."[7]

Meanwhile, supporters were considerably less than enthusiastic.

African American realtors surveyed by the Pittsburgh *Courier*, for example, concluded that the order would have no discernable effect on housing discrimination. Thus, despite tempered praise from such organizations as the NAACP and the Urban League for being a good symbolic first step, editors at the Pittsburgh *Courier* warned, "Negroes are getting very weary of tokenism hailed as victories."[8]

The nine-member President's Committee on Equal Housing, under the leadership of former Pennsylvania Governor David Lawrence, did move to insert nondiscrimination clauses into all new contracts for public housing. They later added these for all urban renewal projects as well. In addition, they occasionally took action against housing contractors who were caught repeatedly discriminating.

In the end, however, the order does not appear to have had much of an impact on either the housing industry or racial residential patterns. By April 1963, a joint statement was issued by the NAACP, the Urban League, the Congress on Racial Equality (CORE), and the National Committee Against Discrimination in Housing. They chastised the Kennedy administration for lax enforcement of Executive Order 11063; afterward, CORE picketed the federal Housing and Home Finance Agency.[9]

THE LAW

Recognizing existing discrimination in housing, Executive Order 11063[10] directed all government departments and agencies with duties relating to housing to take action to end discrimination. They were to "take all actions necessary and appropriate" to prevent discrimination because of race, color, creed, or national origin in the sale or lease of property owned by the federal government or in transactions funded by it. The departments and agencies, specifically the Housing and Home Finance Agency, were directed to take action permitted by law, including litigation, to combat discriminatory practices. They also were given authority to take punitive measures including canceling contracts and withdrawing funding.

This order established the President's Committee on Equal Opportunity in Housing to monitor compliance with the order. Departments and agencies were directed to report to and cooperate with the committee. The committee was given broad authority to implement the objectives of the order.

31. Executive Order 11063

EQUAL OPPORTUNITY IN HOUSING

WHEREAS the granting of Federal assistance for the provision, reha-bilitation, or operation of housing and related facilities from which Americans are excluded because of their race, color, creed, or national origin is unfair, unjust, and inconsistent with the public policy of the United States as manifested in its Constitution and laws; and

WHEREAS the Congress in the Housing Act of 1949 has declared that the general welfare and security of the Nation and the health and living standards of its people require the realization as soon as feasible of the goal of a decent home and a suitable living environment for every American family; and

WHEREAS discriminatory policies and practices based upon race, color, creed, or national origin now operate to deny many Americans the benefits of housing financed through Federal assistance and as a consequence prevent such assistance from providing them with an alternative to substandard, unsafe, unsanitary, and overcrowded housing; and

WHEREAS such discriminatory policies and practices result in segregated patterns of housing and necessarily produce other forms of discrimination and segregation which deprive many Americans of equal opportunity in the exercise of their unalienable rights to life, liberty, and the pursuit of happiness; and

WHEREAS the executive branch of the Government, in faithfully executing the laws of the United States which authorize Federal financial assistance, directly or indirectly, for the provision, rehabilitation, and operation of housing and related facilities, is charged with an obligation and duty to assure that those laws are fairly administered and that benefits thereunder are made available to all Americans without regard to their race, color, creed, or national origin:

NOW, THEREFORE, by virtue of the authority vested in me as President of the United States by the Constitution and laws of the United States, it is ordered as follows:

PART I—PREVENTION OF DISCRIMINATION

SECTION 101. I hereby direct all departments and agencies in the executive branch of the Federal Government, insofar as their functions relate to the provision, rehabilitation, or operation of housing and related facilities, to take all action necessary and appropriate to prevent discrimination because of race, color, creed, or national origin—

(a) in the sale, leasing, rental, or other disposition of residential property and related facilities (including land to be developed for residential use), or in the use or occupancy thereof, if such property and related facilities are—

(i) owned or operated by the Federal Government, or

(ii) provided in whole or in part with the aid of loans, advances, rents, or contributions hereafter agreed to be made by the Federal Government, or

(iii) provided in whole or in part by loans hereafter insured, guaranteed, or otherwise secured by the credit of the Federal Government, or

(iv) provided by the development or the redevelopment of real property purchased, leased, or otherwise obtained from a State or local public agency receiving Federal financial assistance for slum clearance or urban renewal with respect to such real property under a loan or grant contract hereafter entered into; and

(b) in the lending practices with respect to residential property and related facilities (including land to be developed for residential use) of lending institutions, insofar as such practices relate to loans hereafter insured or guaranteed by the Federal Government.

SEC. 102. I hereby direct the Housing and Home Finance Agency and all other executive departments and agencies to use their good offices and to take other appropriate action permitted by law, including the institution of appropriate litigation, if required, to promote the abandonment of discriminatory practices with respect to residential property and related facilities heretofore provided with Federal financial assistance of the types referred to in Section 101 (a) (ii), (iii), and (iv).

PART II—IMPLEMENTATION BY DEPARTMENTS AND AGENCIES

SEC. 201. Each executive department and agency subject to this order is directed to submit to the President's Committee on Equal Opportunity in Housing established pursuant to Part IV of this order (hereinafter sometimes referred to as the Committee), within thirty days from the date of this order, a report outlining all current programs administered by it which are affected by this order.

SEC. 202. Each such department and agency shall be primarily responsible for obtaining compliance with the purposes of this order as the order applies to programs administered by it; and is directed to cooperate with the Committee, to furnish it, in accordance with law, such information and assistance as it may request in the performance of its functions, and to report to it at such intervals as the Committee may require.

SEC. 203. Each such department and agency shall, within thirty days from the date of this order, issue such rules and regulations, adopt such procedures and policies, and make such exemptions and exceptions as may be consistent with law and necessary or appropriate to effectuate [put into effect] the purposes of this order. Each such department and agency shall consult with the Committee in order to achieve such consistency and uniformity as may be feasible.

PART III—ENFORCEMENT

SEC. 302. If any executive department or agency subject to this order concludes that any person or firm (including but not limited to any individual, partnership, association, trust, or corporation) or any State or local public agency has violated any rule, regulation, or procedure issued or adopted pursuant to this order, or any nondiscrimination provision included in any agreement or contract pursuant to any such rule, regulation, or procedure, it shall endeavor to end and remedy such violation by informal means, including conference, conciliation, and persuasion unless similar efforts made by another Federal department or agency have been unsuccessful. In conformity with rules, regulations, procedures, or policies issued or adopted by it pursuant to Section 203 hereof, a department or agency may take such action as may be appropriate under its governing laws, including, but not limited to, the following: It may—

(a) cancel or terminate in whole or in part any agreement or contract with such person, firm, or State or local public agency providing for a loan, grant, contribution, or other Federal aid, or for the payment of a commission or fee;

(b) refrain from extending any further aid under any program administered by it and affected by this order until it is satisfied that the affected person, firm, or State or local public agency will comply with the rules, regulations, and procedures issued or adopted pursuant to this order, and any nondiscrimination provisions included in any agreement or contract;

(c) refuse to approve a lending institution or any other lender as a beneficiary under any program administered by it which is affected by this order or revoke such approval if previously given.

SEC. 303. In appropriate cases executive departments and agencies shall refer to the Attorney General violations of any rules, regulations, or procedures issued or adopted pursuant to this order, or violations of any nondiscrimination provisions included in any agreement or contract, for such civil or criminal action as he may deem appropriate. The Attorney General is authorized to furnish legal advice concerning this order to the Committee and to any department or agency requesting such advice. . . .

PART IV—ESTABLISHMENT OF THE PRESIDENT'S COMMITTEE ON EQUAL OPPORTUNITY IN HOUSING

SEC. 401. There is hereby established the President's Committee on Equal Opportunity in Housing which shall be composed of the Secretary of the Treasury; the Secretary of Defense; the Attorney General; the Secretary of Agriculture; the Housing and Home Finance Administrator; the Administrator of Veterans Affairs; the Chairman of the Federal Home Loan Bank Board; a member of the staff of the Executive Office of the President to be assigned to the Committee by direction of the President, and such other members as the President shall from time to time appoint from the public. The member assigned by the President from the staff of the Executive Office shall serve as the Chairman and Executive Director of the Committee. Each department or agency head may designate an alternate to represent him in his absence. . . .

PART V—POWERS AND DUTIES OF THE PRESIDENT'S COMMITTEE ON EQUAL OPPORTUNITY IN HOUSING

SEC. 501. The Committee shall meet upon the call of the Chairman and at such other times as may be provided by its rules. It shall: (a) adopt rules to govern its deliberations and activities; (b) recommend general policies and procedures to implement this order; (c) consider reports as to progress under this order; (d) consider any matters which may be presented to it by any of its members; and (e) make such reports to the President as he may require or the Committee shall deem appropriate. A report to the President shall be made at least once annually and shall include references to the actions taken and results achieved by departments and agencies subject to this order. The Committee may provide for the establishment of subcommittees whose members shall be appointed by the Chairman.

SEC. 502. (a) The Committee shall take such steps as it deems necessary and appropriate to promote the coordination of the activities of departments and agencies under this order. In so doing, the Committee shall consider the overall objectives of Federal legislation relating to housing and the right of every individual to participate without discrimination because of race, color, creed, or national origin in the ultimate benefits of the Federal programs subject to this order.

(b) The Committee may confer with representatives of any department or agency, State or local public agency, civic, industry, or labor group, or any other group directly or indirectly affected by this order; examine the relevant rules, regulations, procedures, policies, and practices of any department or agency subject to this order and make such recommendations as may be necessary or desirable to achieve the purposes of this order.

(c) The Committee shall encourage educational programs by civic, educational, religious, industry, labor, and other nongovernmental groups to eliminate the basic causes of discrimination in housing and related facilities provided with Federal assistance.

SEC. 503. The Committee shall have an executive committee consisting of the Committee's Chairman and two other members designated by him from among the public members. The Chairman of the Committee shall also serve as Chairman of the Executive Committee. Between meetings of the Committee, the Executive Committee shall be primarily responsible for carrying out the functions of the Committee and may act for the Committee to the extent authorized by it. . . .

JOHN F. KENNEDY
THE WHITE HOUSE,
November 20, 1962.

NOTES

1. See Carl M. Brauer, *John F. Kennedy and the Second Reconstruction* (New York: Columbia University Press, 1977), p. 52.

2. Ibid., p. 85.

3. For example, see Hugh Davis Graham, *Civil Rights and the Presidency* (New York: Oxford University Press, 1992), p. 35.

4. For a fuller discussion of these deliberations, see Brauer, *John F. Kennedy,* pp. 206–7.

5. Ibid., pp. 207–8.

6. Ibid., p. 209.

7. Ibid., p. 209.

8. Ibid.

9. Ibid., p. 210.

10. *Federal Register* (Washington, D.C.: GPO), vol. 27, pp. 11527–30.

32

Twenty-Fourth Amendment to the United States Constitution

1964

The Twenty-Fourth Amendment to the United States Constitution prohibits levying a poll tax in any federal election.

HISTORICAL CONTEXT

Given that blacks were disproportionately poor, the poll tax had been used in the South since the 1890s as a very thinly veiled device to prevent them from voting.[1] In some situations, poor whites escaped when those unable to pay the poll tax had it paid for them or were administered the far more subjective literacy test. In Louisiana, for instance, the combination of poll taxes and literacy tests helped drive down the number of registered blacks from 130,334 in 1896 to 1,342 eight years later.[2]

For decades, civil rights leaders pressured Congress to ban the poll tax. Nevertheless, even though Congress had taken up legislation to eliminate the tax in every Congress since 1939, a statutory ban could not get past Southern-led filibusters in the Senate. The standard argument remained. The federal government was regarded by opponents as lacking the constitutional authority to dictate state voting qualifications.

In 1960 a constitutional amendment to eliminate the poll tax in all federal elections was introduced by Senator Spessard Holland, a conservative Republican from Florida. It gathered momentum in large part because, as a carefully limited constitutional amendment, it did not open the constitutional door to even more federal regulation of state election practices.[3] The amendment passed the Sen-

ate by a vote of 72–16 in 1960, more than enough votes to overcome
any possible filibuster. It was then put on hold, however, while Congress focused on extending presidential voting rights to the residents of Washington, D.C., which was accomplished with the
Twenty-Third Amendment.

When the poll tax amendment was taken up again in 1962, President John F. Kennedy's Justice Department and Emanuel Celler
(Dem., N.Y.), chairman of the House Judiciary Committee, both
endorsed the constitutional route as much more promising than
attaining anti–poll tax legislation. Thus, when Senator Jacob Javits
(Rep., N.Y.) attempted to reintroduce a statutory ban on the poll
tax, that amendment was tabled on a motion from Senate Majority
Leader Mike Mansfield (Dem., Mont.).[4]

The constitutional amendment to ban the poll tax in federal elections then passed both houses of Congress. By 1964, a mere two
years later, it had been ratified by the necessary three-fourths of
the state legislatures. Thus, the Twenty-Fourth Amendment was
added to the Constitution of the United States. It barred "any poll
tax or other tax" from precluding a person from voting in a primary
or general election for federal office.

Nevertheless, it should be noted that at the time of passage, only
Alabama, Arkansas, Mississippi, Virginia, and Texas still levied a poll
tax in federal elections. In addition, even in states that had eliminated the poll tax on their own volition, blacks were still effectively
precluded from voting by a combination of literacy tests and sheer
intimidation.[5] In the end, then, this constitutional amendment
would do little to facilitate black voter registration in those situations. If it had been a statutory law banning poll taxes, and if the
United States Supreme Court had found the federal government
to have the constitutional authority to regulate state voter qualifications in such a manner, it might have established precedent that
would allow additional federal regulation of other discriminatory
state election practices.

In 1966 the United States Supreme Court did rule that requiring
poll taxes in state elections violated the equal protection clause of
the Fourteenth Amendment to the United States Constitution. The
Court declared, "[T]he opportunity for equal participation by all
voters in the election of state legislators is required . . . [and] [w]e
decline to qualify that principle by sustaining this poll tax."[6] By that
time, however, only Alabama, Mississippi, Virginia, and Texas continued to employ the poll tax in their state elections, and the poll

tax was no longer considered a primary impediment to black voting.[7]

THE LAW

The Twenty-Fourth Amendment specifically prohibits the denial of any U.S. citizen's right to vote in federal elections based on the person's failure to pay a poll tax or any other taxes.

32. Twenty-Fourth Amendment

Section 1. The right of citizens of the United States to vote in any primary or other election for President or Vice President, for electors for President or Vice President, or for Senator or Representative in Congress, shall not be denied or abridged by the United States or any State by reason of failure to pay any poll tax or other tax.

Section 2. The Congress shall have power to enforce this article by appropriate legislation.

NOTES

1. For a chronology, see David Goldfield et al., *The American Journey* (Upper Saddle River, N.J.: Prentice-Hall, 1998), pp. 582–83.

2. See C. Vann Woodward, *The Strange Career of Jim Crow* (New York: Oxford University Press, 1966), p. 85.

3. For example, see Carl M. Brauer, *John F. Kennedy and the Second Reconstruction* (New York: Columbia University Press, 1977), pp. 131–32.

4. Ibid., p. 132.

5. See Woodward, *The Strange Career of Jim Crow*, p. 141.

6. *Harper v. Virginia Board of Elections*, 383 U.S. 663 (1966).

7. For example, see Hugh Davis Graham, *Civil Rights and the Presidency* (New York: Oxford University Press, 1992), p. 97.

33

Civil Rights Act

1964

The Civil Rights Act of 1964 directly involved the federal government in the enforcement of an extensive list of civil rights—in both the public and private sector—including voting, public accommodations, public facilities, federally assisted programs, education, and employment.

HISTORICAL CONTEXT

Before the passage of the Civil Rights Act of 1964, several forms of racial segregation remained legal in the United States. Proprietors could and did have white-only lunch counters, and employers could and did post jobs with the notice, "No coloreds need apply." In addition, only a small percentage of Southern blacks were allowed to vote.[1]

The Civil Rights Act of 1964 came into being in the midst of the most extensive, most intense racial unrest in the history of the United States. As rioting spread across many of the nation's large cities, violence was escalating in the South in response to a mounting civil rights movement led by Martin Luther King, Jr. Police brutality in Birmingham, Alabama, where protesting men, women, and children were beaten, was televised to a national audience. Four young, black girls were killed when their Birmingham church was bombed.

President John F. Kennedy, like President Dwight D. Eisenhower before him, was concerned about this expanding unrest. Kennedy responded by addressing a national television audience on June 11, 1963, as he attempted to stir support for his legislative package. He asserted that the extension of equal rights was "as old as the scriptures and . . . as clear as the American Constitution" and it was necessary "if we are to move this problem from the streets to the courts."[2]

Eight days later, Kennedy proposed a major new civil rights law. It was designed to reduce segregation and discrimination in both public accommodations and schools, help mediate local racial disputes, withdraw federal funds from agencies that practiced discrimination, and accelerate the resolution of voter registration challenges. As Kennedy had put it months earlier, "[T]he harmful, wasteful and wrongful results of racial discrimination and segregation still appear in virtually every aspect of national life. . . . The continuing attack on this problem must be equally broad."[3]

Kennedy submitted his bill to Congress in June 1963 as what he called the "fires of frustration and discord" were sweeping the nation.[4] He then made speeches in support of the law, lobbied key congresspersons, and sent his cabinet members up to Capitol Hill to testify on its behalf. Organizations such as the NAACP, the AFL-CIO, the National Council of Churches, and the American Jewish Congress tirelessly lobbied Congress as well. Amidst all this, Martin Luther King, Jr., led the August 28 March on Washington, highlighted by his famous "I Have a Dream" speech.

Yet, it would not be until after Kennedy's assassination in November 1963 that the legislation would gain momentum. Just five days after Kennedy's death, President Lyndon B. Johnson told Congress, "No memorial oration or eulogy could more eloquently honor President Kennedy's memory than the earliest possible passage of the civil rights bill for which he fought so long." Then, in his first State of the Union address, Johnson implored Congress, "Let this session of Congress be known as the session which did more for civil rights than the last hundred sessions combined."[5] Johnson's skillful legislative leadership proved crucial to the legislation's success.

Emanuel Celler (Dem., N.Y.) was chair of the House Judiciary Committee. He received the bill from the House speaker and referred it to subcommittee. Public hearings proceeded for months. Ultimately, an even stronger bill emerged out of subcommittee, and it was passed by the full Judiciary Committee.

The legislation faced far more of an uphill battle in the Senate. Mississippi Democrat James O. Eastland, chair of the Senate Judiciary Committee, did all he could to scuttle it. Only one witness was heard over an eleven-day period, and then the bill was tabled. It was quite clear to proponents that it would be extremely difficult to dislodge the civil rights bill from Eastland's committee.

Hubert Humphrey (Dem., Minn.), the majority whip, and Minority Whip Thomas Kuchel (Rep., Calif.) pressed the case in the Senate. Humphrey, for example, cited statistics demonstrating the economically subordinate position of African Americans. One-fifth of all black females went into domestic service for example, while a black man with a college degree earned less than a white high school dropout. Opponents of the civil rights bill, on the other hand, continued to warn about the risk of a runaway national government encroaching on state, local, and individual prerogatives.

A major debate arose, which split support for the legislation, about whether explicitly to include gender discrimination as well. Organized labor, for instance, attempted to protect women with provisions that would allow women to be required to work fewer hours, do less heavy lifting, and receive maternity leave. Black men were worried about job competition from these women.[6]

Meanwhile, back in the House of Representatives, problems were building as well. Howard Smith (Dem., Va.), chair of the House Rules Committee, refused even to call the committee together. With no rules to govern floor debate, the bill could not go to the House floor where passage actually appeared likely. At that critical juncture, however, John Kennedy was assassinated, and Lyndon Johnson assumed the office of president. Johnson, a former Senate majority leader and a very skillful legislator, moved quickly to dislodge the bill from the House Rules Committee. He organized enough support to allow a parliamentary maneuver to be used that could force the rules consideration out of the Rules Committee to the House floor. Smith finally conceded the inevitable, and the House soon had its rules for the debate of this legislation.

More than eight months after its introduction, the civil rights bill finally reached the House floor. It had undergone eighty-three days of hearings in six separate committees, with 280 witnesses producing more than 6,000 pages of printed testimony. On the House floor, under relatively loose rules, 122 amendments were offered, and nine full days of debate ensued. On February 10, 1964, the marginally amended bill was finally passed by a vote of 290–130.

On the Senate side, there had been no movement in the Judiciary Committee. Consequently, Majority Leader Mike Mansfield

(Dem., Mont.) took a calculated gamble. He circumvented Senator Eastland and took the House-passed bill directly to the Senate floor. The seldom-used parliamentary maneuver was successful, allowing the bill to be debated by the full Senate.[7]

The next obstruction was a Senate filibuster.[8] Southern senators, led by Richard Russell (Dem., Ga.), began to exercise their procedural right to conduct unlimited debate, as Russell put it, to head off "the greatest tragedy ever played out in the Senate."[9] The ensuing filibuster lasted more than eighty days, the longest in Senate history. It added more than 10 million words and 7,000 pages of testimony to the *Congressional Record.*

Needing sixty-seven votes to invoke cloture[10] and end the debate, proponents reached compromises with undecided senators, narrowing the bill's scope and modifying its enforcement components. There were two primary changes. The first required the new Equal Employment Opportunity Commission (EEOC) to seek remedy first through state and local channels; if anyone was to be prosecuted, it was to be done through the attorney general's office. Second, any "affirmative action" was to require evidence of discriminatory intent and not to involve racial quotas or preferential treatment in the resolution.

Cloture was finally imposed on June 10. The vote was 71–29. This marked the first time cloture had been successfully employed to halt a civil rights filibuster since rules allowing limits on debate were passed in 1917. In fact, cloture had been employed only five times over the course of more than fifty years. As Minority Leader Everett Dirksen (Rep., Ill.) put it, "This is an idea whose time has come. It will not be stayed. It will not be denied."[11]

Despite ninety-nine separate attempts at making amendments, only two of which were accepted, the bill came to a final vote on the Senate floor, where it passed 73–27. Because the bill differed from the original House version, however, more delay loomed. Yet, prodded by the all-out lobbying effort of President Johnson, there was enough support in the House to avoid a conference committee and take the matter directly to the House floor. This time the previously defeated chair of the Rules Committee proved more cooperative, and there was a full House vote within a month. Slightly more than a year after it had first been introduced, the civil rights bill, as amended by the Senate, passed the House by a vote of 289–126.[12]

According to historians John Hope Franklin and Alfred Moss,

"The Civil Rights Act of 1964 was the most far-reaching and comprehensive law in support of racial equality ever enacted by Congress."[13] Among its many significant provisions, the bill mandated the desegregation of public schools and set forth provisions for equal employment. Federal aid was to be withheld from state and local governments that discriminated on the basis of "race, color, religion, sex, or national origin." It also prompted the state and federal governments to take "affirmative" steps to address the legacies of past discrimination, and it threatened to withhold federal funds from any schools that continued to segregate by race. It created the EEOC, extended and broadened the role of the Civil Rights Commission, and established a Community Relations Services division in the Commerce Department to mediate local race-related disputes.

The Civil Rights Act also modified the "state" versus "private" distinction, ending racial segregation in public accommodations such as hotels, motels, and restaurants, as well as barring racial discrimination in private-sector employment. This time, however, Congress did not claim authority based on the enforcement clause of the Fourteenth Amendment. The United States Supreme Court had already rejected that approach when it was tried in the Civil Rights Act of 1875. The Fourteenth Amendment was interpreted to restrict only "state action."[14] Instead, Congress grounded the 1964 act in its authority to regulate interstate commerce. Set out in Article 1, Section 8 of the United States Constitution, this provision allows Congress to regulate private companies whose business involves trade with individuals or companies from other states.

As for suffrage, the act required stricter record keeping than was mandated by the Civil Rights Act of 1960, authorized the Commerce Department to compile registration and voting statistics in areas suggested by the Civil Rights Commission, prohibited disenfranchisement owing to minor errors, tightened limitations on literacy tests, and provided a process whereby either the prospective registrant or the attorney general could appeal voter application denials to an independent three-person federal panel.

The bill, signed into law by President Johnson on July 2, 1964, turned out to be even more comprehensive than the one initially proposed by President Kennedy, particularly in the area of employment discrimination. This followed the longest single debate in congressional history, and it was essentially the first major piece of civil rights legislation passed since 1875. Yet, this was not done without cost. As he signed the legislation, Johnson was quoted by aides as saying that the Democratic Party had "just lost the South for a generation."[15]

When tested in the United States Supreme Court, the Court unanimously upheld the constitutionality of key components of the law within five months of passage. Where earlier Courts had rejected federal regulation of private-sector discrimination, for instance, the now more liberal Supreme Court under Chief Justice Earl Warren accepted it within the context of regulation of interstate commerce, which the constitution does not explicitly limit to the public sector.[16]

In a decision concerning resistance by the Heart of Atlanta Motel, for example, the Court ruled that travelers were part of interstate commerce. Therefore, the hotel's refusal to accommodate them amounted to interference with interstate commerce.[17] In an even broader reading of that language, the Court ruled that Birmingham's Ollie's Barbecue would have to serve African Americans as well because a sizable portion of the food served had come from outside the state of Alabama.[18]

Although temporarily overturned by a Court ruling eighteen years later, a 1971 Supreme Court decision created the doctrine of "disparate impact" evidence, allowing discrimination to be demonstrated by numerical imbalances without a clear showing of intent.[19] This essentially gave members of select minority groups a protected legal status, providing a right to sue even without being able to demonstrate discriminatory acts against them personally. This prompted many employers to strive for a race- and gender-balanced workforce out of fear that they might be found to be discriminating if their workforces were too homogenous.

As for affirmative action, the Court upheld the use of race as a school admission criterion. It could be used if there was evidence of past discrimination or a clearly outlined state benefit. If it was used, however, it was only to be one of several factors considered and it was to be applied flexibly.[20]

Overall, however, implementation of the act's eleven broad provisions has been slow and arduous. Short of sending legions of federal observers and law enforcement officials, the implementation of the Civil Rights Act of 1964 was left primarily to state and local administrators, leaving in place an often very cumbersome and resistant process. Literacy tests continued to be unfairly administered, and nothing in the law protected the well-being of the volunteer civil rights workers flowing into the South.[21] Thousands of federal lawsuits continued to be brought each year concerning employment discrimination, and considerable empirical evidence of such discrimination remains.[22] In addition, the United States Supreme Court further narrowed the act's reach in the areas of employment discrimination and affirmative action.[23]

Congress, on the other hand, has acted on occasion to strengthen the law. The Equal Employment Opportunity Act of 1972, for example, amended Title VII to give the EEOC independent commission status. It also granted the EEOC enforcement power to bring federal lawsuits against "patterns or practices" of discrimination by private-sector employees and unions, rather than simply recommending such action to the attorney general of the United States. Lawsuits brought against state and local governments, however, would still have to be brought by the attorney general. Meanwhile, the EEOC saw its staff increase from 359 in 1968 to 1,640 four years later. Over that same time period, its budget increased from $13.2 million to $29.5 million.[24]

Specifically in terms of race, the Civil Rights Restoration Act of 1988 clarified Title VI by allowing federal assistance to be denied to entire institutions if any part of those institutions practiced discrimination.

An amendment was passed in 1991 specifically to correct several Supreme Court interpretations of the 1964 act.[25] In particular, it required employers to justify their job performance criteria if there was clear statistical evidence of job discrimination. It allowed for jury trials and monetary relief provisions, including unlimited back pay, punitive damages, and attorney and expert fees in lawsuits demonstrating discrimination in hirings, promotions, dismissals, or any other terms of employment. In addition, the amendment prohibited litigants from reopening previously settled cases if the litigant had a "reasonable opportunity" to participate in the original case.

By way of compromise, the 1991 act created and specified limits on monetary recovery for "pain and suffering." It explicitly prohibited "race norming," whereby a company uses different standards for different races. It also explicitly outlawed the use of racial "quotas." In addition, it encouraged the use of alternative dispute resolution before litigation.[26] The law is loosely written, inviting lawsuits to determine its exact reach,[27] and it has generally been read narrowly by the United States Supreme Court.[28]

Despite its many impediments, the Civil Rights Act of 1964 has had several significant results. The mere possibility of a jury trial, for example, has caused many companies to alter their business practices and to settle cases rather than risk a larger jury settlement. Denny's Restaurant chain, for example, changed company policies and paid a $45 million settlement to plaintiffs in Maryland and California when evidence revealed a pattern of discriminatory service at several of its restaurants.[29] Black women, with the help of Title VII, have virtually closed the wage gap with white women in the North.[30] In addition, the law has significantly helped guarantee equal treatment in public transportation and hotel accommodations.

THE LAW

The comprehensive Civil Rights Act[31] of 1964 addressed a myriad of civil rights issues including voting, public accommodations, public facilities, federally assisted programs, education, and employment. It directly placed enforcement authority within the responsibility of the Civil Rights Commission and created both the Equal Employment Opportunity Commission and the Community Relations Service to further enforce its provisions.

In regard to voting rights, Title I amends existing voting rights laws. It specifically declares that voting standards must be applied in a like manner to all citizens. The act provides that literacy tests could be employed as long as they were administered in writing, and a copy of the results was given to the individual tested. In addition, the act sets forth that a sixth-grade education, in which instruction was conducted primarily in English, created a presumption of literacy.

The issue of civil rights in public accommodations is addressed in Title II. This section of the act prohibits discrimination and segregation on the basis of race, color, religion, or national origin in public accommodations. The act sets forth an inclusive definition of public accommodations engaged in interstate commerce. Among other establishments, this includes hotels, restaurants, gas stations, theaters, and stadiums. It exempts "private clubs" but does not define that term. Both civil and criminal legal actions are provided as means to enforce the requirements of nondiscrimination in public accommodations.

Title III directs the attorney general to intervene upon receiving a complaint that an individual's right to use a public facility was being denied based on race, color, religion, or national origin. The title specifically authorizes the attorney general to bring a civil lawsuit against the alleged offender.

Title IV requires monitoring of educational equality, with the commissioner of education to report to the president any "lack of availability of equal educational opportunities for individuals by race, color, religion, or national origin in public educational institutions at all levels in the United States." It also authorizes commissioners to offer technical assistance regarding desegregation, to create training institutes to help with the transition to desegregation, and to offer grants to assist with the costs of desegregation. The act authorizes the attorney general to sue communities failing to enforce the desegregation laws themselves. Significantly, the act defines desegregation as "assignment of students to public schools . . . without regard to their race, color, religion, or national origin," but it does not require transportation of students from one school to another to achieve racial balance.

Title V restructures and makes permanent the Civil Rights Commission created in the 1957 Civil Rights Act. This title also sets forth the duties of the commission. The commission is directed to investigate allegations of individuals being denied equal protection or the right to vote.

Title VI declares that no person can be discriminated against in federally assisted programs. It gives each federal agency and department authority to ensure nondiscrimination in these programs.

Title VII prohibits discrimination in employment based on an individual's race, color, religion, or national origin. This title does not require an employer to grant preferential treatment to any individual based on his or her membership in a protected group. The Equal Employment Opportunity Commission (EEOC) was established to ensure compliance with the act. The EEOC was to do this by investigating charges of discrimination. Upon substantiating claims of discrimination, the EEOC was directed to attempt to eliminate the unlawful employment practices in a cooperative manner with the employer. The title authorizes the attorney general to sue if he or she were to find a "pattern or practice" of systematic discrimination. Finally, the title mandates that employers post notices regarding requirements of the law and information pertinent to filing a complaint for violation of the law.

33. Civil Rights Act of 1964

Be it enacted . . . That this Act may be cited as the "Civil Rights Act of 1964".

TITLE I—VOTING RIGHTS

SEC. 101. Section 2004 of the Revised Statutes (42 U.S.C. 1971), as amended by section 131 of the Civil Rights Act of 1957 . . . and as further amended by section 601 of the Civil Rights Act of 1960, . . . is further amended as follows. . . .

(2) No person acting under color of law shall

(A) in determining whether any individual is qualified under State law or laws to vote in any Federal election, apply any standard, practice, or procedure different from the standards, practices, or procedures applied under such law or laws to other individuals within the same county, parish, or similar political subdivision who have been found by State officials to be qualified to vote;

(B) deny the right of any individual to vote in any Federal election because of an error or omission on any record or paper relating to any application, registration, or other act requisite to voting, if such error or omission is not material in determining whether such individual is qualified under State law to vote in such election; or

(C) employ any literacy test as a qualification for voting in any Federal election unless (i) such test is administered to each individual and is conducted wholly in writing, and (ii) a certified copy of the test and of the answers given by the individual is furnished to him within twenty-five days of the submission of his request made within the period of time during which records and papers are required to be retained and preserved pursuant to title III of the Civil Rights Act of 1960. . . .

(3) For purposes of this subsection

(A) the term 'vote' shall have the same meaning as in subsection (e) of this section;

(B) the phrase 'literacy test' includes any test of the ability to read, write, understand, or interpret any matter."

(b) Insert immediately following the period at the end of the first sentence of subsection (c) the following new sentence: "If in any such proceeding literacy is a relevant fact there shall be a rebuttable presumption that any person who has not been adjudged an incompetent and who has completed the sixth grade in a public school in, or a private school accredited by, any State or territory, the District of Columbia, or the Commonwealth of Puerto Rico where instruction is carried on predominantly in the English language, possesses sufficient literacy, comprehension, and intelligence to vote in any Federal election." [For purposes of determining literacy, it is presumed that any person who has completed the sixth grade is literate. This presumption is subject to legal challenge, however.] . . . .

TITLE II—INJUNCTIVE RELIEF AGAINST DISCRIMINATION IN PLACES OF PUBLIC ACCOMMODATION

SEC. 201. (a) All persons shall be entitled to the full and equal enjoyment of the goods, services, facilities, privileges, advantages, and accommodations of any place of public accommodation, as defined in this section, without discrimination or segregation on the ground of race, color, religion, or national origin.

(b) Each of the following establishments which serves the public is a place of public accommodation within the meaning of this title if its operations affect commerce, or if discrimination or segregation by it is supported by State action:

(1) any inn, hotel, motel, or other establishment which provides lodging to transient guests, other than an establishment located within a building which contains not more than five rooms for rent or hire and which is actually occupied by the proprietor of such establishment as his residence;

(2) any restaurant, cafeteria, lunchroom, lunch counter, soda fountain, or other facility principally engaged in selling food for consumption on the premises, including, but not limited to, any such facility located on the premises of any retail establishment; or any gasoline station;

(3) any motion picture house, theater, concert hall, sports arena, stadium or other place of exhibition or entertainment; and

(4) any establishment (A) (i) which is physically located within the premises of any establishment otherwise covered by this subsection, or (ii) within the premises of which is physically located any such covered establishment, and (B) which holds itself out as serving patrons of such covered establishment. . . .

(e) The provisions of this title shall not apply to a private club or other establishment not in fact open to the public, except to the extent that the facilities of such establishment are made available to the customers or patrons of an establishment within the scope of subsection (b).

SEC. 202. All persons shall be entitled to be free, at any establishment or place, from discrimination or segregation of any kind on the ground of race, color, religion, or national origin, if such discrimination or segregation is or purports to be required by any law, statute, ordinance, regulation, rule, or order of a State or any agency or political subdivision thereof.

SEC. 203. No person shall (a) withhold, deny, or attempt to withhold or deny, or deprive or attempt to deprive, any person of any right or privilege secured by section 201 or 202, or (b) intimidate, threaten, or coerce, or attempt to intimidate, threaten, or coerce any person with the purpose of interfering with any right or privilege secured by section 201 or 202, or (c) punish or attempt to punish any person for exercising or attempting to exercise any right or privilege secured by section 201 or 202.

SEC. 204. (a) Whenever any person has engaged or there are reasonable grounds to believe that any person is about to engage in any act or practice prohibited by section 203, a civil action for preventive relief, including an application for a permanent or temporary injunction, restraining order, or other order, may be instituted by the person aggrieved and, upon timely application, the court may, in its discretion, permit the Attorney General to intervene in such civil action if he certifies that the case is of general public importance. Upon application by the complainant and in such circumstances as the court may deem just, the court may appoint an attorney for such complainant and may authorize the commencement of the civil action without the payment of fees, costs, or security. . . .

(c) In the case of an alleged act or practice prohibited by this title which occurs in a State, or political subdivision of a State, which has a State or local law prohibiting such act or practice and establishing or authorizing a State or local authority to grant or seek relief from such practice or to institute criminal proceedings with respect thereto upon receiving notice thereof, no civil action may be brought under subsection (a) before the expiration of thirty days after written notice of such alleged act or practice has been given to the appropriate State or local authority by registered mail or in person, provided that the court may stay proceedings in such civil action pending the termination of State or local enforcement proceedings.

(d) In the case of an alleged act or practice prohibited by this title which occurs in a State, or political subdivision of a State, which has no State or local law prohibiting such act or practice, a civil action may be brought under subsection (a): Provided, That the court may refer the matter to the Community Relations Service established by title X of this Act for as long as the court believes there is a reasonable possibility of obtaining voluntary compliance, but for not more than sixty days: Provided further. That upon expiration of such sixty-day period, the court may extend such period for an additional period, not to exceed a cumulative total of one hundred and twenty days, if it believes there then exists a reasonable possibility of securing voluntary compliance. . . .

SEC. 206. (a) Whenever the Attorney General has reasonable cause to believe that any person or group of persons is engaged in a pattern or practice of resistance to the full enjoyment of any of the rights secured by this title, and that the pattern or practice is of such a nature and is intended to deny the full exercise of the rights herein described, the Attorney General may bring a civil action in the appropriate district court of the United States by filing with it a complaint (1) signed by him (or in his absence the Acting Attorney General), (2) setting forth facts pertaining to such pattern or practice, and (3) requesting such preventive relief, including an application for a permanent or temporary injunction, restraining order or other order against the person or persons responsible for such pattern or practice, as he deems necessary to insure the full enjoyment of the rights herein described. . . .

TITLE III—DESEGREGATION OF PUBLIC FACILITIES

SEC. 301. (a) Whenever the Attorney General receives a complaint in writing signed by an individual to the effect that he is being deprived of or threatened with the loss of his right to the equal protection of the laws, on account of his race, color, religion, or national origin, by being denied equal utilization of any public facility which is owned, operated, or managed by or on behalf of any State or subdivision thereof, other than a public school or public college as defined in section 401 of title IV hereof and the Attorney General believes the complaint is meritorious and certifies that the signer or signers of such complaint are unable, in his judgment, to initiate and maintain appropriate legal proceedings for relief and that the institution of an action will materially further the orderly progress of desegregation in public facilities, the Attorney General is authorized to institute for or in the name of the United States a civil action in any appropriate district court of the United States against such parties and for such relief as may be appropriate, and such court shall have and shall exercise jurisdiction of proceedings instituted pursuant to this section. [The attorney general is directed to bring legal action to enforce individuals' rights to use public facilities.]. . . .

TITLE IV—DESEGREGATION OF PUBLIC EDUCATION DEFINITIONS

SEC. 401. As used in this title—

(a) "Commissioner" means the Commissioner of Education.

(b) "Desegregation" means the assignment of students to public schools and within such schools without regard to their race, color, religion, or national origin, but "desegregation" shall not mean the assignment of students to public schools in order to overcome racial imbalance.

(c) "Public school" means any elementary or secondary educational institution, and "public college" means any institution of higher education or any technical or vocational school above the secondary school level, provided that such public school or public college is operated by a State, subdivision of a State, or governmental agency within a State, or operated wholly or predominantly from or through the use of governmental funds or property, or funds or property derived from a governmental source.

(d) "School board" means any agency or agencies which administer a system of one or more public schools and any other agency which is responsible for the assignment of students to or within such system.

Survey and Report of Educational Opportunities

SEC. 402. The Commissioner shall conduct a survey and make a report to the President and the Congress, within two years of the enactment of this title, concerning the lack of availability of equal educational opportunities for individuals by reason of race, color, religion, or national origin in public educational institutions at all levels in the United States, its territories and possessions, and the District of Columbia.

Technical Assistance

SEC. 403. The Commissioner is authorized, upon the application of any school board, State, municipality, school district, or other governmental unit legally responsible for operating a public school or schools, to render technical assistance to such applicant in the preparation, adoption, and implementation of plans for the desegregation of public schools. Such technical assistance may, among other activities, include making available to such agencies information regarding effective methods of coping with special educational problems occasioned by desegregation, and making available to such agencies personnel of the Office of Education or other persons specially equipped to advise and assist them in coping with such problems.

Training Institutes

SEC. 404. The Commissioner is authorized to arrange, through grants or contracts, with institutions of higher education for the operation of short-term or regular session institutes for special training designed to improve the ability of teachers, supervisors, counselors, and other elementary or secondary school personnel to deal effectively with special educational problems occasioned by desegregation. Individuals who attend such an institute on a full-time basis may be paid stipends for the period of their attendance at such institute in amounts specified by the Commissioner in regulations, including allowances for travel to attend such institute.

Grants

SEC. 405. (a) The Commissioner is authorized, upon application of a school board, to make grants to such board to pay, in whole or in part, the cost of—

(1) giving to teachers and other school personnel inservice training in dealing with problems incident to desegregation, and

(2) employing specialists to advise in problems incident to desegregation. . . .

Suits by the Attorney General

SEC. 407. (a) Whenever the Attorney General receives a complaint in writing

(1) signed by a parent or group of parents to the effect that his or their minor children, as members of a class of persons similarly situated, are being deprived by a school board of the equal protection of the laws, or

(2) signed by an individual, or his parent, to the effect that he has been denied admission to or not permitted to continue in attendance at a public college by reason of race, color, religion, or national origin, and the Attorney General believes the complaint is meritorious and certifies that the signer or signers of such complaint are unable, in his judgment, to initiate and maintain appropriate legal proceedings for relief and that the institution of an action will materially further the orderly achievement of desegregation in public education, the Attorney General is authorized, after giving notice of such complaint to the appropriate school board or college authority and after certifying that he is satisfied that such board or authority has had a reasonable time to adjust the conditions alleged in such complaint, to institute for or in the name of the United States a civil action in any appropriate district court of the United States against such parties and for such relief as may be appropriate, and such court shall have and shall exercise jurisdiction of proceedings instituted pursuant to this section, provided that nothing herein shall empower any official or court of the United States to issue any order seeking to achieve a racial balance in any school by requiring the transportation of pupils or students from one school to another or one school district to another in order to

achieve such racial balance, or otherwise enlarge the existing power of the court to insure compliance with constitutional standards. . . .

TITLE V—COMMISSION ON CIVIL RIGHTS

Rules of Procedure of the Commission Hearings

SEC. 504. (a) Section 104 (a) of the Civil Rights Act of 1957 (42 U.S.C. 1975c (a); 71 Stat. 635), as amended, is further amended to read as follows:

Duties of the Commission

SEC. 104. (a) The Commission shall—

(1) investigate allegations in writing under oath or affirmation that certain citizens of the United States are being deprived of their right to vote and have that vote counted by reason of their color, race, religion, or national origin; which writing, under oath or affirmation, shall set forth the facts upon which such belief or beliefs are based;

(2) study and collect information concerning legal developments constituting a denial of equal protection of the laws under the Constitution because of race, color, religion or national origin or in the administration of justice;

(3) appraise the laws and policies of the Federal Government with respect to denials of equal protection of the laws under the Constitution because of race, color, religion or national origin or in the administration of justice;

(4) serve as a national clearinghouse for information in respect to denials of equal protection of the laws because of race, color, religion or national origin, including but not limited to the fields of voting, education, housing, employment, the use of public facilities, and transportation, or in the administration of justice;

(5) investigate allegations, made in writing and under oath or affirmation, that citizens of the United States are unlawfully being accorded or denied the right to vote, or to have their votes properly counted, in any election of presidential electors, Members of the United States Senate, or of the House of Representatives, as a result of any patterns or practice of fraud or discrimination in the conduct of such election; and

(6) Nothing in this or any other Act shall be construed as authorizing the Commission, its Advisory Committees, or any person under its supervision or control to inquire into or investigate any membership practices or internal operations of any fraternal organization, any college or uni-

versity fraternity or sorority, any private club or any religious organization. . . .

TITLE VI—NONDISCRIMINATION IN FEDERALLY ASSISTED PROGRAMS

SEC. 601. No person in the United States shall, on the ground of race, color, or national origin, be excluded from participation in, be denied the benefits of, or be subjected to discrimination under any program or activity receiving Federal financial assistance.

SEC. 602. Each Federal department and agency which is empowered to extend Federal financial assistance to any program or activity, by way of grant, loan, or contract other than a contract of insurance or guaranty, is authorized and directed to effectuate [put into effect] the provisions of section 601 with respect to such program or activity by issuing rules, regulations, or orders of general applicability which shall be consistent with achievement of the objectives of the statute authorizing the financial assistance in connection with which the action is taken. No such rule, regulation, or order shall become effective unless and until approved by the President. . . .

TITLE VII—EQUAL EMPLOYMENT OPPORTUNITY

Definitions

SEC. 701. For the purposes of this title—

(a) The term "person" includes one or more individuals, labor unions, partnerships, associations, corporations, legal representatives, mutual companies, joint-stock companies, trusts, unincorporated organizations, trustees, trustees in bankruptcy, or receivers.

(b) The term "employer" means a person engaged in an industry affecting commerce who has twenty-five or more employees for each working day in each of twenty or more calendar weeks in the current or preceding calendar year, and any agent of such a person, but such term does not include (1) the United States, a corporation wholly owned by the Government of the United States, an Indian tribe, or a State or political subdivision thereof, (2) a bona fide private membership club (other than a labor organization) which is exempt from taxation under section 501 (c) of the Internal Revenue Code of 1954: . . . Provided further, That it shall be the policy of the United States to insure equal employment opportunities for Federal employees without discrimination because of race, color, religion, sex or national origin and the President shall utilize his existing authority to effectuate this policy.

(c) The term "employment agency" means any person regularly undertaking with or without compensation to procure employees for an employer or to procure for employees opportunities to work for an employer and includes an agent of such a person; but shall not include an agency of the United States, or an agency of a State or political subdivision of a State, except that such term shall include the United States Employment Service and the system of State and local employment services receiving Federal assistance.

(d) The term "labor organization" means a labor organization engaged in an industry affecting commerce, and any agent of such an organization, and includes any organization of any kind, any agency, or employee representation committee, group, association, or plan so engaged in which employees participate and which exists for the purpose, in whole or in part, of dealing with employers concerning grievances, labor disputes, wages, rates of pay, hours, or other terms or conditions of employment, and any conference, general committee, joint or system board, or joint council so engaged which is subordinate to a national or international labor organization. . . .

(f) The term "employee" means an individual employed by an employer.

(g) The term "commerce" means trade, traffic, commerce, transportation, transmission, or communication among the several States; or between a State and any place outside thereof; or within the District of Columbia, or a possession of the United States; or between points in the same State but through a point outside thereof.

(h) The term "industry affecting commerce" means any activity, business, or industry in commerce or in which a labor dispute would hinder or obstruct commerce or the free flow of commerce and includes any activity or industry "affecting commerce" within the meaning of the Labor-Management Reporting and Disclosure Act of 1959.

(i) The term "State" includes a State of the United States, the District of Columbia, Puerto Rico, the Virgin Islands, American Samoa, Guam, Wake Island, the Canal Zone, and Outer Continental Shelf lands defined in the Outer Continental Shelf Lands Act. . . .

Discrimination Because of Race, Color, Religion, Sex, or National Origin

SEC. 703. (a) It shall be an unlawful employment practice for an employer

(1) to fail or refuse to hire or to discharge any individual, or otherwise to discriminate against any individual with respect to his compensation,

terms, conditions, or privileges of employment, because of such individual's race, color, religion, sex, or national origin. . . .

(c) It shall be an unlawful employment practice for a labor organization
(1) to exclude or to expel from its membership, or otherwise to discriminate against, any individual because of his race, color, religion, sex, or national origin. . . .

(d) It shall be an unlawful employment practice for any employer, labor organization, or joint labor-management committee controlling apprenticeship or other training or retraining, including on-the-job training programs to discriminate against any individual because of his race, color, religion, sex, or national origin in admission to, or employment in, any program established to provide apprenticeship or other training.

(e) Notwithstanding any other provision of this title, (1) it shall not be an unlawful employment practice for an employer to hire and employ employees, for an employment agency to classify, or refer for employment any individual, for a labor organization to classify its membership or to classify or refer for employment any individual, or for an employer, labor organization, or joint labor-management committee controlling apprenticeship or other training or retraining programs to admit or employ any individual in any such program, on the basis of his religion, sex, or national origin in those certain instances where religion, sex, or national origin is a bona fide occupational qualification reasonably necessary to the normal operation of that particular business or enterprise, and (2) it shall not be an unlawful employment practice for a school, college, university, or other educational institution or institution of learning to hire and employ employees of a particular religion if such school, college, university, or other educational institution or institution of learning is, in whole or in substantial part, owned, supported, controlled, or managed by a particular religion or by a particular religious corporation, association, or society, or if the curriculum of such school, college, university, or other educational institution or institution of learning is directed toward the propagation of a particular religion. . . .

(h) Notwithstanding any other provision of this title, it shall not be an unlawful employment practice for an employer to apply different standards of compensation, or different terms, conditions, or privileges of employment pursuant to a bona fide seniority or merit system, or a system which measures earnings by quantity or quality of production or to employees who work in different locations, provided that such differences are not the result of an intention to discriminate because of race, color, religion, sex, or national origin, nor shall it be an unlawful employment practice for an employer to give and to act upon the results of any professionally developed ability test provided that such test, its administration or action upon the results is not designed, intended or used to discriminate because of race, color, religion, sex or national origin. . . .

(j) Nothing contained in this title shall be interpreted to require any employer, employment agency, labor organization, or joint labor-management committee subject to this title to grant preferential treatment to any individual or to any group because of the race, color, religion, sex, or national origin of such individual or group on account of an imbalance which may exist with respect to the total number or percentage of persons of any race, color, religion, sex, or national origin employed by any employer, referred or classified for employment by any employment agency or labor organization, admitted to membership or classified by any labor organization, or admitted to, or employed in, any apprenticeship or other training program, in comparison with the total number or percentage of persons of such race, color, religion, sex, or national origin in any community, State, section, or other area, or in the available work force in any community, State, section, or other area. [Employers are not required to grant preferential treatment to individuals based on race, color, sex, or national origin.]. . . .

Equal Employment Opportunity Commission

SEC. 705. (a) There is hereby created a Commission to be known as the Equal Employment Opportunity Commission, which shall be composed of five members, not more than three of whom shall be members of the same political party, who shall be appointed by the President by and with the advice and consent of the Senate. . . . The President shall designate one member to serve as Chairman of the Commission, and one member to serve as Vice Chairman. The Chairman shall be responsible on behalf of the Commission for the administrative operations of the Commission, and shall appoint, in accordance with the civil service laws, such officers, agents, attorneys, and employees as it deems necessary to assist it in the performance of its functions. . . .

(g) The Commission shall have power—

(1) to cooperate with and, with their consent, utilize regional, State, local, and other agencies, both public and private, and individuals;

(2) to pay to witnesses whose depositions are taken or who are summoned before the Commission or any of its agents the same witness and mileage fees as are paid to witnesses in the courts of the United States;

(3) to furnish to persons subject to this title such technical assistance as they may request to further their compliance with this title or an order issued thereunder;

(4) upon the request of (i) any employer, whose employees or some of them, or (ii) any labor organization, whose members or some of them, refuse or threaten to refuse to cooperate in effectuating the provisions of this title, to assist in such effectuation by conciliation or such other remedial action as is provided by this title;

(5) to make such technical studies as are appropriate to effectuate the purposes and policies of this title and to make the results of such studies available to the public;

(6) to refer matters to the Attorney General with recommendations for intervention in a civil action brought by an aggrieved party. . . .

Prevention of Unlawful Employment Practices

SEC. 706. (a) Whenever it is charged in writing under oath by a person claiming to be aggrieved, or a written charge has been filed by a member of the Commission where he has reasonable cause to believe a violation of this title has occurred (and such charge sets forth the facts upon which it is based) that an employer, employment agency, or labor organization has engaged in an unlawful employment practice, the Commission shall furnish such employer, employment agency, or labor organization (hereinafter referred to as the "respondent") with a copy of such charge and shall make an investigation of such charge, provided that such charge shall not be made public by the Commission. If the Commission shall determine, after such investigation, that there is reasonable cause to believe that the charge is true, the Commission shall endeavor to eliminate any such alleged unlawful employment practice by informal methods of conference, conciliation, and persuasion. . . .

(b) In the case of an alleged unlawful employment practice occurring in a State, or political subdivision of a State, which has a State or local law prohibiting the unlawful employment practice alleged and establishing or authorizing a State or local authority to grant or seek relief from such practice or to institute criminal proceedings with respect thereto upon receiving notice thereof, no charge may be filed under subsection (a) by the person aggrieved before the expiration of sixty days after proceedings have been commenced under the State or local law, unless such proceedings have been earlier terminated, provided that such sixty-day period shall be extended to one hundred and twenty days during the first year after the effective date of such State or local law. If any requirement for the commencement of such proceedings is imposed by a State or local authority other than a requirement of the filing of a written and signed statement of the facts upon which the proceeding is based, the proceeding shall be deemed to have been commenced for the purposes of this subsection at the time such statement is sent by registered mail to the appropriate State or local authority.

(c) In the case of any charge filed by a member of the Commission alleging an unlawful employment practice occurring in a State or political subdivision of a State, which has a State or local law prohibiting the practice alleged and establishing or authorizing a State or local authority to grant or seek relief from such practice or to institute criminal proceedings with respect thereto upon receiving notice thereof, the Commission shall, before taking any action with respect to such charge, notify the appropriate State or local officials and, upon request, afford them a reasonable time, but not less than sixty days (provided that such sixty-day period shall be extended to one hundred and twenty days during the first year after the effective day of such State or local law), unless a shorter period is requested, to act under such State or local law to remedy the practice alleged. . . .

(e) If within thirty days after a charge is filed with the Commission or within thirty days after expiration of any period of reference under subsection (c) (except that in either case such period may be extended to not more than sixty days upon a determination by the Commission that further efforts to secure voluntary compliance are warranted), the Commission has been unable to obtain voluntary compliance with this title, the Commission shall so notify the person aggrieved and a civil action may, within thirty days thereafter, be brought against the respondent named in the charge (1) by the person claiming to be aggrieved, or (2) if such charge was filed by a member of the Commission, by any person whom the charge alleges was aggrieved by the alleged unlawful employment practice. Upon application by the complainant and in such circumstances as the court may deem just, the court may appoint an attorney for such complainant and may authorize the commencement of the action without the payment of fees, costs, or security. Upon timely application, the court may, in its discretion, permit the Attorney General to intervene in such civil action if he certifies that the case is of general public importance. Upon request, the court may, in its discretion, stay further proceedings for not more than sixty days pending the termination of State or local proceedings described in subsection (b) or the efforts of the Commission to obtain voluntary compliance.

(f) Each United States district court and each United States court of a place subject to the jurisdiction of the United States shall have jurisdiction of actions brought under this title. . . .

(g) If the court finds that the respondent has intentionally engaged in or is intentionally engaging in an unlawful employment practice charged in the complaint, the court may enjoin the respondent from engaging in such unlawful employment practice, and order such affirmative action as may be appropriate, which may include reinstatement or hiring of employees, with or without back pay (payable by the employer, employment agency, or labor organization, as the case may be, responsible for the unlawful employment practice). Interim earnings or amounts earnable with reasonable diligence by the person or persons discriminated against shall operate to reduce the back pay otherwise allowable. No order of the court shall require the admission or reinstatement of an individual as a member of a union or the hiring, reinstatement, or promotion of an individual as an employee, or the payment to him of any back pay, if such individual was refused admission, suspended, or expelled or was refused employment or advancement or was suspended or discharged for any reason other than discrimination on account of race, color, religion, sex or national origin or in violation of section 704 (a). . . .

SEC. 707. (a) Whenever the Attorney General has reasonable cause to believe that any person or group of persons is engaged in a pattern or practice of resistance to the full enjoyment of any of the rights secured by this title, and that the pattern or practice is of such a nature and is intended to deny the full exercise of the rights herein described, the Attorney General may bring a civil action in the appropriate district court of the United States by filing with it a complaint (1) signed by him . . . (2) setting forth facts pertaining to such pattern or practice, and (3) requesting such relief, including an application for a permanent or temporary injunction, restraining order or other order against the person or persons responsible for such pattern or practice, as he deems necessary to insure the full enjoyment of the rights herein described.

(b) The district courts of the United States shall have and shall exercise jurisdiction of proceedings instituted pursuant to this section, and in any such proceeding the Attorney General may file with the clerk of such court a request that a court of three judges be convened to hear and determine the case. Such request by the Attorney General shall be accompanied by a certificate that, in his opinion, the case is of general public importance. . . .

Notices to be Posted

SEC. 711. (a) Every employer, employment agency, and labor organization, as the case may be, shall post and keep posted in conspicuous places upon its premises where notices to employees, applicants for employment, and members are customarily posted a notice to be prepared or approved by the Commission setting forth excerpts from or, summaries of, the pertinent provisions of this title and information pertinent to the filing of a complaint.

(b) A willful violation of this section shall be punishable by a fine of not more than $100 for each separate offense. . . .

APPROVED July 2, 1964.

NOTES

1. For example, see John Hope Franklin and Alfred A. Moss, Jr., *From Slavery to Freedom: A History of African Americans* (New York: Knopf, 1994), pp. 509–17.

2. Quoted in Steven Lawson, *Running for Freedom* (Philadelphia: Temple University Press, 1991), p. 95.

3. President John F. Kennedy, Special Message to Congress on Civil Rights, February 28, 1963, in John F. Kennedy, *Public Papers of the President* (Washington, D.C.: GPO, 1963), pp. 221–30.

4. Quoted in Bernard Schwartz, ed., *Statutory History of the United States: Civil Rights* (New York: Chelsea House, 1970), pt. 2, p. 1055.

5. Ibid., p. 1018.

6. See Hanes Walton, Jr., and Robert C. Smith, *American Politics and the African American Quest for Universal Freedom* (New York: Longman, 2000), p. 124.

7. Besides employing a procedure that allowed a House bill to avoid committee and move directly to the Senate floor, the public accommodations provisions were routed through the Senate Commerce Committee and arrived on the Senate floor with a positive recommendation.

8. The House of Representatives, with 435 members, operates with a Rules Committee that sets strict rules for floor debates. The Senate, with only 100 members, allows unlimited debate. Unlimited debate, however, can give rise to a filibuster, in which members can prevent consideration of a bill they oppose by speaking continuously until the majority gives up and withdraws the bill in question. (Note 10 describes the parliamentary procedure that allows the Senate to put an end to a particular filibuster.)

9. Schwartz, *Statutory History*, p. 1089.

10. In a cloture vote, a two-thirds majority of the Senate can place a time limit on debate of a given bill, thus forcing an end to any filibuster.

11. For a more detailed discussion of these political compromises, see Hugh Davis Graham, *Civil Rights and the Presidency* (New York: Oxford University Press, 1992), pp. 81–83.

12. For a more detailed analysis of this legislative process, see Charles Whalen and Barbara Whalen, *The Longest Debate: A Legislative History of the 1964 Civil Rights Act* (Cabin John, Md.: Seven Locks Press, 1984); Robert Loevy, ed., *The Civil Rights Act of 1964: The Passage of the Law That Ended Racial Segregation* (Albany: SUNY Press, 1997); Schwartz, *Statutory History*, pt. 2, pp. 1089–1092.

13. Franklin and Moss, *From Slavery to Freedom*, p. 508.

14. See the *Civil Rights Cases* 109 U.S. 3 (1883).

15. Quoted in Walton and Smith, *American Politics and the African American Quest*, p. 206.

16. See *Heart of Atlanta Motel v. United States*, 379 U.S. 241 (1964).

17. Ibid.

18. *Katzenbach v. McClung*, 379 U.S. 294 (1964).

19. See *Griggs v. Duke Power Company*, 401 U.S. 424 (1971).

20. *Regents of the University of California v. Bakke*, 438 U.S. 265 (1978). Also see *United States Steelworkers v. Weber*, 443 U.S. 193 (1979).

21. For example, see Franklin and Moss, *From Slavery to Freedom*, pp. 508–9.

22. For example, see U.S. Civil Rights Commission, *Federal Civil Rights Enforcement Efforts* (Washington, D.C.: U.S. Government Printing Office, 1970); Charles Bullock III and Charles Lamb, *The Implementation of Civil Rights Policy* (Monterey, Calif.: Brooks/Cole, 1984); Loevy, *The Civil Rights Act of 1964*. For ongoing evidence of employment discrimination, see Margery Turner et al., *Opportunities Denied, Opportunities Diminished: Discrimination in Hiring* ('Washington, D.C.: Urban Institute, 1991); Joleen Kirschenman and Kathryn Neckerman, "We'd Love to Hire Them, but . . . The Meaning of Race for Employers," in *The Urban Underclass*, ed. Christopher Jencks and Paul Peterson (Washington, D.C.: Urban Institute, 1991); Rochelle Sharp, "Losing Ground," *Wall Street Journal*, September 14, 1993, p. A14.

23. For example, see *Wards Cove Packing Company v. Antonio*, 490 U.S. 642 (1989); *City of Richmond v. Croson*, 488 U.S. 469 (1989); *Adarand Constructors, Inc. v. Pena*, 115 S.Ct. 2097 (1995).

24. Graham, *Civil Rights and the Presidency*, p. 217.

25. The four primary U.S. Supreme Court decisions at issue were *Lorance v. AT&T Technologies, Inc.*, 490 U.S. 900 (1989); *Martin v. Wilks*, 490 U.S. 755 (1989); *Patterson v. McLean Credit Union* 491 U.S. 164 (1989); and *Wards Cove Packing Company v. Antonio* 490 U.S. 642 (1989).

26. For a fuller discussion of this legislation, see Ronald D. Rotunda, "The Civil Rights Act of 1991: A Brief Introductory Analysis of the Congressional Response to Judicial Interpretation," *Notre Dame Law Review* 68 (1993): 923; David Cathcart et al., *The Civil Rights Act of 1991* (New York: American Law Institute, 1993); Nicole Gueron, "An Idea Whose Time Has Come: A Comparative Procedural History of the Civil Rights Act of 1960, 1964, and 1991," *Yale Law Review* 104 (1995):1201.

27. For example, see Steven Holmes, "Lawyers Expect Ambiguities in New Rights Law to Bring Years of Law Suits," *New York Times*, December 12, 1991.

28. For example, see *St. Mary's Honor Center v. Hicks*, 509 U.S. 502 (1993).

29. See "Denny's to Settle Bias Cases," *Washington Post*, May 24, 1994, p. A1.

30. For example, James D. Smith and Finis Welch, *Closing the Gap* (Santa Monica, Calif.: Rand, 1986); Department of Commerce, Bureau of the Census, *The Black Population of the United States* (Washington, D.C.: U.S. Government Printing Office, 2000); Department of Commerce, Bureau of the Census, *Characteristics of the Black Population* (Washington, D.C.: U.S. Government Printing Office, 2000); Patricia Smith, ed., *Feminist Jurisprudence* (New York: Oxford University Press, 1993).

31. *United States Statutes at Large* (Washington, D.C.: GPO), vol. 78, pp. 241–68.

34

Voting Rights Act

1965

The Voting Rights Act prohibited literacy tests and comparable vote-impeding devices and provided federal examiners to conduct registration and observe voting as needed.

HISTORICAL CONTEXT

After he was elected president in 1964, Lyndon B. Johnson turned his attention to expanding the provisions of the sweeping Civil Rights Act of 1964, this time focusing more closely on effective voter registration. In his 1965 State of the Union address, he declared his intent to "eliminate every remaining obstacle to the right and opportunity to vote."

On March 7, 1965, while Martin Luther King, Jr., was leading his march from Selma to Montgomery, Alabama, peaceful marchers were beaten when they tried to cross the Edmund Pettus Bridge. This incident came to be known as "Bloody Sunday." The Reverend James Reeb and Mrs. Viola Liuzzo, both white civil rights workers, also recently had been murdered.

While the nation watched these events unfold on national television, President Johnson implored Congress to add the force of the national government to this civil rights effort by passing new, stronger voting rights legislation. The president believed that the vote was critical to opening the doors to broader expansions of black civil rights. According to Johnson, "[M]any of the breakthroughs would follow as a consequence of the black man's own legitimate power as an American citizen, not as a gift from the white man."[1]

There were also political advantages to be gained. In 1964, for example, Johnson had lost five key Southern states (Alabama, Georgia, Louisiana, Mississippi, and South Carolina). If the sizable black populations of those states could be registered, the Democratic Party stood to offset the inroads Republican conservatives, such as presidential candidate Barry Goldwater, had made across the South.

By 1965 nearly 60 percent of Southern blacks remained unregistered. Despite the legal authority bestowed by the 1957, 1960, and 1964 Civil Rights Acts, the federal Justice Department had brought only seventy-one voting rights cases to court. The chief justice of the United States Supreme Court, Earl Warren, noted that "case-by-case litigation against voting discrimination" was failing due to the "inordinate amount of time required to overcome the obstructionist tactics invariably encountered in these lawsuits."[2]

Among other things, reformers felt they needed to find a way to wrestle voter registration from the discretion of local registrars and from the slow and resistant local judiciary. To that end, pressure continued to be exerted by such entities as the Civil Rights Commission who sent in federal registrars and tried to eliminate the highly subjective literacy tests entirely.

On March 15, 1965, Johnson lamented to a joint session of Congress that "every device of which human ingenuity is capable has been used to deny this right [to vote]." He called for the passage of legislation needed to "overcome the crippling legacy of bigotry and injustice" with "no delay, no hesitation, no compromise." He concluded by promising, "[W]e shall overcome."[3]

Two days later, he sent to Congress his voting rights measure, which had been formulated with significant input from lawyers in the Justice Department's Civil Rights Division after consultation with Martin Luther King, Jr. Essentially, the president was attempting to end all literacy tests, automatically permit federal registrars to work in resistant areas, and require the Justice Department to approve any new state voting rules to ensure that they did not negatively affect black suffrage. To those ends, Johnson had asked his staff to devise the "goddamnedest, toughest voting rights bill" it could muster.[4]

Amidst televised images from Selma and elsewhere, national public opinion polls indicated a 76 percent nationwide approval for such a bill and a 49 percent approval in the South. Senator Hale

Boggs (Dem., La.), concluded, "I . . . support this bill because I believe the fundamental right to vote must be a part of this great experiment in human progress under freedom which is America."[5]

Statistically, the case was relatively easy to make. Senators Philip Hart (Dem., Mich.) and Jacob Javits (Rep., N.Y.), for instance, presented a barrage of data showing just how few Southern blacks were able to circumvent literacy tests and other devices in order to be able to vote. As Birch Bayh (Dem., Ind.) concluded, "[T]he Fifteenth Amendment . . . has not been in effect for many years, because the average nonwhite man has not been able to vote."[6]

The opposition was led by Senator Sam Ervin (Dem., N.C.) and Senator Herman Talmadge (Dem., Ga.). Opponents once again argued that such regulations amounted to a federal usurpation of states' rights to qualify their own voters. They also contended that the legislation in many ways amounted to a Second Reconstruction of the South. In particular, the bill's automatic "triggering" devices for federal intervention were regarded as based on presumptions that were both arbitrary and discriminatory against specific Southern states. Southern states argued, for instance, that they should have the right to test the literacy of their voters, just as several Northern states were doing. In addition, the bill was considered an unconstitutional "ex post facto law" and a "bill of attainder" in as much as the law essentially punished certain states based on past events and provided them no opportunity to defend themselves at trial.

Nevertheless, under the president's skillful legislative guidance, the Voting Rights Bill literally sailed through the Congress. It passed almost intact in early August, scarcely five months after its introduction. The Senate Judiciary Committee approved the bill within the fifteen-day time limit it was given; cloture was voted before a Southern filibuster took form; and the full Senate then approved the measure by a vote of 79–18. The House acted even more quickly. After just four days of strictly limited debate on the House floor, the bill passed by a vote of 328–74.

President Johnson made a symbolic trip to Capitol Hill to sign the final version on August 6, 1965. At the signing ceremony he asserted,

> The right to vote is the most basic right without which all others are meaningless. It gives people—people as individuals—control over their destinies. . . . The vote is the most powerful instrument ever

devised by man for breaking down injustice and destroying the terrible walls which imprison men because they are different from other men.[7]

Legal historian Bernard Schwartz refers to the Voting Rights Act as "in many ways, the most drastic civil rights statute ever enacted by Congress."[8] Among other things, it provided for federal examiners automatically to conduct registration and observe voting in states or counties demonstrating a pattern of discrimination in the past. It directed the attorney general legally to challenge poll taxes in state elections, and to challenge other practices even if there was only statistical evidence of discrimination. It shifted the burden of proof to the state to defend its laws and actions as nondiscriminatory. And, when a federal suit was pending, federal courts were authorized temporarily to ban the practice alleged to be discriminatory.

In addition, all literacy tests and certain other suspect practices were to be suspended in states where less than half of their eligible voters had registered or turned out in the 1964 presidential election. The law also designated that recalcitrant states could be subject to the requirement of preclearance of all new voting laws to check for possible racial discrimination.

A House amendment to outlaw all poll taxes had been eliminated by the House-Senate conference committee before the bill returned to the Senate. Nevertheless, the United States Supreme Court achieved the same result when it ruled in 1966 that the federal Constitution prohibits the use of such taxes at any level of government.[9] Seven years later, the court all but outlawed literacy tests as well.[10]

The nation's highest court upheld the Voting Rights Act itself as a "rational means to effectuate the constitutional prohibition of racial discrimination in voting." Under the Fifteenth Amendment's enforcement clause, Congress was allowed to provide for "the suspension of voting tests that have been used as notorious means to deny and abridge voting rights on racial grounds." According to Chief Justice Earl Warren, "The Court has recognized that exceptional conditions can justify legislative measures not otherwise appropriate."[11]

Results of the Voting Rights Act and the Supreme Court's decisions were particularly noteworthy among blacks. Hundreds of thousands of African Americans were registered within months after the law's passage. Black registration in the preclearance states had increased to 62 percent by 1968 and nearly to 75 percent a year later. In Mississippi, for instance, it increased from 7 percent in 1964 to 59 percent in 1968. In Dallas County, site of the infamous Selma events, black registration jumped from fewer than 1,000 to more than 8,500 in that same time period. Not surprisingly, the number of black elected officials grew dramatically as well.[12]

The Civil Rights Division of the Justice Department also seized upon its preclearance authority and carefully scrutinized a variety of voting-related state actions, including reapportionment, redistricting, and annexation plans. The division then initiated legal action if necessary in an attempt to stop any such move that threatened to dilute black voting strength.

Nonetheless, pursuing legal remedies is almost always a slow and arduous process. The Southern black vote, for instance, had lost much of its clout by the time full suffrage was finally extended. In 1900 African Americans actually formed a majority of the population in South Carolina and Mississippi. They accounted for less than a third of those electorates by the 1960s. Similar population declines were also recorded in Alabama, Florida, Georgia, and Louisiana.[13]

In addition, much of the original Voting Rights Act of 1965 had to be renewed after five years. In 1970, for instance, President Richard Nixon and the Republican leadership tried to eliminate the intrusive preclearance and oversight triggering devices aimed at Southern states. They justified this by citing the remarkable increase in black registration and voting that had already occurred. They proposed instead to replace them with an end to all literacy tests and with Justice Department authority to pursue voting discrimination anywhere in the nation.

Such alterations were vigorously opposed by civil rights advocates. They noted ongoing resistance to black registration and voting in the South, and they feared dilution of the oversight effort and a return to the even more cumbersome judicial approach of earlier years.[14] Clarence Mitchell, chief lobbyist for the NAACP, argued that the Republican efforts were little more than "a sophisticated, a calculated, incredible effort . . . to make it impossible for us to continue on the constitutional course that we have followed . . . in protecting the right to vote."[15]

Congress rather quickly rejected key Nixon administration proposals and renewed the essence of the Voting Rights Act.[16] The process for assigning federal observers and registrars would remain. Nevertheless, this version applied the law in a more geographically neutral manner. Preclearance was reaffirmed, triggered by a formula that now could extend it to Northern jurisdictions as well. Literacy tests were suspended for another five years, although this time across the entire country. The 1970 Voting Rights extension also granted eighteen-year-olds the right to vote in presidential elections, nationalized absentee balloting procedures, and reduced residency requirements for those elections.[17]

Five years later, in 1975, President Gerald Ford noted that, despite gains, the number of black elected officials in the South remained disproportionately low. While invoking the memory of Dr. Martin Luther King, Jr., on the anniversary of his birthday, President Ford moved for a renewal of the Voting Rights Act. "The right to vote is the very foundation of our American system. There must be no question whatsoever about the right of each eligible American to participate in our electoral process."[18]

Liberals added foreign-language minorities to the coverage and sought renewal for ten years, instead of five. This time, however, there was only token opposition. Bolstered by the strong lobbying effort of the United States Commission on Civil Rights, the ten-year extension sailed through the House, and cloture was imposed in the Senate even before any senator could commence a filibuster. President Ford wavered at the very last minute, temporarily supporting nationwide preclearance. Yet, he reversed course again, and the extension became law.[19]

By 1985 renewal would face a more conservative Republican president, Ronald W. Reagan, and it would be reviewed by a recently elected Republican majority in the United States Senate, the first Republican control of that body in nearly thirty years. Those elections had continued to solidify the South under the banner of the contemporary Republican Party, and affected Southern states continued to seek a reprieve from the years of preclearing all state election laws with the federal government.

The renewal also came on the heels of a restrictive decision made by the United States Supreme Court. A five-vote Court majority had read the Voting Rights Act as requiring clear evidence of intent to discriminate racially before an election rule could be overturned.[20] This posed a particular difficulty in challenging practices such as at-large elections. Established decades earlier for reasons that were race-neutral on their face, such practices clearly hindered black candidates from being elected where blacks did not form an electoral majority.

Anticipating a more prolonged battle, civil rights forces in Congress began the renewal process early. Then they pressed for the renewal of all existing provisions and asked for discriminatory results to be added to discriminatory intent as grounds for reversing disadvantageous election rules. By October 1981, the Democratic majority in the House of Representatives had passed a ten-year renewal, which included an "effects test" for determining illegal black vote dilution. Their argument was that this simply allowed courts to weigh the discriminatory impact of election rules in order to determine whether they illegally discriminated against blacks by substantively reducing their chances of electing blacks to political office.

The Reagan administration and many congressional Republicans were opposed to an effects test for the same reasons they had opposed a variety of race-conscious policies. The president warned that such a results-minded law "would come down to where all of society had to have an actual quota system" for minority representatives.[21] Others opposed what they viewed to be "preferential treatment"; they argued instead for the "color-blind ideal of equal opportunity for all."[22]

A compromise was fashioned by a coalition of Senate Democrats and a group of moderate Republicans lead by Robert Dole (Rep., Kans.). They agreed to a twenty-five-year extension that included a preclearance "bailout" provision for cooperative states, as well as a modified results test that would allow courts to consider the "totality of circumstances" when reviewing election rules that appeared to reduce the electoral opportunities of minorities. The adopted Dole Proviso did not explicitly sanction the principle of "proportional representation" for minorities.

The compromise passed easily when a Senate filibuster attempt made by Jesse Helms (Rep., N.C.) failed to draw even token support. In the end, opponents could only garner four votes in opposition to the renewal bill; even South Carolina Senator Strom Thurmond and Mississippi Senator John Stennis voted in the affirmative. President Reagan then signed the bill into law, praising it as evidence of "our unbending commitment to voting rights."[23] Thereafter, the law's results test was upheld as constitutional by the United States Supreme Court.[24]

Following the 1990 census, this law was invoked to allow the creation of "black majority districts" as a mechanism for increasing black representation in Congress, after years of gerrymandering to maintain "white majority districts" had kept such representation to a minimum. Nonetheless, the United States Supreme Court struck down such a race-conscious solution. Justice Sandra Day O'Connor stated in her majority opinion,

> Racial gerrymandering, even for remedial purposes, may Balkanize us into competing racial factions; it threatens to carry us further from the goal of a political system in which race no longer matters— a goal that the Fourteenth and Fifteenth Amendments embody, and to which the Nation continues to aspire.[25]

Despite that particular setback, the Voting Rights Act has been used by a host of black litigants to challenge legally electoral rules that systematically produce underrepresentation of minority candidates. In cities like Memphis, black voters finally have been able to elect blacks to the city's top elected positions after legal challenges led to the elimination of at-large city council elections and runoff elections for citywide office.[26]

THE LAW

The Voting Rights Act of 1965[27] grants all citizens freedom from voting impediments based on race or color and provides mechanisms to achieve that end.

Specifically, the law directs that, in legal actions instituted by the attorney general to enforce the guarantees of the Fifteenth Amendment, the federal court can appoint examiners and suspend tests being used to deny citizens the right to vote. The act also provides that the federal court can retain the right to review voting practices of a state where the court earlier had found violations of the Fifteenth Amendment.

In order to ensure the right to vote, the act prohibits tests and other devices used to qualify voters in any states or political subdivisions that had utilized such tests or devices and had fewer than half of their eligible voters registered or voting in the most recent presidential election. A state or political subdivision could circumvent this requirement by initiating an action in federal court to determine that the test had been used for the preceding five years without the purpose or effect of denying a citizen's right to vote on account of race or color. Under the act, a state seeking to administer voting qualifications can also request a declaration from the U.S. District Court that the voting qualifications do not have the purpose or would not have the effect of illegally denying a citizen's right to vote.

When required by the federal court, or deemed necessary by the attorney general, the act declares that the Civil Service Commission must appoint as many examiners as required to enforce the Fifteenth Amendment. The law provides guidelines for the examiners to use in determining whether individuals are qualified to vote. The act grants the attorney general the authority to send federal election observers to political subdivisions as necessary. In addition, it sets forth Congress's declaration that poll taxes are unconstitutional and directs the attorney general to take action necessary to eliminate such taxes.

Finally, the act declares that no person can interfere with a citizen's right to vote. Any such interference could subject the wrongdoer to fines and imprisonment.

34. Voting Rights Act of 1965

Be it enacted . . . That this Act shall be known as the "Voting Rights Act of 1965."

SEC. 2. No voting qualification or prerequisite to voting, or standard, practice, or procedure shall be imposed or applied by any State or political subdivision to deny or abridge the right of any citizen of the United States to vote on account of race or color.

SEC. 3. (a) Whenever the Attorney General institutes a proceeding under any statute to enforce the guarantees of the fifteenth amendment in any State or political subdivision the court shall authorize the appointment of Federal examiners by the United States Civil Service Commission in accordance with section 6 to serve for such period of time and for such political subdivisions as the court shall determine is appropriate to enforce the guarantees of the fifteenth amendment (1) as part of any interlocutory order [pronounced during the course of the proceeding] if the court determines that the appointment of such examiners is necessary to enforce such guarantees or (2) as part of any final judgment if the court finds that violations of the fifteenth amendment justifying equitable relief have occurred in such State or subdivision: Provided, That the court need not authorize the appointment of examiners if any incidents of denial or abridgement of the right to vote on account of race or color (1) have been few in number and have been promptly and effectively corrected by State or local action, (2) the continuing effect of such incidents has been eliminated, and (3) there is no reasonable probability of their recurrence in the future.

(b) If in a proceeding instituted by the Attorney General under any statute to enforce the guarantees of the fifteenth amendment in any State or political subdivision the court finds that a test or device has been used for the purpose or with the effect of denying or abridging the right of any citizen of the United States to vote on account of race or color, it shall suspend the use of tests and devices in such State or political subdivisions as the court shall determine is appropriate and for such period as it deems necessary.

(c) If in any proceeding instituted by the Attorney General under any statute to enforce the guarantees of the fifteenth amendment in any State or political subdivision the court finds that violations of the fifteenth amendment justifying equitable relief have occurred within the territory of such State or political subdivision, the court, in addition to such relief as it may grant, shall retain jurisdiction for such period as it may deem appropriate. . . .

SEC. 4. (a) To assure that the right of citizens of the United States to vote is not denied or abridged on account of race or color, no citizen shall be denied the right to vote in any Federal, State, or local election because of his failure to comply with any test or device in any State with respect to which the determinations have been made under subsection (b) or in any political subdivision with respect to which such determinations have been made as a separate unit, unless the United States District Court for the District of Columbia in an action for a declaratory judgment brought by such State or subdivision against the United States has determined that no such test or device has been used during the five years preceding the filing of the action for the purpose or with the effect of denying or abridging the right to vote on account of race or color. . . .

(b) The provisions of subsection (a) shall apply in any State or in any political subdivision of a state which (1) the Attorney General determines maintained on November 1, 1964, any test or device, and with respect to which (2) the Director of the Census determines that less than 50 per cent of the persons of voting age residing therein were registered on November 1, 1964, or that less than 50 per cent of such persons voted in the presidential election of November 1964. . . .

(c) The phrase "test or device" shall mean any requirement that a person as a prerequisite for voting or registration for voting (1) demonstrate the ability to read, write, understand, or interpret any matter, (2) demonstrate any educational achievement or his knowledge of any particular subject, (3) possess good moral character, or (4) prove his qualifications by the voucher of registered voters or members of any other class.

(d) For purposes of this section no State or political subdivision shall be determined to have engaged in the use of tests or devices for the purpose or with the effect of denying or abridging the right to vote on account of race or color if (1) incidents of such use have been few in number and have been promptly and effectively corrected by State or local action, (2) the continuing effect of such incidents has been eliminated, and (3) there is no reasonable probability of their recurrence in the future. . . .

SEC. 5. Whenever a State or political subdivision with respect to which the prohibitions set forth in section 4 (a) are in effect shall enact or seek to administer any voting qualification or prerequisite to voting, or standard, practice, or procedure with respect to voting different from that in force or effect on November 1, 1964, such State or subdivision may institute an action in the United States District Court for the District of Columbia for a declaratory judgment [a ruling of the court] that such qualification, prerequisite, standard, practice, or procedure does not have the purpose and will not have the effect of denying or abridging the right to vote on account of race or color, and unless and until the court enters such judgment no person shall be denied the right to vote for failure to comply with such qualification, prerequisite, standard, practice, or procedure. . . .

SEC. 6. Whenever (a) a court has authorized the appointment of examiners pursuant to the provisions of section 3 (a), or (b) unless a declaratory judgment has been rendered under section 4 (a), the Attorney General certifies with respect to any political subdivision named in, or included within the scope of, determinations made under section 4 (b) that (1) he has received complaints in writing from twenty or more residents of such political subdivision alleging that they have been denied the right to vote under color of law on account of race or color, and that he believes such complaints to be meritorious, or (2) that in his judgment (considering, among other factors, whether the ratio of nonwhite persons to white persons registered to vote within such subdivision appears to him to be reasonably attributable to violations of the fifteenth amendment or whether substantial evidence exists that bona fide efforts are being made within such subdivision to comply with the fifteenth amendment), the appointment of examiners is otherwise necessary to enforce the guarantees of the fifteenth amendment, the Civil Service Commission shall appoint as many examiners for such subdivision as it may deem appropriate to prepare and maintain lists of persons eligible to vote in Federal, State, and local elections. . . .

SEC. 7. (a) The examiners for each political subdivision shall, at such places as the Civil Service Commission shall by regulation designate, examine applicants concerning their qualifications for voting. An application to an examiner shall be in such form as the Commission may require and shall contain allegations that the applicant is not otherwise registered to vote.

(b) Any person whom the examiner finds, in accordance with instructions received under section 9 (b), to have the qualifications prescribed by State law not inconsistent with the Constitution and laws of the United States shall promptly be placed on a list of eligible voters. . . .

SEC. 8. Whenever an examiner is serving under this Act in any political subdivision, the Civil Service Commission may assign, at the request of the Attorney General, one or more persons, who may be officers of the United States, (1) to enter and attend at any place for holding an election in such subdivision for the purpose of observing whether persons who are entitled to vote are being permitted to vote, and (2) to enter and attend at any place for tabulating the votes cast at any election held in such subdivision for the purpose of observing whether votes cast by persons entitled to vote are being properly tabulated. Such persons so assigned shall report to an examiner appointed for such political subdivision, to the Attorney General, and if the appointment of examiners has been authorized pursuant to section 3 (a), to the court. . . .

SEC. 10. (a) The Congress finds that the requirement of the payment of a poll tax as a precondition to voting (i) precludes persons of limited means from voting or imposes unreasonable financial hardship upon such persons as a precondition to their exercise of the franchise, (ii) does not bear a reasonable relationship to any legitimate State interest in the conduct of elections, and (iii) in some areas has the purpose or effect of denying persons the right to vote because of race or color. Upon the basis of these findings, Congress declares that the constitutional right of citizens to vote is denied or abridged in some areas by the requirement of the payment of a poll tax as a precondition to voting.

(b) In the exercise of the powers of Congress under section 5 of the fourteenth amendment and section 2 of the fifteenth amendment, the Attorney General is authorized and directed to institute forthwith in the name of the United States such actions, including actions against States or political subdivisions, for declaratory judgment [binding ruling of the court] or injunctive relief [remedy issued by the court forbidding some act] against the enforcement of any requirement of the payment of a poll tax as a precondition to voting, or substitute therefor enacted after November 1, 1964, as will be necessary to implement the declaration of subsection (a) and the purposes of this section. . . .

SEC. 11. (a) No person acting under color of law shall fail or refuse to permit any person to vote who is entitled to vote under any provision of this Act or is otherwise qualified to vote, or willfully fail or refuse to tabulate count, and report such person's vote.

(b) No person, whether acting under color of law or otherwise, shall intimidate, threaten, or coerce, or attempt to intimidate, threaten, or coerce any person for voting or attempting to vote, or intimidate, threaten, or coerce, or attempt to intimidate, threaten, or coerce any person for urging or aiding any person to vote or attempt to vote, or intimidate, threaten, or coerce any person for exercising any powers or duties under section 3(a), 6, 8, 9, 10, or 12(e).

(c) Whoever knowingly or willfully gives false information as to his name, address, or period of residence in the voting district for the purpose of establishing his eligibility to register or vote, or conspires with another individual for the purpose of encouraging his false registration to vote or illegal voting, or pays or offers to pay or accepts payment either for registration to vote or for voting shall be fined not more than $10,000 or imprisoned not more than five years, or both: Provided, however, That this provision shall be applicable only to general, special, or primary elections held solely or in part for the purpose of selecting or electing any candidate for the office of President, Vice President, presidential elector, Member of the United States Senate, Member of the United States House of Representatives, or Delegates or Commissioners from the territories or possessions, or Resident Commissioner of the Commonwealth of Puerto Rico.

(d) Whoever, in any matter within the jurisdiction of an examiner or hearing officer knowingly and willfully falsifies or conceals a material fact, or makes any false, fictitious, or fraudulent statements or representations, or makes or uses any false writing or document knowing the same to contain any false, fictitious, or fraudulent statement or entry, shall be fined not more than $10,000 or imprisoned not more than five years, or both.

SEC. 12. (a) Whoever shall deprive or attempt to deprive any person of any right secured by section 2, 3, 4, 5, 7, or 10 or shall violate section 11 (a) or (b), shall be fined not more than $5,000, or imprisoned not more than five years, or both.

(b) Whoever, within a year following an election in a political subdivision in which an examiner has been appointed (1) destroys, defaces, mutilates, or otherwise alters the marking of a paper ballot which has been cast in such election, or (2) alters any official record of voting in such election tabulated from a voting machine or otherwise, shall be fined not more than $5,000, or imprisoned not more than five years, or both. . . .

APPROVED August 6, 1965.

NOTES

1. Quoted in Steven Lawson, *Black Ballots: Voting Rights in the South, 1944–1969* (New York: Columbia University Press, 1976), p. 300.

2. *South Carolina v. Katzenbach*, 383 U.S. 301 (1966). Also see the House Judiciary Committee, "The Voting Rights Bill," 89th Cong., 1st sess., H. Rept. 439 (Washington, D.C.: U.S. Government Printing Office, 1965).

3. Quoted in Bernard Schwartz, ed., *Statutory History of the United States Civil Rights*, Part 2 (New York: Chelsea House, 1970), pp. 1507, 1509.

4. Quoted in Abigail M. Thernstrom, *Whose Votes Count?* (Cambridge, Mass.: Harvard University Press, 1987), p. 15. For a more detailed discussion of the thinking that went into the formulation of this bill, see Hugh Davis Graham, *Civil Rights and the Presidency* (New York: Oxford University Press 1992), pp. 93–96.

5. Quoted in Lawson, *Black Ballots*, p. 320.

6. Quoted in Schwartz, *Statutory History of the United States*, pt. 2, p. 1471.

7. Lyndon Johnson, *The Vantage Point: Perspectives of the Presidency, 1963–1969* (New York: Holt, Rinehart and Winston, 1971), p. 161.

8. Schwartz, *Statutory History of the United States*, pt. 2, p. 1469.

9. *Harper v. Virginia Board of Elections*, 383 U.S. 663 (1966). It should be noted that only four states still had functioning poll taxes at this time: Alabama, Mississippi, Texas, and Virginia. In addition, no racial disenfranchisement could be specifically attributed to the poll tax alone. See Graham, *Civil Rights and the Presidency*, p. 97.

10. *Gaston County v. United States*, 411 U.S. 525 (1973).

11. *South Carolina v. Katzenbach*, 383 U.S. 301 (1966). Also see the expansive reading the Court gave the law in *Allen v. State Board of Elections*, 393 U.S. 544 (1969).

12. For example, see Frank R. Parker, *Black Votes Count* (Chapel Hill: University of North Carolina Press, 1990); Lawson, *Black Ballots*; Bernard Grofman and Chandler Davidson, eds., *Controversies in Minority Voting: The Voting Rights Act in Perspective* (Washington, D.C.: Brookings Institute, 1992); John Mack Farragher et al., *Out of Many* (Upper Saddle River, N.J.: Prentice-Hall, 2000), p. 870; James Roark et al., *The American Promise* (Boston: Bedford Books, 1998), pp. 1120–21.

13. For example, see Howard Ball et al., *Compromised Compliance: Implementation of the 1965 Voting Rights Act* (Westport, Conn.: Greenwood Press, 1982).

14. For example, see U.S. Commission on Civil Rights, *Political Participation* (Washington, D.C.: U.S. Commission on Civil Rights, 1968), pp. 21–84; Steven Lawson, *In Pursuit of Power* (New York: Columbia University Press, 1985), chap. 5.

15. Quoted in Lawson, *In Pursuit of Power*, pp. 137–138.

16. For a more detailed discussion of the politics leading to this decision, see Lawson, *In Pursuit of Power*, chap. 5; Graham, *Civil Rights and the Presidency*, pp. 129–157.

17. Because the United States Supreme Court ruled in *Oregon v. Mitchell*, 400 U.S. 112 (1970), that Congress could only change voter qualifications for federal elections, the Twenty-Sixth Amendment was added to the United States Constitution, extending the franchise to eighteen-year-olds in state elections as well.

18. Quoted in Lawson, *In Pursuit of Power*, p. 253.

19. For more discussion of these events, see "110 Years of Voting Rights Legislation," *Congressional Quarterly Weekly Report* (April 11, 1981): 634; Lawson, *In Pursuit of Power*, chap. 8.

20. *City of Mobile v. Bolden*, 446 U.S. 55 (1980).

21. Quoted in Steven Lawson, *Running for Freedom* (Philadelphia: Temple University Press, 1991), p. 209.

22. Assistant Attorney General William Bradford Reynolds, head of the Civil Rights Division, speech to the Delaware Bar Association, February 22, 1982, reprinted in the House Committee on the Judiciary, *Hearings on Department of Justice Authorization for Fiscal Year 1983*, 97th Cong., 2d sess., 1982, p. 92.

23. Quoted in Lawson, *In Pursuit of Power*, p. 292. For a more detailed discussion of these events, see ibid., pp. 282–93.

24. *Thornburgh v. Gingles*, 478 U.S. 30 (1986).

25. *Shaw v. Reno*, 509 U.S. 630 (1993).

26. For example, see Marcus D. Pohlmann and Michael P. Kirby, *Racial Politics at the Crossroads: Memphis Elects Dr. W.W. Herenton* (Knoxville: University of Tennessee Press, 1996), chap. 5. More generally, see Bernard Grofman et al., *Minority Representation and the Quest for Voting Equality* (New York: Cambridge University Press, 1992); Lawson, *In Pursuit of Power*.

27. *United States Statutes at Large* (Washington, D.C.: GPO), vol. 79, pp. 437–46.

35

Executive Order 11246

1965

Most notably, President Lyndon Johnson's Executive Order 11246 prohibited discrimination by federal contractors and required them to take positive steps to hire and promote qualified minorities and women.

HISTORICAL CONTEXT

President Lyndon B. Johnson delivered the commencement address at Howard University in June 1965. Among other things, the president stated,

> You do not take a person who, for years, has been hobbled by chains and liberate him, bring him to the starting line of a race and then say, "You are free to compete with all the others," and still justly believe that you have been completely fair.
>
> Thus it is not enough just to open the gates of opportunity. All our citizens must have the ability to walk through those gates.
>
> This is the next and more profound stage of the battle for civil rights. We seek not just legal equity but human ability, not just equality as a right and a theory but equality as a fact and equality as a result.[1]

Executive Order 11246 was issued by President Johnson on September 24, 1965, a little more than three months after he delivered his speech at Howard University. The order was to be administered by the Labor Department's new Office of Contract Compliance, and it was to be enforced by the Equal Employment Opportunity Commission of the Justice Department. The goal was to guarantee that protected groups were hired, trained, and promoted fairly by employers in both government jobs and in government-related private employment. In terms of private-sector employers, the order prohibited employment discrimination on the basis of race, color, religion, sex, or national origin by any federal contractor with fifty or more employees and federal contracts worth more than $50,000. In practice, it covered roughly one-third of the U.S. workforce.[2]

This executive order was to go beyond the monitoring and contract reviews mandated by the previous orders of Presidents Roosevelt, Truman, and Kennedy. As President Johnson had indicated in his Howard commencement speech, he felt even more was required to guarantee equal opportunity. Given entrenched prejudices and the history of past discrimination, the Johnson executive order required employers receiving sizable federal contracts to take positive steps to hire and promote qualified minorities and women. This "affirmative action" was to be overseen by the Department of Labor.[3]

The construction industry was the biggest challenge. According to political historian Hugh Graham, "Construction was a fluid, ad hoc, contract-chasing enterprise where construction companies bid competitively for projects, and winning low bidders then obtained their workers from hiring-halls bound by union contracts."[4] The challenge, then, was to police a very decentralized hiring process that was filling some 20 million federally financed jobs at that time.[5]

Late in the Johnson administration, a detailed "Cleveland Plan" was developed as an implementation device by Edward Sylvester, the director of the Labor Department's Office of Contract Compliance. The plan, designed to spur minority employment in the construction industry in Cleveland, Ohio, required construction companies with federal contracts to develop written plans detailing precisely how many blacks they were going to try to hire at each phase of construction. The goal of the Johnson administration at that point was "increasing materially the utilization of minorities and women."[6]

The Council of Economic Advisors recently had estimated the economic cost of such underutilization. They concluded that racial discrimination alone was costing the nation more than $17 billion in potential production each year, or more than 3 percent of the existing gross national product. This occurred when skills were both underdeveloped and underutilized.[7]

Despite nearly universal recognition of ongoing job discrimination and its costs to both the individuals involved and the nation as a whole, the Cleveland Plan was opposed on almost every political front, including opposition from both employers and organized labor. In particular, it was seen as requiring "quotas"[8] and moving the nation down the path of "reverse discrimination."[9] The comptroller general ultimately determined it to be illegal, but on more technical grounds. The plan deviated from standard contract bidding practices inasmuch as it explicitly used race as a selection factor rather than merely accepting the lowest bid.

The essence of the Cleveland Plan reemerged as an antidiscrimination proposal under the Nixon administration. It was spurred by the efforts of Secretary of Labor George Shultz, Assistant Secretary of Labor Arthur Fletcher, and John Wilks, the director of the Office of Contract Compliance. This time it was entitled the "Philadelphia Plan,"[10] and, even though it still required detailed racial hiring strategies, it took more care to conform to standard bidding practices. For example, it asked for target ranges instead of specific numerical targets, and it requested these after the bid had been accepted and the contract provisionally extended. Nevertheless, opposition remained widespread, and, according to the comptroller general, it remained illegal as it would "require hiring, firing, or promotion of employees in order to meet a racial 'quota' or to achieve a certain racial balance."[11]

The decision of the comptroller general was rejected by the president, however, and Richard Nixon claimed it was within his constitutional authority to reject it. Therefore, Lyndon Johnson's earlier Cleveland Plan was finally revised and employed by Richard Nixon in 1971. It required specific affirmative action goals and timetables for hiring and training blacks and other minorities.

The United States Senate initially balked at the Nixon decision and passed a law siding with the comptroller general's ruling.[12] At that point, President Nixon and his secretary of labor initiated an intense lobbying effort in the House of Representatives. There they prevailed by a vote of 208–156, as the House defeated the same measure that had passed in the Senate. They managed to hold together three-quarters of the Republican minority and then split the Democratic majority, with civil rights liberals opposing Southern Democrats and supporters of organized labor.[13]

The Philadelphia Plan then came to be the model for affirmative action plans across the country. As reworked by Secretary Shultz, it ultimately was extended to all federal contractors. They were to file an affirmative action plan within 120 days of winning a contract. The plan was first to assess whether various minority groups were underutilized compared to what "would be reasonably expected by their availability . . . in the immediate labor area." If underutilization was found, the contractor was then to submit "specific goals and timetables . . . to correct any identifiable deficiencies" or risk being excluded from consideration for future federal contracts.[14]

President Nixon also utilized a variation of this approach to address such discrimination in the federal government itself. Executive Order 11478, announced in August 1969, formally superseded parts of President Johnson's Executive Order 11246. It guaranteed equal employment opportunity in all direct federal employment, including the utilization of affirmative action plans. The onus was placed on each federal department and agency to cultivate a larger minority presence in its area by emphasizing innovative recruitment and training efforts. The Civil Service Commission was designated as the primary coordinator and enforcement agent.

In its *Regents of the University of California v. Bakke* decision, the United States Supreme Court ruled on the essence of the Philadelphia Plan. In that 1978 decision involving admission to medical school, the Court allowed race to be used as a governmental selection factor. According to Justice Blackman, "In order to get beyond racism, we must first take race into account." If it was to be used, however, there needed to be either evidence of past discrimination or a clearly outlined state benefit. Even then, race could be only one of several factors considered, and it had to be flexibly applied.[15]

THE LAW

Executive Order 11246[16] stated a policy of nondiscrimination on the basis of race, creed, color, or national origin in federal employment. It directed executive departments and agencies to establish programs of equal employment opportunity. The Civil Service Commission was required to supervise these programs and review all complaints of discrimination.

The order also addressed government contracts, including federally assisted construction contracts. Pursuant to the order, all contractors agreed to include certain provisions in their government contracts. In these required provisions, contractors agreed not to discriminate on the basis of race, creed, color, or national origin. Furthermore, the contracts provided that the contractors would take affirmative action in the employment process. The contractors also were required to post notices in conspicuous places setting forth their obligations and to notify applicants of their nondiscriminatory practices. If the contractors violated the nondiscriminatory clauses of the agreements, their contracts could be terminated, and the contractor could be declared ineligible for future government contracts.

Government contractors were required to comply with the rules and regulations of the secretary of labor, who was charged with investigating the employment practices of the contractors. To carry out the requirements of the order, the secretary of labor was granted authority to hold hearings and issue sanctions and penalties. Likewise, government contracting agencies were given the authority to impose sanctions and penalties under this order.

Executive Order 11246 superseded several previous presidential orders and abolished the President's Committee on Equal Employment Opportunity.

35. Executive Order 11246

EQUAL EMPLOYMENT OPPORTUNITY

. . . it is ordered as follows:

PART I—NONDISCRIMINATION IN GOVERNMENT EMPLOYMENT

SECTION 101. It is the policy of the Government of the United States to provide equal opportunity in Federal employment for all qualified persons, to prohibit discrimination in employment because of race, creed, color, or national origin, and to promote the full realization of equal employment opportunity through a positive, continuing program in each executive department and agency. The policy of equal opportunity applies to every aspect of Federal employment policy and practice.

SEC. 102. The head of each executive department and agency shall establish and maintain a positive program of equal employment opportunity for all civilian employees and applicants for employment within his jurisdiction in accordance with the policy set forth in Section 101.

SEC. 103. The Civil Service Commission shall supervise and provide leadership and guidance in the conduct of equal employment opportunity programs for the civilian employees of and applications for employment within the executive departments and agencies and shall review agency program accomplishments periodically. In order to facilitate the achievement of a model program for equal employment opportunity in the Federal service, the Commission may consult from time to time with such individuals, groups, or organizations as may be of assistance in improving the Federal program and realizing the objectives of this Part.

SEC. 104. The Civil Service Commission shall provide for the prompt, fair, and impartial consideration of all complaints of discrimination in Federal employment on the basis of race, creed, color, or national origin. Procedures for the consideration of complaints shall include at least one impartial review within the executive department or agency and shall provide for appeal to the Civil Service Commission. . . .

PART II—NONDISCRIMINATION IN EMPLOYMENT BY GOVERNMENT CONTRACTORS AND SUBCONTRACTORS

Subpart B—Contractors' Agreements

SEC. 202. Except in contracts exempted in accordance with Section 204 of this Order, all Government contracting agencies shall include in every Government contract hereafter entered into the following provisions: During the performance of this contract, the contractor agrees as follows:

(1) The contractor will not discriminate against any employee or applicant for employment because of race, creed, color, or national origin. The contractor will take affirmative action to ensure that applicants are employed, and that employees are treated during employment, without regard to their race, creed, color, or national origin. Such action shall include, but not be limited to the following: employment, upgrading, demotion, or transfer; recruitment or recruitment advertising; layoff or termination; rates of pay or other forms of compensation; and selection for training, including apprenticeship. The contractor agrees to post in conspicuous places, available to employees and applicants for employment, notices to be provided by the contracting officer setting forth the provisions of this nondiscrimination clause.

(2) The contractor will, in all solicitations or advertisements for employees placed by or on behalf of the contractor, state that all qualified applicants will receive consideration for employment without regard to race, creed, color, or national origin.

(3) The contractor will send to each labor union or representative of workers with which he has a collective bargaining agreement or other contract or understanding, a notice, to be provided by the agency con-

tracting officer, advising the labor union or workers' representative of the contractor's commitments under Section 202 of [this executive order], and shall post copies of the notice in conspicuous places available to employees and applicants for employment.

(4) The contractor will comply with all provisions of [this executive order], and of the rules, regulations, and relevant orders of the Secretary of Labor.

(5) The contractor will furnish all information and reports required by [this executive order], and by the rules, regulations, and orders of the Secretary of Labor, or pursuant thereto, and will permit access to his books, records, and accounts by the contracting agency and the Secretary of Labor for purposes of investigation to ascertain [determine] compliance with such rules, regulations, and orders.

(6) In the event of the contractor's noncompliance with the nondiscrimination clauses of this contract or with any of such rules, regulations, or orders, this contract may be canceled, terminated or suspended in whole or in part and the contractor may be declared ineligible for further Government contracts in accordance with procedures authorized in [this executive order], and such other sanctions may be imposed and remedies invoked as provided in [this order], or by rule, regulation, or order of the Secretary of Labor, or as otherwise provided by law. . . .

Subpart C—Powers and Duties of the Secretary of Labor and the Contracting Agencies

SEC. 205. Each contracting agency shall be primarily responsible for obtaining compliance with the rules, regulations, and orders of the Secretary of Labor with respect to contracts entered into by such agency or its contractors. All contracting agencies shall comply with the rules of the Secretary of Labor in discharging their primary responsibility for securing compliance with the provisions of contracts and otherwise with the terms of this Order and of the rules, regulations, and orders of the Secretary of Labor. . . . They are directed to cooperate with the Secretary of Labor and to furnish the Secretary of Labor such information and assistance as he may require in the performance of his functions under this Order. They are further directed to appoint or designate, from among the agency's personnel, compliance officers. It shall be the duty of such officers to seek compliance with the objectives of this Order by conference, conciliation, mediation, or persuasion.

SEC. 206. (a) The Secretary of Labor may investigate the employment practices of any Government contractor or subcontractor, or initiate such investigation by the appropriate contracting agency, to determine whether or not the contractual provisions specified in Section 202 of this Order have been violated. Such investigation shall be conducted in accordance with the procedures established by the Secretary of Labor and the investigating agency shall report to the Secretary of Labor any action taken or recommended.

(b) The Secretary of Labor may receive and investigate or cause to be investigated complaints by employees or prospective employees of a Government contractor or subcontractor which allege discrimination contrary to the contractual provisions specified in Section 202 of this Order. . . .

SEC. 207. The Secretary of Labor shall use his best efforts, directly and through contracting agencies, other interested Federal, State, and local agencies, contractors, and all other available instrumentalities to cause any labor union engaged in work under Government contracts or any agency referring workers or providing or supervising apprenticeship or training for or in the course of such work to cooperate in the implementation of the purposes of this Order. . . .

SEC. 208. (a) The Secretary of Labor, or any agency, officer, or employee in the executive branch of the Government designated by rule, regulation, or order of the Secretary, may hold such hearings, public or private, as the Secretary may deem advisable for compliance, enforcement, or educational purposes. . . .

Subpart D—Sanctions and Penalties

SEC. 209. (a) In accordance with such rules, regulations, or orders as the Secretary of Labor may issue or adopt, the Secretary or the appropriate contracting agency may:

(1) Publish, or cause to be published, the names of contractors or unions which it has concluded have complied or have failed to comply with the provisions of this Order or of the rules, regulations, and orders of the Secretary of Labor.

(2) Recommend to the Department of Justice that, in cases in which there is substantial or material violation or the threat of substantial or material violation of the contractual provisions set forth in Section 202 of this Order, appropriate proceedings be brought to enforce those provisions. . . .

(3) Recommend to the Equal Employment Opportunity Commission or the Department of Justice that appropriate proceedings be instituted under Title VII of the Civil Rights Act of 1964.

(4) Recommend to the Department of Justice that criminal proceedings be brought for the furnishing of false information to any contracting agency or to the Secretary of Labor as the case may be.

(5) Cancel, terminate, suspend . . . for failure of the contractor or subcontractor to comply with the non-discrimination provisions of the contract. . . .

(6) Provide that any contracting agency shall refrain from entering into further contracts, or extensions or other modifications of existing contracts, with any noncomplying contractor, until such contractor has satisfied the Secretary of Labor that such contractor has established and will carry out personnel and employment policies in compliance with the provisions of this Order.

(b) Under rules and regulations prescribed by the Secretary of Labor, each contracting agency shall make reasonable efforts within a reasonable time limitation to secure compliance with the contract provisions of this Order by methods of conference, conciliation, mediation, and persuasion before proceedings shall be instituted under Subsection (a)(2) of this Section, or before a contract shall be canceled or terminated in whole or in part under Subsection (a)(5) of this Section for failure of a contractor or subcontractor to comply with the contract provisions of this Order. . . .

PART III—NONDISCRIMINATION PROVISIONS IN FEDERALLY ASSISTED CONSTRUCTION CONTRACTS

SEC. 301. Each executive department and agency which administers a program involving Federal financial assistance shall require as a condition for the approval of any grant, contract, loan, insurance, or guarantee thereunder, which may involve a construction contract, that the applicant for Federal assistance undertake and agree to incorporate, or cause to be incorporated, into all construction contracts paid for in whole or in part with funds obtained from the Federal Government or borrowed on the credit of the Federal Government pursuant to such grant, contract, loan, insurance, or guarantee, or undertaken pursuant to any Federal program involving such grant, contract, loan, insurance, or guarantee, the provisions prescribed for Government contracts by Section 202 of this Order . . . preserving in substance the contractor's obligations thereunder, as may be approved by the Secretary of Labor, together with such additional provisions as the Secretary deems appropriate to establish and protect the interest of the United States in the enforcement of those obligations. . . .

SEC. 303. (a) Each administering department and agency shall be responsible for obtaining the compliance of such applicants with their undertakings under this Order. Each administering department and agency is directed to cooperate with the Secretary of Labor, and to furnish the

Secretary such information and assistance as he may require in the performance of his functions under this Order.

(b) In the event an applicant fails and refuses to comply with his undertakings, the administering department or agency may take any or all of the following actions: (1) cancel, terminate, or suspend in whole or in part the agreement, contract, or other arrangement with such applicant with respect to which the failure and refusal occurred; (2) refrain from extending any further assistance to the applicant under the program with respect to which the failure or refusal occurred until satisfactory assurance of future compliance has been received from such applicant; and (3) refer the case to the Department of Justice for appropriate legal proceedings. . . .

PART IV—MISCELLANEOUS

SEC. 403. (a) Executive Orders Nos. 10590 (January 19, 1955), 10722 (August 5, 1957), 10925 (March 6, 1961) [discussed in Chapter 29], 11114 (June 22, 1963), and 11162 (July 28, 1964), are hereby superseded and the President's Committee on Equal Employment Opportunity established by Executive Order No. 10925 is hereby abolished. All records and property in the custody of the Committee shall be transferred to the Civil Service Commission and the Secretary of Labor, as appropriate. . . .

LYNDON B. JOHNSON
THE WHITE HOUSE,
September 24, 1965.

NOTES

1. June 4, 1965. Quoted in Charles V. Hamilton, *American Government* (Chicago: Scott, Forseman, 1982), p. 532.

2. See James L. Roark et al., *The American Promise* (Boston: Bedford Books, 1998), p. 1122.

3. For example, see Richard T. Seymour, "A Point of View: Why Executive Order 11246 Should Be Preserved," *Employee Relations Law Journal* 11, no. 4 (Spring 1986): 568–84.

4. Hugh Davis Graham, *Civil Rights and the Presidency* (New York: Oxford University Press, 1992), p. 154.

5. Ibid., p. 155.

6. Quoted in Hamilton, *American Government*, p. 535.

7. Study discussed in John Hope Franklin and Alfred A. Moss, Jr., *From Slavery to Freedom: A History of African Americans* (New York: Knopf, 1994), pp. 513–14.

8. A quota requires a fixed number be selected from a particular demographic group.

9. Reverse discrimination is discrimination against one group as a result of providing preferential treatment for another group.

10. Actually, this was the second Philadelphia Plan. The first Philadelphia Plan, like the Cleveland Plan, was developed by Edward Sylvester during the Johnson years.

11. Comptroller General Elmer Staats to Secretary of Labor George Shultz, August 5, 1969, GAO; 49 Comp. Gen. 59 (1969).

12. The Senate actually passed it as an amendment to a minor supplemental appropriation bill meant for victims of Hurricane Camille.

13. For a fuller discussion, see Graham, *Civil Rights and the Presidency*, pp. 155–69; Hanes Walton, Jr., and Robert C. Smith, *American Politics and the African American Quest for Universal Freedom* (New York: Longman, 2000), pp. 208–9.

14. CFR Part 60–62 (1970).

15. *Regents of the University of California v. Bakke*, 438 U.S. 265 (1978).

16. *Federal Register* (Washington, D.C.: GPO), vol. 30, pp. 12319–25.

36

Fair Housing Act

1968

The Fair Housing Act barred racial discrimination in the advertising, sale, rental, or financing of most housing units.

HISTORICAL CONTEXT

President John F. Kennedy's Executive Order 11063 (1962) banned racial discrimination only in housing where federal funds were involved, leaving the large majority of sale and rental decisions to occur outside federal regulation.

In 1966 Martin Luther King, Jr., led the Chicago Freedom Movement. The specific goal was to open white neighborhoods to black residents and to force landlords to meet health and safety regulations. More broadly, it was an attempt to focus the city and the nation's attention on the continuing problem of racial discrimination in the housing market.

Housing discrimination, however, remained a highly volatile national issue because racial segregation was deeply entrenched across the United States. Some of that residential segregation was by individual choice. Much of it, on the other hand, resulted from the discriminatory practices of sellers and their real estate agents. The government also contributed by following such practices as racial segregation in local public housing. Nevertheless, the overall issue was so pervasive and so volatile that even the Civil Rights Act of 1964 avoided the subject.

By 1966 President Lyndon B. Johnson was pressing for a legislative package that would outlaw housing discrimination and protect civil rights workers in the North and South. To this end, he offered fair housing legislation in both 1966 and 1967. The measures both stalled in Congress because the political climate was no longer nearly as conducive to the passage of sweeping new civil rights initiatives.

Most Republicans opposed the fair housing measures in large part because they would give the federal government power to police the motivations of people in selling and renting their own residences. In addition, the national mood had shifted. Urban rioting was at its zenith, and the rhetoric of ever more militant black activists was now joined by a growing backlash among whites. It had become increasingly difficult to pass any new civil rights legislation in this atmosphere. The coalition of liberal Democrats and moderate Republicans—the group that had been the driving force behind much of the era's civil rights legislation—had begun to unravel.[1]

During President Johnson's State of the Union address given on January 17, 1968, the Congress largely fell silent when he mentioned his civil rights agenda, although meeting of riot control garnered hearty applause.[2] Despite the absence of congressional enthusiasm for his civil rights proposals, the president persisted. In his January 24 civil rights message to Congress, he argued for a fair housing bill because such legislation "is decent and right." He also argued that "the criminal conduct of some must not weaken our resolve to deal with the real grievances of all those suffering discrimination."[3]

A very limited civil rights bill had passed in the House of Representatives in August 1967. Adopted by the Committee of the Whole after only three hours of debate, it made racially motivated violence directed at blacks and civil rights workers a federal crime. Yet, as Representative Robert Kastenmeier (Dem., Wis.) put it, "Passage of this bill will have little or no effect on the average American Negro."[4]

As moderate as the legislation was, however, Senator Sam Ervin (Dem., N.C.) still led a successful filibuster. That filibuster lasted for thirty-three days and survived three separate cloture votes. On February 19, the *Wall Street Journal* declared the very modest House bill to be "almost certainly doomed."[5] Yet, the president pressed on. In particular, he reached out to organizations like the NAACP and the Leadership Conference on Civil Rights. Together they lobbied furiously.[6]

The pivotal revision was offered by Minority Leader Everett Dirksen (Rep., Ill.) after he was informed that the majority of his party wanted passage of some type of civil rights bill.[7] The housing issue then reemerged in the Senate as an amendment to the House bill. As such, it was never subjected to the normal route through the labyrinth of House and Senate committees. In his speech to Congress introducing his amendment, Dirksen justified his own reversal: "There are only two categories of people who do not change their minds in the face of reality. One group is sacredly embalmed. . . . The other . . . [have] problems . . . that have committed them to mental institutions."[8]

Although very definitely open housing legislation, the Dirksen amendment did exempt single-family owner-occupied housing if the family sold or rented the property on its own, not using a real estate company. This reduced coverage from 90 percent to 80 percent of all housing. In addition, the compromise relied on local judges to punish those caught discriminating, with the burden of proof falling on those bringing the lawsuit. The Department of Housing and Urban Development could only hold hearings and try to mediate disputes. The attorney general, on the other hand, would be authorized to bring suit on behalf of individuals, if there was an identifiable "pattern or practice" of such discrimination.

Opposition quickly reemerged, led again by Senator Ervin, who called Dirksen's housing initiative an effort "to rob Americans of their precious freedom to control the use and disposition of their privately-owned property."[9] Once again, a Southern-led filibuster developed.

This time, however, sufficient compromises had been reached. With the support of the leadership of both political parties, cloture was voted on March 4. Such bipartisan support had been spurred in part by the release of the *Kerner Commission Report on Civil Disorder*, which cited housing discrimination as an underlying cause of racial unrest in the nation's cities.

Nonetheless, forty-three amendments were offered during the one hour of Senate floor debate. The most noteworthy amendment to pass, offered by Senator Strom Thurmond (Dem., S.C.), strengthened the bill's antirioting provisions. Rioters, for example, were to be subjected to the same penalties as those convicted of harming civil rights workers, and it became a federal crime to teach someone to use firearms or explosives for rioting purposes. Amendments to soften the bill's fair housing provisions, however, were defeated.

The amended bill passed the full Senate by a vote of 71–20 on

March 11, endorsed by the Republican Party's two leading presidential candidates, Richard M. Nixon and Nelson Rockefeller. Once again, it stalled when it returned to the House. The House Rules Committee, for instance, voted to postpone even considering the bill until April 9, after Congress returned from its Easter recess.

It was the assassination of Martin Luther King, Jr., on April 4 that appeared to do more than anything else to turn the tide.[10] President Johnson, who had announced his intention not to seek a second term, urged Congress to honor King's memory by passing "legislation so long delayed and so close to fulfillment."[11]

As urban rioting spread following the assassination, the Senate bill passed rapidly through the House. The Rules Committee recommended approval on April 9, the day of King's funeral. There was to be one hour of debate, and no amendments were to be allowed. Without amendment, then, the full House adopted the bill on April 10 by a vote of 229–195. President Johnson signed the bill the day after passage. At the signing ceremony, he declared that the "only real road to progress for free people is through the process of law."[12]

Representative John Anderson (Rep., Ill.) explained his support by stating, "I seek to reward those Negroes who can become responsible leaders of our society and diminish the influence of black racists and preachers of violence."[13] Meanwhile, opponents had expressed concern for the haste with which the bill had been considered, as well as for the loss of individual freedom inherent in the bill. John Ashbrook (Rep., Ohio), for example, decried "the Reichstag-type rubberstamp process" and concluded, "The whole concept of freedom and private property are at stake here."[14]

Titles eight and nine of the 1968 Civil Rights Act, also known as either the Fair Housing Act or the Open Housing Act, prohibited discrimination on the basis of race, sex, national origin, color, religion, handicap, and familial status in the sale, rental, financing, or advertising of housing, with a few minor exceptions for owner-occupied homes sold or rented without a real estate agent. Violators faced significant penalties. The Department of Housing and Urban Development was given the authority to initiate complaints. Meanwhile, the Department of Justice was granted litigation authority. Yet, the burden of proof remained on the complainant, and that person had to seek local remedies first. The act also included a punitive antirioting provision and barred discrimination in jury selection.[15]

In June 1968, the United States Supreme Court broadened legal coverage, ruling that the Civil Rights Act of 1866 already banned racial discrimination in the sale and rental of all residential housing.[16] Earlier, the court had struck down racial zoning and refused to allow judicial enforcement of restrictive covenants—legal agreements that required homeowners to sell on the basis of race.[17] In handing down these decisions, the nation's highest court was attempting to eliminate the racial discrimination that "herds men into ghettos and makes their ability to buy property turn on the color of their skin."[18]

The pronouncements were sweeping, but the enforcement mechanisms were weak. Individuals had to file suit themselves and then had the burden of proof, even though such discrimination is often subtle and hard to pinpoint. Fair housing groups attempted to help, but little actually changed as a result of this original law. The 1988 Fair Housing Amendments Act strengthened enforcement procedures and allowed the Department of Housing and Urban Development to initiate legal action. Nonetheless, most U.S. cities remained heavily segregated by race.[19]

THE LAW

Titles VIII and IX of the 1968 Civil Rights of Act,[20] commonly referred to as the Fair Housing Act, barred discriminatory practices in the advertising, sale, rental, or financing of most dwellings. The act specifically prohibited discrimination on the basis of race, color, religion, or national origin. Injuring, intimidating, or interfering with individuals attempting to exercise rights to fair housing was specifically prohibited by the act and punishable by fines and imprisonment.[21]

Authority for administration of the Fair Housing Act was given to the secretary of housing and urban development, who was also charged with the responsibility of commencing educational and cooperative activities to further the purposes of the act. The secretary was encouraged to cooperate with state and local agencies involved in the administration of fair housing laws. Executive departments and agencies of the Federal government were directed to administer their housing-related programs in accordance with the act and to cooperate with the secretary.

The enforcement provisions of the Fair Housing Act required individuals to file a written complaint with the secretary. Upon receipt of the complaint, the secretary was required to investigate and determine whether to attempt to resolve the dispute. The act directed the Secretary to attempt to eliminate discriminatory housing practices "by informal methods of conference, conciliation, and persuasion." If the aggrieved party was not satisfied with the resolution of the matter, the individual could file a lawsuit in United States district court. In such action, the burden of proof was placed on the party filing the complaint.

36. Civil Rights Act of 1968

Be it enacted . . .

TITLE VIII—FAIR HOUSING POLICY

SEC. 801. It is the policy of the United States to provide, within constitutional limitations, for fair housing throughout the United States.

Definitions

SEC. 802. As used in this title—

(a) "Secretary" means the Secretary of Housing and Urban Development.

(b) "Dwelling" means any building, structure, or portion thereof which is occupied as, or designed or intended for occupancy as, a residence by one or more families, and any vacant land which is offered for sale or lease for the construction or location thereon of any such building, structure, or portion thereof.

(c) "Family" includes a single individual.

(d) "Person" includes one or more individuals, corporations, partnerships, associations, labor organizations, legal representatives, mutual companies, joint-stock companies, trusts, unincorporated organizations, trustees, trustees in bankruptcy, receivers, and fiduciaries.

(e) "To rent" includes to lease, to sublease, to let and otherwise to grant for a consideration the right to occupy premises not owned by the occupant.

(f) "Discriminatory housing practice" means an act that is unlawful under section 804, 805, or 806.

(g) "State" means any of the several States, the District of Columbia, the Commonwealth of Puerto Rico, or any of the territories and possessions of the United States. . . .

Discrimination in the Sale or Rental of Housing

SEC. 804. . . . [I]t shall be unlawful—

(a) To refuse to sell or rent after the making of a bona fide offer, or to refuse to negotiate for the sale or rental of, or otherwise make unavailable or deny, a dwelling to any person because of race, color, religion, or national origin.

(b) To discriminate against any person in the terms, conditions, or privileges of sale or rental of a dwelling, or in the provision of services or facilities in connection therewith, because of race, color, religion, or national origin.

(c) To make, print, or publish, or cause to be made, printed, or published any notice, statement, or advertisement, with respect to the sale or rental of a dwelling that indicates any preference, limitation, or discrimination based on race, color, religion, or national origin, or an intention to make any such preference, limitation, or discrimination.

(d) To represent to any person because of race, color, religion, or national origin that any dwelling is not available for inspection, sale, or rental when such dwelling is in fact so available.

(e) For profit, to induce or attempt to induce any person to sell or rent any dwelling by representations regarding the entry or prospective entry into the neighborhood of a person or persons of a particular race, color, religion, or national origin.

Discrimination in the Financing of Housing

SEC. 805. After December 31, 1968, it shall be unlawful for any bank, building and loan association, insurance company or other corporation, association, firm or enterprise whose business consists in whole or in part in the making of commercial real estate loans, to deny a loan or other financial assistance to a person applying therefor for the purpose of purchasing, constructing, improving, repairing, or maintaining a dwelling, or to discriminate against him in the fixing of the amount, interest rate, duration, or other terms or conditions of such loan or other financial assistance, because of the race, color, religion, or national origin of such person or of any person associated with him in connection with such loan or other financial assistance or the purposes of such loan or other financial assistance, or of the present or prospective owners, lessees, tenants, or occupants of the dwelling or dwellings in relation to which such loan or other financial assistance is to be made or given. . . .

Discrimination in the Provision of Brokerage Services

SEC. 806. After December 31, 1968, it shall be unlawful to deny any person access to or membership or participation in any multiple-listing service, real estate brokers' organization or other service, organization, or facility relating to the business of selling or renting dwellings, or to discriminate against him in the terms or conditions of such access, membership, or participation, on account of race, color, religion, or national origin.

Exemption

SEC. 807. Nothing in this title shall prohibit a religious organization, association, or society, or any nonprofit institution or organization operated, supervised or controlled by or in conjunction with a religious organization, association, or society, from limiting the sale, rental or occupancy of dwellings which it owns or operates for other than a commercial purpose to persons of the same religion, or from giving preference to such persons, unless membership in such religion is restricted on account of race, color, or national origin. Nor shall anything in this title prohibit a private club not in fact open to the public, which as an incident to its primary purpose or purposes provides lodgings which it owns or operates for other than a commercial purpose, from limiting the rental or occupancy of such lodgings to its members or from giving preference to its members.

Administration

SEC. 808. (a) The authority and responsibility for administering this Act shall be in the Secretary of Housing and Urban Development. . . .

(d) All executive departments and agencies shall administer their programs and activities relating to housing and urban development in a manner affirmatively to further the purposes of this title and shall cooperate with the Secretary to further such purposes.

(e) The Secretary of Housing and Urban Development shall—

(1) make studies with respect to the nature and extent of discriminatory housing practices in representative communities, urban, suburban, and rural, throughout the United States;

(2) publish and disseminate reports, recommendations, and information derived from such studies;

(3) cooperate with and render technical assistance to Federal, State, local, and other public or private agencies, organizations, and institutions which are formulating or carrying on programs to prevent or eliminate discriminatory housing practices;

(4) cooperate with and render such technical and other assistance to the Community Relations Service as may be appropriate to further its activities in preventing or eliminating discriminatory housing practices; and

(5) administer the programs and activities relating to housing and ur-

ban development in a manner affirmatively to further the policies of this title.

Education and Conciliation

SEC. 809. Immediately after the enactment of this title the Secretary shall commence such educational and conciliatory activities as in his judgment will further the purposes of this title. He shall call conferences of persons in the housing industry and other interested parties to acquaint them with the provisions of this title and his suggested means of implementing it, and shall endeavor with their advice to work out programs of voluntary compliance and of enforcement. . . . He shall consult with State and local officials and other interested parties to learn the extent, if any, to which housing discrimination exists in their State or locality, and whether and how State or local enforcement programs might be utilized to combat such discrimination in connection with or in place of, the Secretary's enforcement of this title. The Secretary shall issue reports on such conferences and consultations as he deems appropriate.

Enforcement

SEC. 810. (a) Any person who claims to have been injured by a discriminatory housing practice or who believes that he will be irrevocably injured by a discriminatory housing practice that is about to occur (hereafter "person aggrieved") may file a complaint with the Secretary. Complaints shall be in writing and shall contain such information and be in such form as the Secretary requires. Upon receipt of such a complaint the Secretary shall furnish a copy of the same to the person or persons who allegedly committed or are about to commit the alleged discriminatory housing practice. Within thirty days after receiving a complaint . . . the Secretary shall investigate the complaint and give notice in writing to the person aggrieved whether he intends to resolve it. If the Secretary decides to resolve the complaint, he shall proceed to try to eliminate or correct the alleged discriminatory housing practice by informal methods of conference, conciliation, and persuasion. Nothing said or done in the course of such informal endeavors may be made public or used as evidence in a subsequent proceeding under this title without the written consent of the persons concerned. . . .

(b) A complaint under subsection (a) shall be filed within one hundred and eighty days after the alleged discriminatory housing practice occurred. Complaints shall be in writing and shall state the facts upon which the allegations of a discriminatory housing practice are based. Complaints may be reasonably and fairly amended at any time. A respondent may file an answer to the complaint against him and with the leave of the Secretary, which shall be granted whenever it would be reasonable and fair to do so, may amend his answer at any time. . . .

(c) Wherever a State or local fair housing law provides rights and remedies for alleged discriminatory housing practices which are substantially equivalent to the rights and remedies provided in this title, the Secretary shall notify the appropriate State or local agency of any complaint filed under this title which appears to constitute a violation of such State or local fair housing law, and the Secretary shall take no further action with respect to such complaint if the appropriate State or local law enforcement official has, within thirty days from the date the alleged offense has been brought to his attention, commenced proceedings in the matter, or, having done so, carries forward such proceedings with reasonable promptness. In no event shall the Secretary take further action unless he certifies that in his judgment, under the circumstances of the particular case, the protection of the rights of the parties or the interests of justice require such action. [Deference is given to state enforcement, and the Secretary is not to intervene unless the state fails to protect individual rights or the broader interests of justice.]

(d) If within thirty days after a complaint is filed with the Secretary or within thirty days after expiration of any period of reference under subsection (c), the Secretary has been unable to obtain voluntary compliance with this title, the person aggrieved may, within thirty days thereafter, commence a civil action in any appropriate United States district court, against the respondent named in the complaint, to enforce the rights granted or protected by this title, insofar as such rights relate to the subject of the complaint: Provided, That no such civil action may be brought in any United States district court if the person aggrieved has a judicial remedy under a State or local fair housing law which provides rights and remedies for alleged discriminatory housing practices which are substantially equivalent to the rights and remedies provided in this title. [Individuals are precluded from bringing federal action if a legal redress exists under state law.] Such actions may be brought without regard to the amount in controversy in any United States district court for the district in which the discriminatory housing practice is alleged to have occurred or be about to occur or in which the respondent resides or transacts business. If the court finds that a discriminatory housing practice has occurred or is about to occur, the court may, subject to the provisions of section 812, enjoin the respondent from engaging in such practice or order such affirmative action as may be appropriate. [Court is granted authority to stop discriminatory practices.]

(e) In any proceeding brought pursuant to this section, the burden of proof shall be on the complainant. [Aggrieved person is required to prove discriminatory housing practices.]

(f) Whenever an action filed by an individual, in either Federal or State court, pursuant to this section or section 812, shall come to trial the Secretary shall immediately terminate all efforts to obtain voluntary compliance. . . .

Enforcement by Private Persons

SEC. 812. (a) The rights granted by sections 803, 804, 805, and 806 may be enforced by civil actions in appropriate United States district courts without regard to the amount in controversy and in appropriate State or local courts of general jurisdiction. A civil action shall be commenced within one hundred and eighty days after the alleged discriminatory housing practice occurred: Provided, however, That the court shall continue such civil case brought pursuant to this section or section 810 (d) from time to time before bringing it to trial if the court believes that the conciliation efforts of the Secretary or a State or local agency are likely to result in satisfactory settlement of the discriminatory housing practice complained of in the complaint made to the Secretary or to the local or State agency and which practice forms the basis for the action in court: protects the same rights as are granted by this title; but any law of a State, a political subdivision, or other such jurisdiction that purports to require or permit any action that would be a discriminatory housing practice under this title shall to that extent be invalid. . . .

Interference, Coercion, or Intimidation

SEC. 817. It shall be unlawful to coerce, intimidate, threaten, or interfere with any person in the exercise or enjoyment of, or on account of his having exercised or enjoyed, or on account of his having aided or encouraged any other person in the exercise or enjoyment of, any right granted or protected by section 803, 804, 805, or 806. This section may be enforced by appropriate civil action. . . .

TITLE IX—PREVENTION OF INTIMIDATION IN FAIR HOUSING CASES

SEC. 901. Whoever, whether or not acting under color of law, by force or threat of force willfully injures, intimidates or interferes with, or attempts to injure, intimidate or interfere with—

(a) any person because of his race, color, religion or national origin and because he is or has been selling, purchasing, renting, financing, occupying, or contracting or negotiating for the sale, purchase, rental, financing or occupation of any dwelling, or applying for or participating in any service, organization, or facility relating to the business of selling or renting dwellings; or

(b) any person because he is or has been, or in order to intimidate such person or any other person or any class of persons from—

(1) participating, without discrimination on account of race, color, religion or national origin, in any of the activities, services, organizations or facilities described in subsection 901 (a); or

(2) affording another person or class of persons opportunity or protection so to participate; or

(c) any citizen because he is or has been, or in order to discourage such citizen or any other citizen from lawfully aiding or encouraging other persons to participate, without discrimination on account of race, color, religion or national origin, in any of the activities, services, organizations or facilities described in subsection 901 (a), or participating lawfully in speech or peaceful assembly opposing any denial of the opportunity to so participate—shall be fined not more than $1,000, or imprisoned not more than one year, or both; and if bodily injury results shall be fined not more than $10,000, or imprisoned not more than ten years, or both; and if death results shall be subject to imprisonment for any term of years or for life. . . .

APPROVED April 11, 1968.

NOTES

1. For example, see Hugh Davis Graham, *Civil Rights and the Presidency* (New York: Oxford University Press, 1992), p. 127.

2. Steven F. Lawson, *In Pursuit of Power* (New York: Columbia University Press, 1985), p. 81.

3. Ibid., p. 82.

4. Bernard Schwartz, ed., *Statutory History of the United States: Civil Rights* (New York: Chelsea House, 1970), pt. 2, p. 1667.

5. Cited in Graham, *Civil Rights and the Presidency*, p. 128.

6. Lawson, *In Pursuit of Power* p. 87.

7. Ibid., p. 85.

8. Schwartz, *Statutory History of the United States*, pt. 2, p. 1682.

9. Quoted in ibid., p. 1630.

10. For example, see ibid., pp. 1631–32.

11. Quoted in Lawson, *In Pursuit of Power*, p. 86.

12. Quoted in ibid., p. 87.

13. Ibid.

14. Schwartz, *Statutory History of the United States*, pt. 2, pp. 1793, 1797.

15. For more detail, see Schwartz, *Statutory History of the United States*, pt. 2, pp. 1627–1837; Lawson, *In Pursuit of Power*, pp. 81–88; Graham, *Civil Rights and the Presidency*, pp. 127–131.

16. In *Jones v. Alfred H. Mayer Co.*, 392 U.S. 409 (1968), the Court found the congressional authority to regulate such private decisions in the enforcement clause of the Thirteenth Amendment. Combatting housing discrimination was regarded as eradicating what Justice John Marshall Harlan had called one of the "badges and incidents" of slavery in his dissenting opinion in the 1883 Civil Rights Cases.

17. See *Buchanan v. Warley*, 245 U.S. 60 (1971) and *Shelly v. Kramer*, 334 U.S. 1 (1948), respectively, where such decisions are seen as extensions of "state action" and thus bound by Fourteenth Amendment guarantees of equal protection and due process of law.

18. Quoted in Schwartz, *Statutory History of the United States*, pt. 2, p. 1814.

19. For example, see Douglass S. Massey and Nancy A. Denton, *American Apartheid: Segregation and the Making of the Underclass* (Cambridge, Mass.: Harvard University Press, 1993), especially chap. 7; John Hope Franklin and Alfred A. Moss, Jr., *From Slavery to Freedom: A History of African Americans* (New York: Knopf, 1994), pp. 471–72.

20. *United States Statutes at Large* (Washington, D.C.: GPO), vol. 82, pp. 73–92.

21. Title I of the Civil Rights Acts prohibits injuring, intimidating, or interfering by force or threat of force, whether or not acting under the color of law, with individuals engaging in other federally protected activities. It also provides for fines and imprisonment, but it does not create a right to sue for damages.

Bibliography

Blaustein, Albert, and Robert Zangrando. *Civil Rights and the Black American*. New
    York: Washington Square Press, 1968.
Branch, Taylor. *Parting the Waters: America in the King Years, 1954–1963*. New York:
    Simon and Schuster, 1988.
Brauer, Carl M. *John F. Kennedy and the Second Reconstruction*. New York: Columbia
    University Press, 1977.
Bullock, Charles III, and Charles Lamb. *The Implementation of Civil Rights Policy*.
    Monterey, Calif.: Brooks/Cole, 1984.
Corwin, Edward S. *The Constitution and What It Means Today*. Princeton; N.J.: Prince-
    ton University Press, 1978.
Davis, David Brian. *The Problem of Slavery in the Age of Revolution, 1770–1823*. Ithaca,
    N.Y.: Cornell University Press, 1975.
Divine, Robert, et al. *America: Past and Present*. New York: Longman, 1999.
Faragher, John Mack, et al. *Out of Many*. Upper Saddle River, N.J.: Prentice-Hall,
    2000.
Farrand, Max. *The Framing of the Constitution of the United States*. New Haven, Conn.:
    Yale University Press, 1913.
Foner, Eric. *Reconstruction: America's Unfinished Revolution, 1863–1877*. New York:
    Harper and Row, 1988.
Franklin, John Hope, ed. *Race and History: Selected Essays, 1938–1988*. Baton Rouge:
    Louisiana State University Press, 1994.
Franklin, John Hope, and Alfred A. Moss, Jr. *From Slavery to Freedom: A History of
    African Americans*. New York: Knopf, 1994.
Frazier, E. Franklin. *The Negro in the United States*. New York: Macmillan, 1957.
Goldfield, David, et al. *The American Journey*. Upper Saddle River, N.J.: Prentice-
    Hall, 1998.
Graham, Hugh Davis. *Civil Rights and the Presidency*. New York: Oxford University
    Press, 1992.
———. *The Civil Rights Era*. New York: Oxford University Press, 1990.
Johnson, Paul. *A History of the American People*. New York: HarperCollins, 1997.
Key, V.O. *Southern Politics*. New York: Knopf, 1949.

Lawson, Steven. *Black Ballots: Voting Rights in the South, 1944–1969.* New York: Columbia University Press, 1976.
———. *In Pursuit of Power.* New York: Columbia University Press, 1985.
———. *Running for Freedom.* Philadelphia: Temple University Press, 1991.
Legal Information Institute. *Historic Supreme Court Decisions.* Available online: http://supct.law.cornell.edu/supct/cases/topic.htm#Topic_C-E.
Library of Congress. *African American Odyssey.* Available online: http://lcweb2.loc.gov/ammem/aaohtml/.
Morrison, Samuel Eliot, and Henry Steele Commager. *The Growth of the American Republic.* Oxford, England: Oxford University Press, 1962.
Nelson, William E. *The 14th Amendment.* Cambridge, Mass.: Harvard University Press, 1995.
Nieman, Donald. *Promises to Keep: African-Americans and the Constitutional Order, 1776 to the Present.* New York: Oxford University Press, 1991.
O'Brien, David. *Constitutional Law and Politics: Civil Rights and Civil Liberties.* New York: Norton, 2000.
Roark, James, et al. *The American Promise.* Boston: Bedford Books, 1998.
Schultz, Jeffrey, et al., eds. *Encyclopedia of Minorities in American Politics: African Americans and Asian Americans,* vol. 1. Westport, CT: Oryx Press, 2000.
Schwartz, Bernard, ed. *Statutory History of the United States: Civil Rights,* pt. 1. New York: Chelsea House, 1970.
Sitkoff, Harvard. *The Struggle for Black Equality 1954–1980.* New York: Hill and Wang, 1981.
Walton, Hanes, Jr., and Robert C. Smith. *American Politics and the African American Quest for Universal Freedom.* New York: Longman, 2000.
Woodward, C. Vann. *The Strange Career of Jim Crow.* New York: Oxford University Press, 1966.

Index

Abolitionists, 13, 23, 28–29, 47, 56, 62–63, 65–66
Ackerman, Amos T., 117
Acts of Congress, 130–132
Adams, Abigail, 10
Adams, John, 10
Affirmative action, 96–97, 131, 183, 185, 187, 213, 215, 251–253
Aid to Families with Dependent Children (AFDC), 131
Amnesty Act of 1898, 109
Anderson, John, 264
Antibusing legislation, 131
Antidiscrimination laws, 129
Antilynching laws, 70, 94–95, 129, 140
Antislavery movement, 13, 23, 28–29, 47, 56, 62–63, 65–66
Antiterrorism law, 116
Arensault, Raymond, 124
Arthur, Chester, 124
Articles of Confederation (1766), 1, 3–6; historical context of, 3–5; the law, 5–6
Ashbrook, John, 264
Atchison, David, 48

Badge of servitude, 83, 125
Barbour, John, 134
Barnett, Ross, 194–196
Battle of Antietam, 64

Bayh, Birch, 237
Bidwell, Barnabas, 28
Bill of Rights, 16, 92, 95
Bingham, John, 83, 103, 106
Birmingham (AL) church bombing, 210
Black, Hugo, 194
Black codes, 82, 87, 92, 123
Black majority districts, 242
Blackman, Harry, 253
Blaine, James, 103, 124
"Bleeding Kansas," 48
Bloody Sunday (March 7, 1965), 235
Boggs, Hale, 237
Bradley, Joseph, 125
Bradley, Stephen, 28
Brauer, Carl, 196, 200
Brooks, Preston, 48
Brotherhood of Sleeping Car Porters, 129, 134, 152
Brown, Prentiss, 134
Brown v. Board of Education, 98, 130, 157–159, 165
Brownell, Herbert, 164
Burke, Thomas, 4
Butler, Andrew, 48
Butler, Benjamin, 116

Calhoun, John, 41
Capper, Arthur, 134

Carpenter, Matthew, 107
Carpetbaggers, 74, 88
Celler, Emanuel, 174, 208, 211
Chase, Salmon, 42
Chicago Freedom Movement, 261
Child labor, 131
Churchill, John, 107
Civil disobedience, 153
Civil rights, 139–140, 163–164, 199
Civil Rights Act (1866), 70, 82–84, 87,
   92, 117, 265; historical context of,
   82–83; the law, 83–84
Civil Rights Act (1870), 107, 109–113
Civil Rights Act (1871). See Klan Act
   (1871)
Civil Rights Act (1875), 70, 123–127,
   214; historical context of, 123–126;
   the law, 126
Civil Rights Act (1957), 104, 131, 163–
   171, 173–176, 218; historical context
   of, 163–166; the law, 166–167
Civil Rights Act (1960), 131, 166, 173–
   181, 214; historical context of, 173–
   175; the law, 176
Civil Rights Act (1964), 104, 125–126,
   131, 166, 210–233; historical context
   of, 210–217; the law, 217–218; Title
   I, 217, 219–220; Title II, 217, 220–
   222; Title III, 217–218, 222; Title IV,
   218, 222–225; Title V, 218, 225–226;
   Title VI, 216, 218, 226; Title VII,
   216, 218, 226–233
Civil Rights Act (1968), Title VIII &
   IX. See Fair Housing Act
Civil Rights Act (1988), 132
Civil Rights Act (1991), 132
Civil Rights Commission, 131, 142, 163–
   164, 166, 174, 214, 217–218, 236
Civil Rights era, 129–132; Acts of
   Congress, 130–132; Civil Rights Act
   (1957), 104, 131, 163–171, 173–176,
   218; Civil Rights Act (1960), 131,
   166, 173–181; Civil Rights Act
   (1964), 104, 125–126, 131, 166, 210–
   233; Executive Order(s), 129–130;
   Executive Order 8802 (1941), 130,
   133–137; Executive Order 9808
   (1946), 130, 139–143; Executive

Order 9980 (1948), 130, 145–150;
   Executive Order 9981 (1948), 130,
   152–155; Executive Order 10730
   (1957), 130, 157–162; Executive
   Order 10925 (1961), 130, 183–192;
   Executive Order 11053 (1962), 130,
   194–198; Executive Order 11063
   (1962), 130, 199–206, 261; Executive
   Order 11246 (1965), 130, 250–259;
   Fair Housing Act (1968), 131–132,
   166, 261–272 Twenty-fourth
   Amendment (1964), 104, 131, 207–
   209; Voting Rights Act (1965), 104,
   131–132, 166 235–248
Civil rights movement, 173, 210, 235,
   262
Civil Rights Restoration Act of 1988,
   216
Civil Service Commission, 146, 148,
   243, 253
Civil War, 2, 57, 62–65, 71, 79
Clark, Joseph, 175
Clay, Henry, 36–37, 41
Cleveland Plan, 251–252
Cloture, 213, 237, 262–263
Coffin, Levi, 25
Collective bargaining, 131
Commerce regulation, 18, 214–215,
   217
Committee on Fair Employment
   Practices, 133, 136
Common Sense (Paine), 8
Community Relations Service, 217
Compelling state interest, 96
Compromise of 1850, 1, 40–45;
   historical context of, 40–42; the law,
   42–43
Compromise of 1877, 108, 124
Confiscation Acts (1861 and 1862), 2,
   56–61; historical context of, 56–57;
   the law, 58
Congress on Racial Equality (CORE),
   201
Conkling, Roscoe, 63
Constitution of the Confederate States
   of America (1861), 1, 52–55;
   historical context of, 52–54; the law,
   54

Constitutional Convention, 16, 27
Continental Congress, 3, 10, 14
Corwin Amendment. *See* Thirteenth
   Amendment
Cotton gin, 27
Council of Economic Advisors, 251

Davis, Henry, 85
Davis, Jefferson, 53, 65
Declaration of Independence (1776),
   1, 8–12, 53; historical context of, 8–
   11; the law, 11
Delany, Martin, 65
Department of Housing and Urban
   Development, 263–265
Desegregation, 98, 123–124, 129–131,
   163, 214, 218; U.S. military service,
   146, 152–155. *See also* School
   desegregation
Dickinson, John, 3
Dirksen, Everett, 174, 213, 262–263
Discrimination: gender discrimination,
   212; housing discrimination, 130,
   147, 164, 174, 199–201, 261–263;
   patterns or practices of, 216, 218,
   263; private-sector discrimination,
   215; reverse discrimination, 252;
   voting discrimination, 102–103, 140.
   See also Employment discrimination;
   Racial discrimination
Discriminatory intent, 213
Disenfranchisement, 70, 88, 140. *See
   also* Right to vote
Disparate impact, 97, 215
Dixiecrats, 145–146
Dixon, Jeremiah, 35
Dole, Robert, 241
Douglas, Paul, 166
Douglas, Stephen, 41, 46–48
Dred Scott decision (1857), 37, 70, 82,
   93
Due process of law, 69, 93, 95–96, 118

Eastland, James O., 165, 174, 211–213
Eisenhower, Dwight D., 130, 157–160,
   164–166, 173–174, 184, 210
Eldredge, Charles, 107–108
Eliot, Thomas Dawes, 71

Ellsworth, Oliver, 18
Emancipation Proclamation (1863), 2,
   57, 62–67, 78; historical context of,
   62–66; the law, 66
Emancipation society, 56
Emerson, John, 37
Employment discrimination, 164, 174,
   216, 218; Cleveland Plan, 251–252;
   defense industry/vocational training,
   133–135; federal contractors, 250,
   253–254; federal employment, 130,
   146–147; state vs. private, 214
Enforcement Act (1870), 70, 104, 106–
   114, 116, 167; historical context of,
   106–109; the law, 109
Equal Employment Opportunity Act of
   1972, 216
Equal Employment Opportunity
   Commission (EEOC), 213–214, 216–
   218, 251
Equal protection under the law, 69–
   70, 83, 86, 92–93, 95–96, 107, 115–
   116, 123–124, 157, 167
Ervin, Sam, 165, 237, 262–263
Executive Order, 129–130
Executive Order 8802 (1941), 130, 133–
   137; historical context of, 133–135;
   the law, 135–136
Executive Order 9808 (1946), 139–143;
   historical context of, 139–142; the
   law, 142
Executive Order 9980 (1948), 145–
   150, 153; historical context of, 145–
   147; the law, 147–148
Executive Order 9981 (1948), 130, 152–
   155; historical context of, 152–154;
   the law, 154
Executive Order 10730 (1957), 130,
   157–162; historical context of, 157–
   160; the law, 160
Executive Order 10925 (1961), 183;
   historical context of, 183–186; the
   law, 186–187
Executive Order 11053 (1962), 194;
   historical context of, 194–196; the
   law, 196–197
Executive Order 11063 (1962), 130,

199–206, 261; historical context of,
   199–201; the law, 210
Executive Order 11246 (1965), 130,
   250–259; historical context of, 250–
   253; the law, 253–254
Executive Order 11478 (1969), 253

Fahy, Charles, 153
Fair Employment Board, 130, 145–146,
   148, 153
Fair employment practices, 145, 147
Fair Employment Practices
   Commission (FEPC), 130, 134–135,
   146, 152, 185
Fair Housing Act (1968), 131–132,
   166, 261–272; historical context of,
   261–265; the law, 265–266; Title
   VIII, 266–271; Title IX, 271–272
Faubus, Orval, 158–159
Favoritism, 125
Federal contractors, 250, 253–254
Federal employment, 146–147, 184–
   187, 251, 253
Federal government, 20; implied
   powers of, 4
Federal ratio, 17
Federalism, 93
Federalist Paper No. 54 (Madison), 17
Federally assisted programs, 218
Fifteenth Amendment (1870), 70, 80,
   95, 102–105, 107–109, 117, 164, 237–
   238, 242; historical context of, 102–
   104; the law, 105
Fifth Amendment, 37
Filibuster, 213, 240–241, 262–263
First Amendment, 95
Fletcher, Arthur, 252
Force Act (1871), 108
Ford, Gerald, 240
Forrest, William Bedford, 115
Forrestal, James, 152
Fortas, Abe, 184
"Forty acres and a mule," 73–74
Fourteenth Amendment (1868), 60,
   80, 83, 87, 89, 92–101, 103, 106–107,
   116–118, 125–126, 164, 214; due
   process clause, 95; equal protection
   clause, 96, 123–124, 157, 208;

historical context of, 92–98; the law,
   98–99; privileges or immunities
   clause, 94–95
Franklin, Benjamin, 18
Franklin, John Hope, 28, 213
Free individuals, 4–5
Free states, 35, 41–42
Freedmen's Bureau (1865), 69, 71–77,
   87; historical context of, 71–75; the
   law, 75
Freedom to Serve, 153
Fugitive Slave Act (1793), 1–2, 22–25,
   40–42, 49, 56–57; historical context
   of, 22–23; the law, 23–25
Fugitive slaves, 5, 19, 42–43
Fugitives from justice, 23–24
Fulbright, J. William, 174
Full and equal enjoyment, 123, 126

Garfield, James, 124
Gender discrimination, 212
George III, King of England, 8–11
Gerrymandering, 242
Goldwater, Barry, 236
Gomillion, Charles, 166
Gordon, John B., 115
Government by injunction, 165
Graham, Hugh, 251
Grandfather clauses, 93, 95, 104
Granger, Lester, 152–153
Grant, Ulysses S., 116–118, 124
Great Depression (1930s), 70, 129, 131
Greeley, Horace, 62

Harlan, John Marshall, 125
Hart, Philip, 237
Hayes, Rutherford B., 108, 124
Hays compromise (1876), 70
Helms, Jesse, 241
Henson, Josiah, 23
Holland, Spessard, 207
Hoover, J. Edgar, 164
Hopper, Isaac, 22
Housing and Home Finance Agency,
   201
Housing discrimination, 130, 147, 164,
   174, 199–201, 261–263
Howard, General Oliver Otis, 71–74

Howard University, 73, 250
Humphrey, Hubert, 212

Implied powers, 4
Individual equality, 9
International slave trading, 27–28
Interstate commerce, 18, 214–215, 217

Javits, Jacob, 200, 208, 237
Jefferson, Thomas, 8–10, 13, 28, 37
Jim Crow laws, 157, 184, 200. *See also*
   Black codes
Job discrimination. *See* Employment
   discrimination
Johnson, Andrew, 72–74, 82–83, 86–
   87, 92, 103
Johnson, Cave, 42
Johnson, Frank, 175
Johnson, Lyndon B., 130, 165, 174,
   184–185, 211–215, 235–237, 250–
   252, 261–262, 264
Johnson, Paul, 195
Jury duty, 70, 123
Justice Department, 147, 164, 175, 185,
   195, 200, 208, 236, 239, 251, 264

Kansas-Nebraska Act (1854), 46;
   historical context of, 46–49; the law,
   49
Kastenmeier, Robert, 174, 262
Kelly, William, 79
Kennedy, John F., 130, 160, 183–186,
   194–196, 199–200, 208, 210–212,
   214, 251, 261
Kennedy, Robert, 184–185, 195
*Kerner Commission Report on Civil
   Disorder,* 263
King, Coretta Scott, 183
King, Martin Luther, Jr., 163–164, 183,
   210–211, 235–236, 240, 261, 264
King, Rufus, 17
Klan Act (1871), 70, 115–123;
   historical context of, 115–118; the
   law, 118; Section 1983, 117
Knox, William, 134
Ku Klux Klan, 115–118
Kuchel, Thomas, 212

Labor Department, 251; Office of
   Contract Compliance, 250–251
Labor laws, 131
LaGuardia, Fiorello, 134
Land ordinances, 14
Langston, John Mercer, 72
Lawrence, David, 201
Lee, Robert E., 80
Letters for a Farmer in Pennsylvania
   (Dickinson), 3
Lincoln, Abraham, 52–53, 57, 62–64,
   66, 69, 71, 78–80, 85–87
Literacy tests, 104, 131, 207–208, 215,
   217, 235–240
Liuzzo, Viola, 235
Louisiana Purchase, 13, 35–36, 40
Loyalty oath, 58, 86, 88

McClellan, George, 64
McPherson, James, 125
Madison, James, 16–17
Mansfield, Mike, 208, 212
March on Washington, 129, 134, 211
Marshall, Thurgood, 175
Martial law, 116, 118
Mason, Charles, 35
Mason, George, 18
Mason, John, 23
Mason-Dixon line, 35
Meredith, James, 194–196
Merit system of hiring, 70
Mexican-American War, 40
Minimum wage, 131
Missouri Compromise (1820), 1, 35–
   40, 46–47, 49; historical context of,
   35–38; the law, 38
Mitchell, Clarence, Jr., 163, 239
Mitchell, William, 166, 174–175
Montgomery bus boycott, 163, 173
Morris, Governour, 18
Moss, Alfred, 28, 213

National Association for the
   Advancement of Colored People
   (NAACP), 131, 133, 139, 147, 153,
   163, 201, 211, 239, 262
National citizenship, 83, 94, 102

National Committee Against
Discrimination in Housing, 201
National Guard, 157–160
National Urban League, 152–153
Nebraska Territory, 46
New Deal, 129, 131
Nixon, Richard M., 164, 183–184, 239,
252–253, 264
Nonviolent protest, 173
Northwest Ordinance (1787), 1, 13–
15, 40, 79; historical context of, 13–
14; the law, 14–15

O'Brien, Lawrence, 199
O'Connor, Sandra Day, 242
O'Donnell, Kenneth, 199
Open Housing Act. See Fair Housing
Act (1968)

Paine, Thomas, 8
Patterns or practices of discrimination,
216, 218, 263
Pendleton Act (1883), 70, 146
Philadelphia Plan, 252–253
Pierce, Franklin, 47
Pinckney, Charles Cotesworth, 18, 22
Political rights, 102
Polk, James, 40
Poll taxes, 104, 131, 207–209, 238
Postwar Reconstruction era, 69–70;
Civil Rights Act (1866), 70, 82–84,
265; Civil Rights Act (1875), 70, 123–
127; Enforcement Act (1870), 70,
104, 106–114, 167; Fifteenth
Amendment (1870), 70, 80, 95, 102–
105, 107–109, 117, 164, 237–238,
242; Fourteenth Amendment
(1868), 69, 80, 83, 87, 89, 92–101,
103, 106–107, 116–118, 123–126,
157, 164, 208; Freedmen's Bureau
(1965), 69, 71–77; Klan Act (1871),
70, 115–123; Reconstruction Act
(1867), 70, 85–91; Thirteenth
Amendment (1865), 69, 78–81, 83,
86, 92, 125
Preferential treatment, 213
President's Committee on Civil Rights,
130, 139

President's Committee on Equal
Opportunity in Housing, 200–201
President's Committee on Equality of
Treatment and Opportunity in the
Armed Services, 153–154
President's Equal Employment
Opportunity Committee (EEOC),
130, 183–187 254
Prigg v. Pennsylvania, 23
Private clubs, 217
Private-sector discrimination, 215
Privileges and immunities clause, 37,
69, 93–95
Proclamation of Amnesty and
Reconstruction (1863), 79
Public accommodations, 80, 87, 123,
164, 174, 199, 210–211, 214, 217

Quitman, John 23
Quotas, 213, 216, 252

Race norming, 216
Racial discrimination, 125, 130–131,
133, 184, 199; disparate impact, 97–
98; right to vote, 70, 104, 108, 140,
166
Racial quotas, 213, 216, 252
Racial rioting, 210, 262, 264
Racial segregation, 70, 123, 140, 152,
210
Randolph, A. Phillip, 129, 134, 152–
153
Reagan, Ronald, 132, 240–241
Reconstruction Act (1867), 70, 82–91;
historical context of, 85–88; the law,
88–89
Reconstruction Bill (1864), 87
Reeb, James, 235
Regents of the University of California v.
Bakke, 253
Repeal Act of 1894, 108–109
Republican Party, 88, 107, 117, 240
Restrictive covenants, 147, 265
Reverse discrimination, 252
Rhett, Robert Barnwell, 47, 53
Ridgeway, Matthew, 154
Right to vote, 70, 88, 102–104, 164–
167, 173–176, 210; grandfather

clauses, 93, 95, 104; literacy tests, 104, 131, 207–208, 215, 217, 235–240. *See also* Civil Rights Act (1960); Enforcement Act (1870); Fifteenth Amendment (1870); Voting Rights Act (1965)
Rockefeller, Nelson A., 264
Roosevelt, Eleanor, 134
Roosevelt, Franklin D., 129, 133–136, 145–146, 184, 251
Runaway slaves, 1, 13, 15, 22–23, 42. *See also* Fugitive Slave Act (1793)
Russell, Richard, 165, 199, 213
Rutledge, Edward, 4

Safe houses, 22
Scalawags, 88
School desegregation, 164–165, 174, 184, 199, 214, 218; antibusing legislation, 131; *Brown v. Board of Education*, 98, 130, 157–159, 165; University of Mississippi at Oxford riots, 194–196
Schwartz, Bernard, 238
Scott, Dred, 37
Scott, Robert, 75
Secession, 52–53
Secret Service, 117
Section 1983, 117
Selective incorporation, 95
Sengstacke, John, 153
Separate but equal, 98, 126, 157
Seward, William, 47, 64–65
Sherman, Roger, 19
Sherman, William T., 73–74
"Sherman grants," 73–74
Shultz, George, 252–253
Sixteenth Amendment, 16–17
Slave Importation Act (1807), 1, 27–34; excerpt from, 30–34; historical context of, 27–29; the law, 29–30
Slave states, 35, 41–42
Slave trade, 27–28
Slavery period, 1–2; Articles of Confederation (1766), 1, 3–6; Compromise of 1850 (1850), 1, 40–45; Confiscation Acts (1861 and 1862), 2, 56–51; Constitution of the

Confederate States of America (1861), 1, 52–55; Declaration of Independence (1776), 1, 8–12; Emancipation Proclamation (1863), 2, 62–67; Fugitive Slave Act (1793), 1–2, 22–25; Kansas-Nebraska Act (1854), 1, 46–50; Missouri Compromise (1820), 1, 35–39; Northwest Ordinance (1787), 1, 13–15; Slave Importation Act (1807), 1, 27–34; United States Constitution (1787), 1, 16–21
Smith, Howard, 212
Social Security System, 131
Southern Christian Leadership Conference, 163, 173
Southern Homestead Act (1866), 73
Southern Manifesto on Integration, 158, 165
Southwest Ordinance (1790), 14
Sparkman, John, 199
Squatters' rights, 40
State action, 107, 214
State citizenship, 94
State vs. private distinction, 214
States' rights, 83, 165
Stennis, John, 241
Stevens, Thaddeus, 85
Stewart, William, 104
Stimson, Henry, 134
Stoughton, William, 116
Strict scrutiny test, 96–97
Substantive due process, 95–97
Sumner, Charles, 48–49, 80, 85, 123–124
Supreme Court. *See* United States Supreme Court
Sylvester, Edward, 251

Tallmadge, James, Jr., 36
Talmadge, Herman, 237
Tenth Amendment, 4
Thirteenth Amendment (1865), 69, 78–81, 83, 86, 92, 125; historical context of, 78–80; the law, 80–81
Thomas, Clarence, 132
"3/5 compromise," 17
Thurmond, Strom, 146–147, 241, 263

To Secure These Rights, 140
Transcontinental railroad, 46
Treason, 58
Treaty of Guadalupe Hidalgo (1848), 40
Truman, Harry S, 130, 139–142, 145–147, 152–153, 163–164, 184, 251
Trumball, Lyman, 82–83
Tubman, Harriet, 23
Tuskegee Civic Association, 175
Twenty-fourth Amendment (1964), 104, 131, 207–209
Twenty-third Amendment, 208

Underground Railroad, 22–23, 29
Unemployment compensation, 131
Union Leagues, 88
Unionization, 131
United States Colored Troops, 65
United States Constitution (1787), 1, 16–21, 28, 96; historical context of, 16–19; the law, 19–20. *See also specific amendment*
United States military, 65, 146, 152–155
United States Supreme Court, 41, 70, 80, 92, 132, 194, 240; *Brown v. Board of Education*, 98, 157–159, 165, 210; Civil Rights Act (1875), 125; Civil Rights Act (1964), 215–216; Dred Scott decision (1857), 37, 70, 82; equal protection clause, 97–98, 208; Fifteenth Amendment, 104, 108, 238; Fourteenth Amendment, 93–94, 96, 208, 214; Klan Act, 118; literacy tests, 238; Philadelphia Plan, 253;

racial gerrymandering, 242; restrictive covenants, 147, 265
University of Mississippi at Oxford riots, 194–196
Urban League, 201

Vigilance committees, 23
Vote dilution, 241
Voter registration, 174–176, 184, 208, 211, 214, 235, 238–239
Voting discrimination, 102, 140
Voting rights, 217
Voting Rights Act (1965), 104, 131–132, 166, 235–248; historical context of, 235–242; the law, 242–243

Wade, Benjamin, 85
Wade-Davis bill, 69, 86
Wagner, Robert, 129, 133–134
Warner, Willard, 103
Warren, Earl, 215, 236, 238
Webster, Daniel, 41
Whigs, 47
White, Walter, 139
White Citizens' Councils, 163
White-only primary elections, 104
Whitney, Eli, 27
Wilks, John, 252
Williamson, Hugh, 17
Wilmot, David, 40
Wilmot Proviso, 40
Wilson, James, 78
Winstead, William, 165
Wood, Fernando, 79
Woolworth sit-in, 173
Wright, Fielding, 146
Writ of habeas corpus, 116, 118

Yancey, William, 53

About the Authors

MARCUS D. POHLMANN is currently the chairman of the Department of Political Science at Rhodes College. He has published widely in the field of African-American Politics, including *Black Politics in Conservative America* and *Racial Politics at the Crossroads*.

LINDA VALLAR WHISENHUNT is Legal Fellow in the Richard W. Riley Institute of Government Politics and Public Leadership at Furman University where she instructs students in trial advocacy. She is also of counsel to the law firm of Douglas A. Churdar, P.C. and has practiced in the area of labor and employment law.